Trend, Magnitude and Dimensions of Inequality in Post-Reform India

About the Centre

Nabakrushna Choudhury Centre for Development Studies (NCDS), Bhubaneswar, Odisha, is an inter-disciplinary social science research institute, set up by the Government of Odisha in 1987 in collaboration with the Indian Council of Social Science Research (ICSSR) under the Ministry of Human Resource Development, Government of India. Since its inception, the Centre has been playing a proactive role in promoting multi-disciplinary social science research and helping the State Government and Central Government in their development planning, policy formulation, programme evaluations and monitoring. Besides the Centre is involved in conducting different training programmes in collaboration with different national and state level institutions. It is also providing Ph.D. Programme for research scholars under ICSSR Fellowship.

About the Editors

Professor Raj Kishore Panda is the Director, Nabakrushna Choudhury Centre for Development Studies, Bhubaneswar, Odisha.

Dr. Rajkishor Meher is Reader in Industrial Sociology, Nabakrushna Choudhury Centre for Development Studies, Bhubaneswar, Odisha.

Trend, Magnitude and Dimensions of Inequality in Post-Reform India

Edited by
Rajkishore Panda
Rajkishor Meher

Published for
Nabakrushna Choudhury Centre for Development Studies,
Bhubaneswar-751013
by
CONCEPT PUBLISHING COMPANY PVT. LTD.
NEW DELHI-110059

ISBN-13 : 978-93-5125-138-5

First Published 2015

Published and Printed by

Concept
Since 1974

Concept Publishing Company Pvt. Ltd.
A/15-16, Commercial Block, Mohan Garden
New Delhi-110059 (India)
T: 25351460, 25351794, *F*: 091-11-25357109
E: publishing@conceptpub.com, W: www.conceptpub.com
Editorial Office: H-13, Bali Nagar, New Delhi-110 015, India.

Cataloging in Publication Data—*Courtesy:* D.K. Agencies (P) Ltd. <docinfo@dkagencies.com>

National Seminar on "Trend, Magnitude and Dimensions of Inequality in Post-Reform India" (2012 : Bhubaneswar, India)
Trend, magnitude and dimensions of inequality in post-reform india / edited by Rajkishore Panda, Rajkishor Meher.
pages ; cm
Includes bibliographical references and index.
ISBN 9789351251385

1. Economic development—India—Congresses. 2. Economic development—India—Orissa—Congresses. 3. Equality—India—Congresses. 4. Equality—India—Orissa—Congresses. 5. India—Economic policy—1991- —Congresses. I. Panda, R. K., 1950-, editor. II. Meher, Rajkishore, editor. III. Nabakrushna Choudhury Centre for Development Studies.organizer. IV. Title.

DDC 338.954 23

Preface

The post-reform India presents a scenario of higher economic growth with appreciable reduction in poverty. However, as has been observed by many through various statistical analyses the post-reform scenario is marked by greater regional inequality resulting poverty reduction remaining uneven across states. On the extent of inequality observation at the all-India level differs from that at the state and sub-state levels. More so, inequality across regions differs on the basis of indicators used and statistical tools applied in measuring inequality. There is often debate among academicians, policy makers and non-government agencies in reducing inequality in the country.

The present National Seminar on "Trend, Magnitude and Dimensions of Inequality in Post-Reform India" organised by Nabakrushna Choudhury Centre for Development Studies, Odisha on the occasion of its Silver Jubilee Celebration is an outcome of the issues agitating the minds of Economists, Social Scientists, Planners and Policymakers in the context of rising inequality in the country in recent years. The seminar by way of discussion and interaction intends to examine the issues and challenges of inequality and explore the ways to contain this evil at a faster pace in the country. The seminar discussed various issues under six broad sub-themes: (i) Economic Development vis-à-vis Trend and Magnitudes of Inequality in Contemporary India, (ii) Genesis of Inequality in Indian Society : Economic, Social, Cultural, Religious and Political, (iii) Dimensions of Inequalities in Post Reform Era :

Income, Health, Education, Gender-based and Ethnic-based, (iv) Spatial and Sectoral Aspects of Inequality: Interstate, Intrastate, Rural-Urban, Agricultural, Manufacturing and Tertiary Sector, Organized/Formal *versus* Unorganized/Informal Sector, (v) Inequality, Quality of Life and Environment, and (vi) Process and Measurement of Inequality: Policy Issues, Measures and Implementation. A number of eminent social scientists and scholars all over the country presented their papers and participated in the discussion during the two days on 28th and 29th September, 2012.

At the outset we express our deep sense of gratitude to most respected Professor Baidyanath Misra, eminent Economist and former Academic Chairman and Founder Director of the Centre for inaugurating the Seminar as the Chief Guest. We are grateful to Professor Santosh Chandra Panda, Director, Delhi School of Economics, University of Delhi, who presented his Keynote Paper in the inaugural session of the seminar. We are highly grateful to our Honourable Minister, Higher Education Shri Badri Narayan Patra for his Valedictory Address. We are also grateful to Dr. R.N. Senapati, IAS, Development Commissioner-cum-Additional Chief Secretary, Government of Odisha for addressing in the Valedictory Function as the Guest of Honour. We owe deeply to Professor M.N. Panini, former Professor of Sociology, JNU, New Delhi for delivering the Valedictory Lecture.

We are grateful to all the esteemed Chairpersons of the Technical Sessions, Prof. G.C Kar, Prof. Basudeb Sahoo, Prof. Madhusudan Ghosh, Prof. Kailas Sarap, Prof. D.K.Verma, and Prof. Santosh Panda for excellently conducting the discussion in different technical sessions. We convey our sincere thanks to all the paper writers for the trouble they have taken in writing the papers and participating in the seminar. We also convey our sincere thanks to all the participants for kindly accepting our invitation and participating in different technical sessions. The rapporteurs of the technical sessions, Sri Biswadas Patra, Mrs. Anita Samal, Dr. N. Panigrahi, Dr. Shibalal Meher deserve our thanks for the trouble they have taken for summarizing the deliberations of different speakers and discussions. The seminar would not have been successful without the discussion and deliberation of different distinguished members and in this context, we owe a lot to Prof. K.K. Mohanti, Prof. Adwait Mohanty, Prof. Sudhakar Panda, Prof. R.M. Mallik, Prof. K.C. Samal, Prof. Padmaja Mishra, Prof. B.

Sen, Prof. Bhagabata Patro, Prof. Sailabala Devi for sharing their valued opinion during the discussion.

All the office staff of the Centre deserve thanks in managing different activities of the seminar. Research Scholars of the Centre rendered valuable service during the seminar and all of them deserve our praise. Without their support, the seminar could not have been organised.

We hope the papers listed here will be of great help to the researchers and policy makers for some more thinking in reducing inequality in the country.

Rajkishore Panda
Rajkishor Meher

Contents

List of Contributors

Amarendra Das, Lecturer, Department of Analytical & Applied Economics, Utkal University, Bhubaneswar.

Baidyanath Misra, Former Chairman and Founder Director, Nabakrushna Choudhury Centre for Development Studies (NCDS), Bhubaneswar.

Bibhunandini Das, Research Scholar, Centre for Development Studies, Thiruvananthapuram.

Bimal K. Mohanty, Professor of Economics (Retd.), Ravenshaw University, Cuttack.

Biswajit Ghosh, Professor of Sociology, The University of Burdwan, Burdwan.

D.K. Verma, Professor & Head, Department of SC, ST & OBC Development, Dr. Babasaheb Ambedkar National Institute of Social Sciences (BANISS), Mhow.

Kalpana Sahoo, Research Scholar, Department of Humanities and Social Sciences, National Institute of Technology (NIT), Rourkela.

Madhusudan Ghosh, Professor of Economics, Department of Economics & Politics, Visva-Bharati, Santiniketan, Birbhum, West Bengal.

Prakash Sarangi, Professor of Political Science, University of Hyderabad, Hyderabad.

R.K. Panda, Director, Nabakrushna Choudhury Centre for Development Studies (NCDS), Bhubaneswar.

Ranjan Kumar Nayak, Research Scholar, School of Social Sciences, University of Hyderabad.

Santanu Ray Chaudhuri, Assistant Professor of Economics, Symbiosis School of Economics, Symbiosis International University, Pune.

Santosh Chandra Panda, Director, Delhi School of Economics, Delhi University.

Shibalal Meher, Sr. Lecturer in Economics, Nabakrushna Choudhury Centre for Development Studies (NCDS), Bhubaneswar.

Shovan Ray, Professor, Indira Gandhi Institute of Development Research (IGIDR), Mumbai.

1
Structural Change and Inclusive Growth in India

Baidyanath Misra

Change in occupational structure in a country generally reflects its degree of economic development. Even though India is still regarded as a developing country, it partakes some of the characteristics of developed countries of the world. Take the case of occupational structure. Although agriculture including allied activities provided employment for 58.2 per cent of people according to the 2001 census, its share in GDP at constant (2004-05) prices in 2011-12 has come down to 14.1 per cent (Government of India, 2013). This declining share of the agriculture and allied sector in the country's GDP is consistent with normal development trajectory of most of the developed countries. As a matter of fact in most of the developed countries, the share of agriculture in GDP has come down to the level of 3 to 5 per cent along with a change in employment pattern consistent with the level of income pattern. What is more important is that in spite of declining income level in agriculture, agricultural growth in India remains vital for jobs, income and food security in India.

In most of the developed countries, after a decline in agriculture, there is an increase in industrial development. This is the pattern of structural change which has been followed more or less in most of the developed countries as per the analysis of Simon Kuznets (1966). Generally, when there is decrease in income of agricultural sector, there is increase in unemployment or underemployment for people who were depending on agricultural sector. Most of them try to shift to the manufacturing sector which can provide them better employment opportunities with additional income. As per the analysis of W. Arthur Lewis, this is a source of capital formation in the industrial sector without much additional cost (Lewis, 1954). But in India, before we have been able to accelerate the process of development in industrial sector, we have jumped to service sector. The industrial sector which comprises manufacturing, mining, electricity and construction contributed only 27.7 per cent of the total GDP (Gross Domestic Product) in the year 2011. As against that the share of employment of this sector excluding construction was about 12 per cent in 2009-10 (Government of India, 2013: 216). On the other hand, the share of service sector as per cent of GDP in 2011 had reached to 58.2 per cent. If we include construction in the service sector at factor cost the share of this sector in the year 2011 comes to 64.8 per cent of GDP. The total share of the services and construction sector in employment was 25.30 per cent in 2009-10 and the construction alone registered an increase of 9.60 per cent and services only by 3.12 per cent during 1993-94 to 2009-10 (Papola and Sahu, 2012).

Reason for Structural Change

What is the main reason for such a structural change in India? Though neoclassical economists did not attach any importance to structural change in the process of economic development, Simon Kuznets (1966) demonstrated that growth is brought about by changes in sectoral composition. The reason for this is that along with growth, income elasticity of demand for agricultural products becomes low, while there is increase in demand for manufacturing goods and more so for services. Along with this, there is also difficulty in increasing the supply of agricultural commodities since agriculture being mainly dependent on a fixed factor like land where operation of law of diminishing returns is mostly applicable. In manufactured goods on the other hand, supply can easily be augmented with the help of capital and technology, the only factor which may constrain expansion is labour supply which can, of course, be overcome through technological changes. In services also, technologies may provide sufficient scope for expansion of different types of services. In an industrial economy, services assume great importance leading to larger requirements of transport, storage and communication along with personal services like education, health, recreation and so on. While Kuznets (1966) emphasizes income elasticity of demand as the primary reason for changes in economic structure, Kaldor (1967) on the other hand emphasizes supply side which implies that requirements of expanding industrial sector and rising levels of income increase the demand for more services.

Structural Change in UK and China

Before we analyze economic effects of structural change in India, we may make some comparison with structural position of India with one developed country like United Kingdom (UK) and another developing country like China. Take the case of UK. Before 1800 in UK, agriculture accounted for a half to two-thirds of total output. But gradually it went on decreasing along with the development of industries. By 1950s, industries grew steadily and industrial output reached a level of almost 50 per cent of GDP. This was more or less same with regard to most of the developed countries. Along with the increase in industrial development, the share of agriculture came down while the role of services assumed more importance to meet the demands of industrial development. Then a period of deindustrialization started where the share of industrial output came down to the level of 25 per cent of GDP while services dominated the economy. This is generally called post-industrial society and if we take the example of 2002, we find that in United Kingdom, output share of agriculture declined to the level of one per cent and industry 26 per cent while the share of services increased to 73 per cent. The share of employment was found to be similar as that of national product – for example, shares in employment in percentages came to 1.00 in agriculture, 25.00 in industry and 74.00 in services. The World Development Indicators, 2004 shows that most of the developed countries have more or less the same level of shares of output and employment (World Bank, 2004).

We take only one developing country in Asia, i.e. China which is often compared with India. The sectoral shares of China in 1960 for agriculture, industry and services were 30 per cent, 49 per cent and 21 per cent respectively. All these shares in 2002 changed to

15 per cent for agriculture, 45 per cent for industry and 34 per cent for services. If we compare India with China, we find great differences which really did not help in increasing employment in India. In India, the shares of agriculture, industry and services in the year 1960 were 55 per cent, 16 per cent and 29 per cent respectively. In 2002 the sectoral composition of shares in agriculture came down to 24 per cent (as compared to 15% in China), whereas in the case of industry it increased to 25 per cent (as compared to 51% in China) and in services it was 51 per cent (as compared to 34% in China). Thus, we find that while the Indian industrial sector is almost half of China, our service sector is one and half times more than that of China. We also have more disadvantages in employment pattern. We only take one year, i.e. 2002. In this year while our services sector GDP was 51 per cent, as compared to China's 34 per cent, India's employment share in services was only 22 per cent, as compared to 31 per cent in China. That means we had more income derived from services sector, but less employment while just the opposite happened in China (World Bank, 2004 and 2006).

Changes in Economic Structure of India and their Effects

In the context of above structural change, we may consider the following five issues, i.e. the rate of growth of the economy, changes in poverty structure, scope for additional employment opportunities, the extent of inequality and the level of human development. On the basis of our findings, we may make a few suggestions for securing inclusive growth. We start with economic growth in the country. The entire period from 1951 to 1979-80 was a period of sluggish growth. The growth rate on average per year was 3.5 per cent which was designated as 'Hindu Rate of Growth'. Some economists criticized the period as largely a product of a highly interventionist state with import trading regime which hindered growth rate. Probably, such measures were necessary at that stage to consolidate the economy, build necessary institutions to prepare for an overall change in the economic system and prevent foreign competition. In 1991, because of the economic crisis arising from excessive foreign debt, fiscal deficit and inflationary spiral, the Government adopted a pre-market strategy that liberalized its internal regulatory framework, reduced tariffs, adopted appropriate exchange rate policies and allowed foreign investors to play a significant role in the economy. Even though a full-fledged liberalization started from 1990s, Rajiv Gandhi also took some measures to decentralize the economy in 1980s and adopted some liberal measures to increase the pace of growth. The acceleration in the growth in the 1980s was in fact quite modest. Once we exclude the years 1988-1991, growth in the remaining years – 1980-81 to 1987-88 – turned out to be just 4.6 per cent. After the plan holiday of two years (1990-1992) due to political uncertainty, we have covered four plans, namely Eighth Plan, Ninth Plan, Tenth Plan and Eleventh Plan. During Eighth and Ninth Plans, the rate of growth was 6.5 per cent and 5.5 per cent respectively. Both in the 10th and 11th Plans, the rate of growth almost approached 8 per cent on average per year except in the last year when it was reduced to less than 6 per cent due to prevailing international recession and a number of financial difficulties in the country. The Planning Commission aims at attaining a rate of growth of eight per cent with an inclusive growth in the 12th Plan. We can say that without any hesitation that India has more or less performed well on the growth front.

Increase in the rate of growth of income was crucial for attaining higher per capita income and consumption which contributed to some extent for reducing poverty. It has been estimated in the Economic Survey 2011-12 (Government of India, 2012) that it took 40 years for the real per capita income to double from the level achieved in 1950-51. However, it increased 2.5 times in the next 20 years in the post-reform period. Along with increase in per capita income, there was increase in consumption and since poverty is measured on the level of consumption, there is some decrease in poverty. The Planning Commission has accepted the methodology of Tendulkar Committee for measuring poverty. On the basis of the recommendation of Tendulkar Committee, poverty in India has been reduced from 45.3 per cent in the year 1993-94 to 37.2 per cent in 2004-05 and further to 32 per cent in the year 2009-10 (Tentative). There was decrease in poverty ratio in spite of rise in population. It is also noticed that whenever there is increase in the rate of growth, reduction of poverty becomes higher. For example, poverty figures based on the latest survey, conducted in 2009-10, a period during which growth accelerated to 8.5 per cent, has indeed accelerated over what had been achieved between 1993-94 and 2004-05. Data show that poverty reduction during

2004-05 to 2009-10 was 1.5 percentage points per year compared with just 0.74 percentage points per year between 1993-94 and 2004-05 (Bhagwati and Panagariya, 2012: 42). Bhagwati and Panagariya's (2012) study points out that there is no doubt that there are many that are still poor today. According to them one cannot rule out the possibility that reforms have impoverished some individuals, such as those who were displaced from land to make way for alternative activities without proper compensation.

Why Business and Services not Creating Adequate Productive Jobs

One question which is raised by many scholars – why has not poverty reduced in the same proportion as the rise in income? The answer is given in Economic Survey of India 2012-13 (Government of India, 2013). Both business and services are not creating enough jobs. Let us take the case of business. Business is supposed to create productive jobs. But we do not find productive jobs there. In India, too many small firms stay small and unproductive and not allowed to die gracefully. Too many large profitable firms prefer relying on temporary contract labour and machines than on training workers for longer term jobs. As a group, it is estimated that micro, small and medium enterprises (MSMEs) employ 81 million people in 36 million units across the country, yet many of these firms are unable to grow and/or even shut down. Too many firms in India stay small, unregistered, unincorporated, largely informal, or in the unorganized sector because they can avoid regulations. These firms have little incentive to invest in upgrading skills of largely temporary workers or investing in capital equipment that could bring them into tax net, so their productivity stays low. Low productivity gives them little incentive to grow, completing the vicious circle. The obvious reasons for this are: (a) government regulations are too many with a number of clearances which delay the process, (b) the financial institutions are wary of lending to MSMEs because they lack adequate credit histories or collateral, and (c) difficulty to get access to quality infrastructure.

If the MSMEs find difficulty in improving their productivity, why is large organized manufacturing not creating more jobs? A substantial body of evidence suggests that rigid labour regulations have played a significant role in explaining low organized manufacturing output and employment and high informal manufacturing output. When labour laws constrain firms: (a) they rely more on capital instead of labour, (b) resort to informal arrangements/limiting their scale in order to remain outside of the formal sector altogether and/or (c) hiring contractual labour. Do strict labour laws help labour or increase employment? It is observed that labour regulations offer impediments to manufacturing growth. The Economic Survey points out that the Labour Laws in India are more rigid than in most countries. But very few workers are actually covered by those laws. 'Indeed India suffers from the consequences of strong protection (low flexibility for employers and strong reluctance to offer workers formal jobs) without giving most workers the benefits. As a matter of fact, roughly 85 per cent of workforce in India is engaged in the informal sector. The prevalence of informal employment (workers in either in the informal sector or in the formal sector but lacking employment or social security benefits) is even higher, 95 per cent jobs are informal and 80 per cent of non-agricultural wage workers work without a contract (Papola, 2006).

All this means 'India is not creating enough productive jobs. Moreover, India has the dubious distinction of having some of the most comprehensive labour laws in the world, even while having one of the largest fractions of the working population unprotected' (Government of India, 2013: 48).

While businesses are creating many unproductive jobs, the service sector does not create adequate number of jobs. Excessive regulations, lack of funding and poor infrastructure are common features both in business and services. For example, 27 per cent of retail stores in India report labour regulation as a hindrance in creating jobs. But what is important in case of services that those require better education and skilling. For example information technology, software development and finance not only require higher education but a particular type of qualification. Any graduate cannot handle such jobs. Even mid-level of services like retail trade, hotels and restaurants require particular types of skill. Such training is now available in many parts of India. There is a continuing mismatch between employer's needs and worker's capabilities. It is appropriately stated in Economic Survey that India has to focus on an agenda to create productive jobs outside of agriculture, which will help us reap the demographic dividend and also improve livelihood in agriculture.

Why is there so much Inequality in India?

Creation of productive jobs outside agriculture will usher in a new era of development by improving livelihoods of people who are either unemployed or partially employed. But, it cannot altogether eliminate inequality in the society. Simon Kuznets's (1966) curve hypothesis explains that as a country experiences income growth, there is a secular cycle of economic inequality – an inverted U-shaped curve relating to per capita income with inequality. That secular cycle of economic inequality still continues in India. As has been pointed out by Joseph E. Stiglitz (2012), three forces determine inequality. These forces are market, politics and rent seeking. Even though, the government has a lot of control in the economy, in major fields of economy, we have free enterprise, the profit motive and a freely operating price system. This provides excessive gain to the producers. Further we also see that market forces in some cases are shaped by political processes. Markets are shaped by laws, regulations and institutions. And every law, every regulation, every institutional arrangement has distributive consequences – and the way we have been determining India's economy, it works to the advantage at the top and to the disadvantage of the rest. Another important element of inequality is rent-seeking behaviour of influential people. If an influential man secures a state asset (such as a coal or an iron mine) at below fair market prices, it helps the man to increase his wealth and perpetuates inequality in the society. For example, if the government sells a coal mine for 10 million rupees which is worth 100 million rupees, it is easy to get rich by getting a state asset at a discount. Many of India's current billionaires obtained their business by buying state assets at below market prices and then ensuring continuing profits through monopoly power. Every Indian knows, from the 17th century to the 19th, the British granted the East India Company a monopoly on trade with India, which enriched Britain at the cost of India. We have many examples of market forces, political power and monopoly rents increasing inequality in India.

What are the Factors which Influence Inclusive Growth?

Inclusive Growth does not only depend on poverty reduction, it also depends on human development and gender development. As per the latest available Human Development Report (HDR) 2011 published by the UNDP, the HDI (Human Development Index) for India was 0.547 in 2011 with an overall global ranking of 134 (out of 187 countries). In regard to gender inequality index (GII) which captures the loss in achievement due to gender disparities in the areas of reproductive health, empowerment and labour force participation, the value is 0.617. This is though higher than that of the world average (which is 0.492), unfortunately our performance in this regard is relatively worse than our neighbours like Pakistan, Bangladesh and Sri Lanka. A lot more has to be done in India both in respect of HDI and GII (UNDP, 2011).

All this means when we think of inclusive development, we have to improve poverty alleviation (which is now 29.8 per cent in 2009-10), increase productive employment opportunities (employment growth in the organized sector, public and private combined has increased by 1.0 per cent in 2011 as against 1.9 per cent in 2010), accelerate investment in health, education and other social services (Total expenditure in State and Centre combined in BE 2012-13 comes to 1.36, 3.31 and 2.42 percentage points of GDP respectively) and many other factors which can bring in an overall change both in economic and social sphere.

What Can be Done?

Instead of discussing in detail the needs of different types of activities to ensure inclusive growth, we note down following points in a summary form only as reference:

1. Agriculture at the present stage cannot provide much additional employment. But we have to increase the productivity of agriculture by changing cropping pattern so as to increase the livelihood of all those who pursue agriculture and allied activities. Additional investment in agriculture will reduce poverty much more than any other sector with the same amount of investment.
2. At the same time we should try to establish a large number of manufactured industries in rural areas so that all those who are left out from agriculture can be absorbed in such industries. But manufacturing sector can only improve

provided there is more investment in infrastructure like roads, electricity, sanitation, drinking water, banking facility and so on. Further all these industries should be modernized so as to successfully compete with mega industrial products.

3. This means people who are unemployed and willing to work in such industries must be properly trained to operate such industries. General education will increase awareness, but technical education will provide the necessary qualification to handle such operations.
4. As emphasized in India's Tryst with Destiny, rising inequalities highlight what is wrong with India's growth trajectory, driven as it is by elite consumption and sectoral imbalances, which exclude disadvantaged groups from the benefit of rising GDP, while aggravating income disparities (Bhagwati and Panagariya, 2012: 4). We have already discussed the adverse effect of monopoly power in increasing inequality. Atul Kohli (2012) in his 'Poverty Amid Plenty in the New India' has discussed in detail how monopoly power in India has degenerated India's social and economic framework and suggested a number of measures to control such powerful influences. It all depends as it is now called e-governance. At the same time, it is also necessary to provide direct assistance with the help of creation of productive assets for all those disadvantaged groups to derive benefit from economic development that is pursued in the plan period.
5. Finally, we may mention that there is not only a great deal of exploitation, but also colossal corruption. When Mikhail Kalecki visited Indian Statistical Institute in 1962, he said, "there were too many exploited and too few exploiters". This is mainly because democracy has failed to ensure e-governance, instead of both becoming complementary, have become antithetical to each other. That is the main reason why there is so much corruption in India – more than 50 per cent of GDP. Mark Tully, a BBC correspondent who has written a book entitled 'India in Slow Motion' where he has analyzed corruption from 'Top to Tail' has given an example of an American industrialist of Indian origin who told him, 'I want to invest in my country but I

> go to south-east Asia. There you pay a bribe but you know you will get what you paid for. In India people come out of the woodwork demanding money, one after another and there is no end to it, and no one, not even the Minister, can guarantee that your investment will be cleared.' That is not the end of it. He further adds, "These bastards, it is a disgrace, they are ruining the country. Wherever you go here it's a jungle, with everyone wanting to eat money and everyone saying if you don't give it they can stop your project."

We have quoted such a long statement just to indicate that unless you control such exploiters, you cannot develop the country, reduce poverty or increase inclusive growth. So long this continues our republic will face a crisis and the poor people will remain as poor as they are today. This is a major work which should be done at any cost so that we can have higher economic growth along with equity both in economic and social sphere.

REFERENCES

Bhagwati, Jagdish and Arvind Panagariya (2012). *India's Tryst with Destiny*. Noida, India: Collins Business.

Government of India (2013). *Economic Survey 2012-13*. New Delhi: Ministry of Finance, Department of Economic Affairs, Economic Division and Oxford University Press.

Government of India (2012). *Economic Survey 2011-12*. New Delhi: Ministry of Finance, Department of Economic Affairs, Economic Division and Oxford University Press.

Kaldor, N. (1967). *Strategic Factors in Economic Development*. Ithaca, N.Y.: Cornell University Press.

Kohli, Atul, (2012). *Poverty amid Plenty in the New India*. Cambridge: Cambridge University Press.

Kuznets, S. (1966). *Modern Economic Growth: Rate, Structure and Spread*. New Haven: Yale University Press.

Lewis, W.A. (1954). 'Economic Growth with Unlimited Supply of Labour', *Manchester School*, 22 (May): 139-91.

Papola, T.S. (2006). 'Emerging Structure of Indian Economy: Implications of Growing Intersectoral Imbalances', *Indian Economic Journal*, Vol. 54(1), April-June.

Papola, T.S. and Partha Pratim Sahu (2012). *Growth and Structure of*

Employment in India: Long Term and Post Reform Performance and the Emerging Challenge. New Delhi: Institute for Studies in Industrial Development (ISID). http://isidev.nic.in/pdf/ICSSR_TSP_PPS.pdf

Stiglitz, Joseph E. (2012). *The Price of Inequality*. New York & London: W. Norton & Company.

Tully, Mark (2003). *India in Slow Motion*. New Delhi: Penguin India Limited.

UNDP (2011). *Human Development Report 2011—Sustainability and Equity: A Better Future for All*. New York: UNDP and Oxford University Press.

World Bank (2004). *World Development Indicators 2004*. Washington DC: The World Bank.

World Bank (2006). *World Development Report 2006—Equity and Development*. New York: The World Bank and Oxford University Press.

2

Economic Growth, Inequality and Poverty in Odisha, 1993-2010

Santosh Chandra Panda

Introduction

It is well known now that after decades of stagnation, Odisha has been growing at an average rate of nearly 9 per cent since 2003-04. This is somewhat higher than the national average. When we look at the data on State Domestic Product, either Gross or Net, we see wild fluctuations in SDP till 2003-04. After that the growth rate becomes higher and stable. One doesn't see as much fluctuation in SDP as one observes prior to 2003.

In this context, the first question we ask is whether the recent changes in the growth rate of SDP is statistically significant? This is important since we need to know if the recent upward change in the growth rate is random or robust enough to stand a test of statistical significance. Next we look at the contribution of various sectors to growth and undertake the same statistical significance test as well.

It is natural to ask if the state has done well on growth front, how it has affected the poor and how the income distribution in the state has changed. So, we look at the estimates of economic inequality and poverty during 1993-2010.

It may be appropriate to justify the years chosen (1993-2010) for this analysis. For estimating inequality and poverty, the only data source is NSS data on consumer expenditure. As we know, in

NSS, the data is collected under 'Uniform Reference Period (URP)' and 'Mixed Reference Period (MRP)'. In URP, the recall period is one month for all consumable items and under MRP, the recall period is one month for frequently consumed item (e.g. food) and one year for durables. It is not difficult to see that MRP data is more realistic and likely to capture true consumer expenditure. However, NSS started collecting data under MRP in 1993 only. That is the primary reason why we start our analysis starting 1993-94. We use the thick rounds of NSS which is done every five years. So we use NSS quinquennial rounds of 1993-94, 2004-05, 2009-10, i.e. 50th, 61st and 66th rounds under MRP. The 56th round (1999-2000) of NSS became controversial due to some flaws in the data collection method and has been left out from our analysis. The last thick round was in 2009-10, which is the terminal year in our analysis.

The paper is arranged as follows. In section 2, we look at Odisha's growth performance. Section 3 looks at the estimates of inequality in rural and urban Odisha. Section 4 considers poverty estimates in rural and urban Odisha taking Tendulkar's poverty line and using NSS data under MRP. We conclude in Section 5.

Odisha's Growth Story

The net state domestic product at constant prices in Odisha has grown at an average of 3.2 per cent from 1980-81 till 2002-03 and from 2003-04 till 2009-10 it has grown at a rate of 8.4 per cent. Looking at the growth rates for the relevant period in our paper, we find wild fluctuation in the growth rate (see Table 2.1 and Figures 2.1 and 2.2) till 2003-04 after which it somewhat stabilizes.

To minimize the fluctuations, we take a three-year moving average and the result is presented in Figure 2.3.

Looking at Table 2.1, one gets a feeling that 2003-04 may serve as a pivotal year. Starting 2003-04, the growth rate in the state picks up and the momentum stays till 2009-10. The average rate of growth in the state compares favourably with the national average.

Given the fact that growth rate from 2003-04 has been significantly higher than the previous decades, one would like to know whether this spurt in the growth rate is statistically significant or not. If it is statistically significant, what could be the possible explanation of this strong economic performance?

Table 2.1: Growth Rates in NSDP at Factor Cost

Year	*Growth rate*
1994-95	4.9
1995-96	4.6
1996-97	– 6.9
1997-98	14.4
1998-99	3.1
1999-00	6.3
2000-01	– 2.6
2001-02	6.1
2002-03	– 0.7
2003-04	14.6
2004-05	13.1
2005-06	4.4
2006-07	12.5
2007-08	8.8
2008-09	5.4
2009-10	8.5

Source: Central Statistical Office as reported in RBI website.

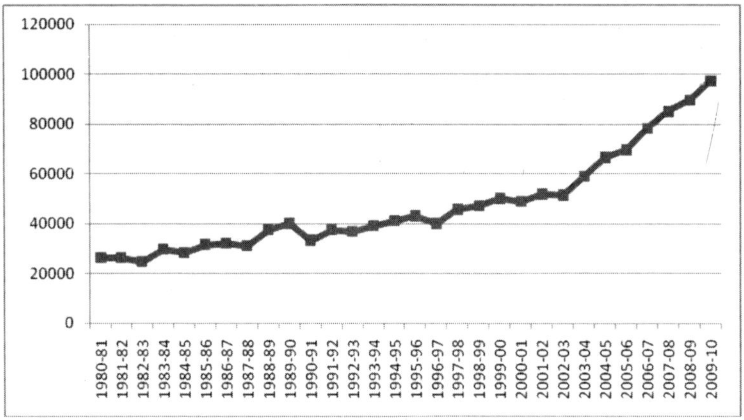

Fig. 2.1: NSDP of Odisha

To test for the statistical significance, we estimate the following regression equation:

$$\log y_t = \alpha_0 + \alpha_1 D_t + \beta_0 t + \beta_1 t * D_t$$

where

y_t = net state domestic product
t = trend variable

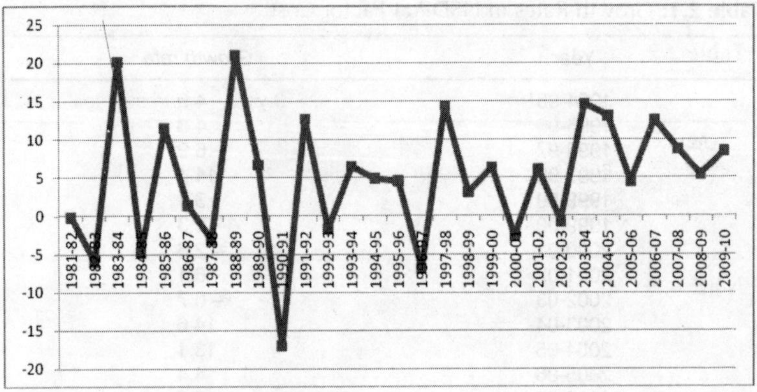

Fig. 2.2: Growth Rate of NSDP

To minimize the fluctuations, we take a three-year moving average and the restult is presented in Figure 2.3.

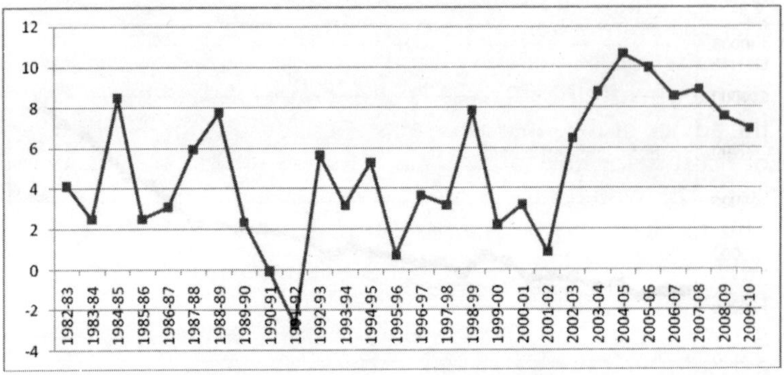

Fig. 2.3: Growth Rate of NSDP (3-year Moving Average)

D_t is the dummy variable which takes value 0 up to 2002-03 and 1 from 2003-04 onwards

$t * D_t$ = represents the dummy variable multiplied with the trend variable.

The growth rate is given by $\frac{\partial \log y_t}{\partial t} = \beta_0 + \beta_1 D_t$. If $D_t = 0$, growth rate is β_0 and if $D_t = 1$, growth rate is $\beta_0 + \beta_1$. The change in rate of growth is presented by β_1. The estimation shows that value of β_1 is statistically significant at 5 per cent level of significance, using Newey-West Standard Errors. The results are summarized in Table 2.2.

Table 2.2: Growth Rate of NSDP[1]

Level			*3-year moving average*		
Up to 2002-03 β_0	*2003-04 onwards* $\beta_0+\beta_1$	*Change* β_1	*Up to 2002-03* β_0	*2003-04 onwards* $\beta_0+\beta_1$	*Change* β_1
3.2	8.4	5.2	3.4	8.6	5.2

Note: The change in rate of growth (β_1) are significant at 5 per cent level of significance.

To understand what might have triggered this upsurge in rate of growth, let us keep in mind that the country followed a policy of economic liberalization since 1991. Industrial licensing was mostly abolished and new enterprise was being encouraged. In Odisha, the benefits of liberalization were implemented rather late and around this time there was a spurt in manufacturing activity. Many industrial houses were invited to establish manufacturing units in steel, ferro-alloys, aluminium and so on. This would have contributed to the increase in growth rate. Secondly, following the advice of the Finance Commission, the state followed a path of fiscal discipline and Odisha is turned into a revenue surplus state. This would have created a congenial atmosphere for growth. Thirdly, there was a major programme on irrigation which would have contributed to agricultural growth. In fact, in the following pages, when we look at the sectoral contribution of the economic growth, the contribution of registered manufacturing and agricultural growth turns out to be significant.

We now turn to the sectoral contribution to economic growth in Odisha. The data source is CSO and we use the data on Gross State Domestic Product at factor cost from 1994-95 to 2009-10. We use the same regression equation used earlier and the results are presented in Table 2.3.

Table 2.3: Growth Rates of GSDP Sector-wise

Sector	*Level*			*3-year moving average*		
	Up to 2002-03	*2003-04 onwards*	*Change*	*Up to 2002-03*	*2003-04 onwards*	*Change*
Primary	1.0	4.4	3.4	1.4	5.0	3.7
Secondary	1.9	9.9	8.0	2.0	10.2	8.2
Tertiary	6.1	9.9	3.8	6.1	9.9	3.8

Figures 2.4 to 2.8 below give a visual representation of performance of various sectors during this period.

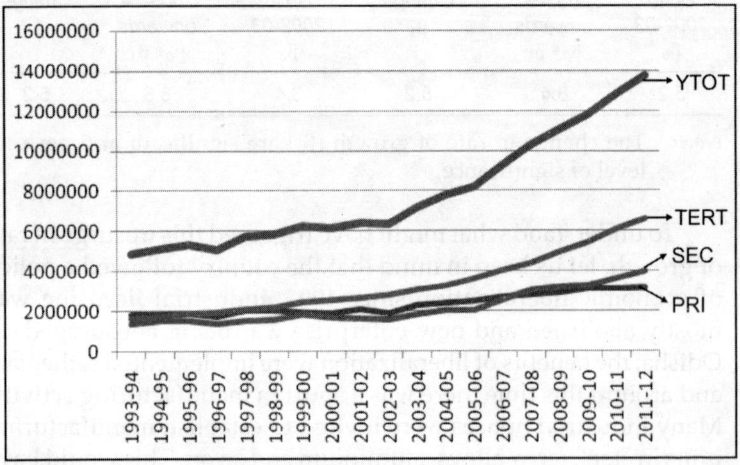

Fig. 2.4: Movement of SDP Sector-wise

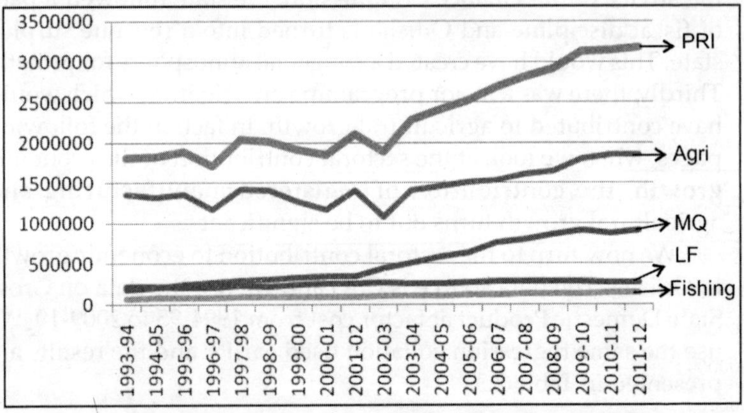

Fig. 2.5: Movement of Primary Sector SDP Component-wise

What is to be noted is that within primary sector, contribution of agriculture has been significant. Within secondary sector, contributions of registered manufacturing and construction activity have played a major role in boosting economic growth. Similarly, within tertiary sector, the contribution of trade, hotels and restaurants and transport and communication has been

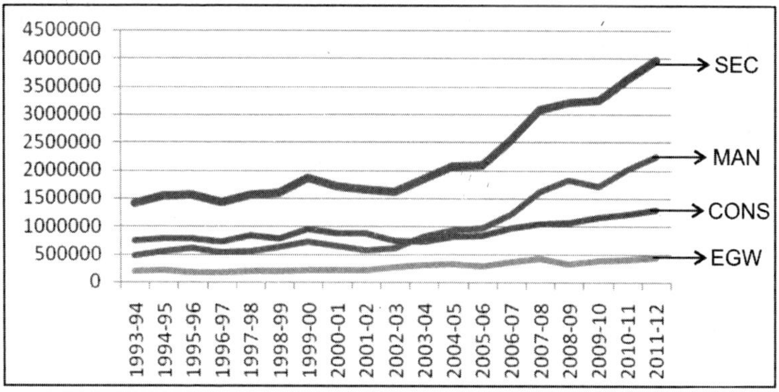

Fig. 2.6: Movement of Secondary Sector SDP Component-wise

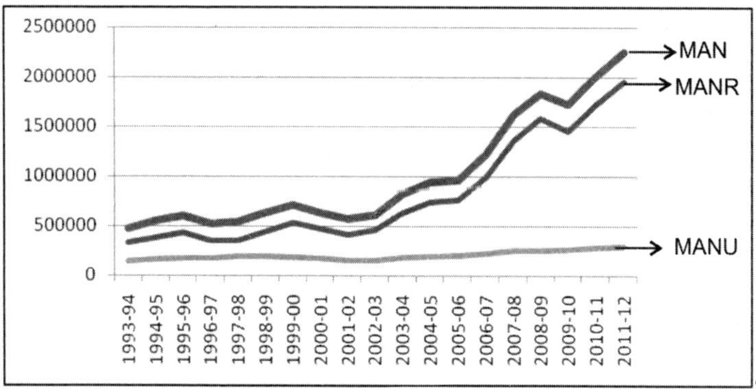

Fig. 2.7: Manufacturing Registered and Unregistered

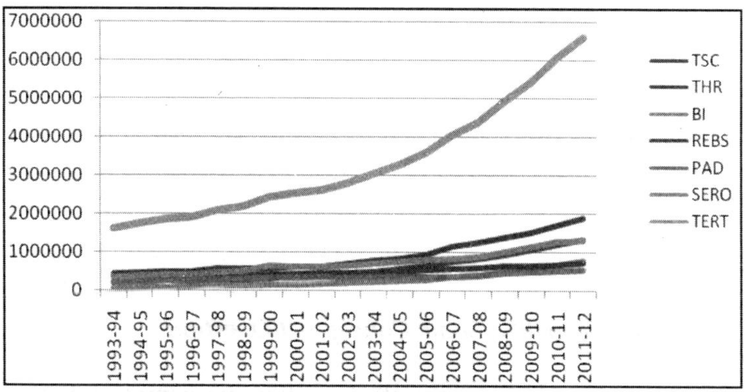

Fig. 2.8: Movement of Tertiary Sector SDP Component-wise

substantial. This is summarized in Table 2.4. We see that tertiary sector is contributing 53.4 per cent to GSDP and primary sector's contribution is only 15.9 per cent.

Table 2.4: Major Drivers of Growth (Shares of Growth since 2003-04)

Sector	*Contribution to Growth (%)*
Primary	15.9
Secondary	30.6
• Manufacturing	15.9
• Registered	12.9
• Construction	10.1
Tertiary	53.4
• Transport, Storage and Communication	10.5
• Trade, Hotels and Restaurants	15.1

Even though the State has been growing at an appreciable rate, the per capita income in Odisha has remained way below the per capita income in the country. If we look at Figure 9 below, where we compare per capita income of Odisha with all India, we see that the gap has widened, rather than the two curves converging. This shows that whatever has been achieved in the state on growth front is still not enough and there is no scope for complacency.

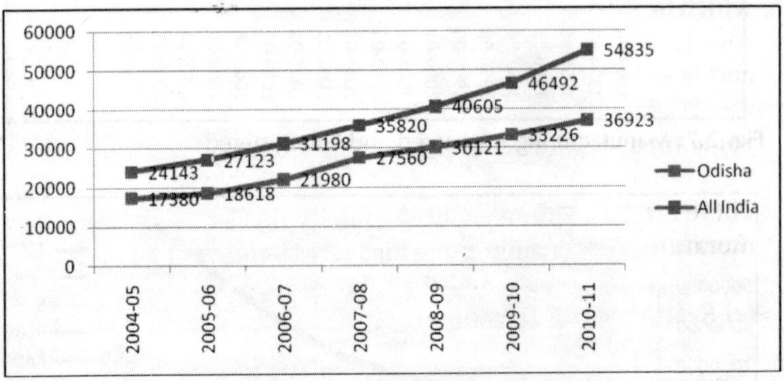

Fig. 2.9: Movement of per capita NNP

Inequality

Economic Inequality: Some Conceptual Questions

Inequality in our society exists since time immemorial. Extreme inequalities in societies have led to social unrest and revolutions in the past and a glance through world history makes it clear that extreme form of inequality had undesirable consequences and hence should be avoidable. The other extreme is to attain perfect equality in a society. Is perfect equality feasible or desirable? The classic paper by Scitovsky (1963) titled "Equity" discusses this issue. Scitovsky observes, and we agree, that as long as we get 'economic incentives' to produce the national product, inequality results since human abilities are unequal. He observes that society is more likely to tolerate inequalities, if these are correlated with merit or people's contribution to society and its values. Inequalities are more acceptable to a person who feels that he has equal chances with others of reaching the top. Also, a society will more easily tolerate inequalities if those at the bottom are provided with subsistence and necessities of life. Therefore, inequality is always linked to poverty, which we analyze in the next section.

While talking about inequalities, one can talk about inequality in income, inequality in wealth, inequality in nutrition, inequality in opportunities and so on. While these are all interesting questions, data on these attributes are difficult to obtain. The NSS data gives us the 'per capita consumption expenditure' and we use this data to measure inequality in Odisha. Therefore, in effect, what we measure here is inequality in per capita consumption expenditure, which is conceptually different from say inequality in wealth in a society. But as we explained above, we have to rely on NSS data and hence have to accept this limitation.

Some Inequality Measures

There are large numbers of inequality measures available in the literature. We consider three measures here:

(a) Relative Mean Deviation

Consider distributions of income over n persons, $i = 1 \ldots n$. Let y_i be the income of person i and let the average level of income be μ. Then,

$$D = \frac{\sum_{i=1}^{n} |\mu - y_i|}{n\mu} = \frac{\text{sum of absolute value of deviations}}{\text{Total income}}$$

(b) Gini Coefficient

Gini coefficient is one of the most popular measures of inequality. This is measured as $G = 1 - 2$ [Area under the Lorenz Curve].

The figure below and the explanation following that explain the Lorenz curve and calculation of Gini coefficient.

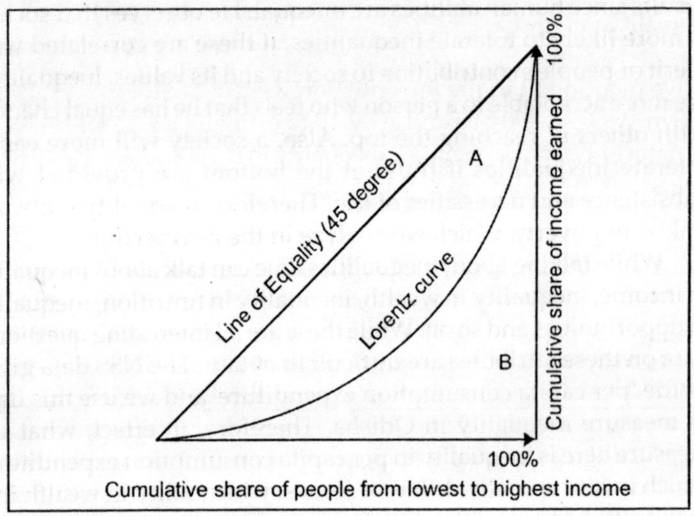

Fig. 2.10: Lorenz Curve and Gini Coefficient

Calculation of Gini Coefficient

Gini Coefficient or Gini Index is defined as a ratio of the areas on the Lorenz Curve diagram. If the area between the line of perfect equality and the Lorenz curve is *A*, and the area under the Lorenz curve is *B*, then the Gini index is $A/(A + B)$. Since $A + B = 0.5$, the Gini index, $G = 2A = 1 - 2B$.

If the Lorenz curve is represented by the function $Y = L(X)$, the value of *B* can be found with integration and

$$G = 1 - 2 \int_0^1 L(X)\,.\,dx$$

(c) Kakwani Measure of Inequality

Let *l* be the length of the Lorenz curve. *l* will always lie between $\sqrt{2}$ and 2.

Then $K = \dfrac{l-\sqrt{2}}{2-\sqrt{2}}$

Out of the three measures listed here, Gini coefficient is the most popular, despite some shortcomings. We use all the three measures to estimate inequality in Odisha.

Inequality in Odisha

As we mentioned in the introduction we use the thick rounds of NSS in 1993-94, 2004-05 and 2009-10 to estimate inequality. Given the nature of data, we estimate inequality in rural and urban Odisha separately. The following tables present the results.

Table 2.5: Inequality in Rural Odisha

Inequality Measures	*1993-94*	*2004-05*	*2009-10*
Relative Mean Deviation	0.155	0.189	0.178
Gini Coefficient	0.223	0.265	0.253
Kakwani Measure	0.047	0.065	0.059

Table 2.6: Inequality in Rural Odihsa by Social Groups (Gini Coefficient)

Social Groups		*1993-94*	*2004-05*	*2009-10*
ST		0.202	0.220	0.221
SC		0.200	0.226	0.213
OBC		—	0.244	0.231
Others	Including OBC	0.219	0.256	0.242
	Excluding OBC	—	0.264	0.256

The results on inequality in rural Odisha are something to cheer about. We see that inequality in rural Odisha increased between 1993-94 and 2004-05 but it shows a decline between 2004-05 and 2009-10. Point to note is that this has been the period of high growth. Contrary to the popular belief that higher growth is always associated with higher inequality, results from rural Odisha show that higher growth can be associated with reduction in inequality also. This result, in a way, corroborates the findings of a cross country analysis by Bruno, Ravallion and Squire (1996) where they conclude that there is no correlation between growth and inequality. In case of rural Odisha, the decline in inequality occurs, no matter which measure of inequality we take.

It will be useful to analyze what could have possibly contributed to the decline in inequality in rural Odisha. We may take note of the fact that various redistribution schemes such as MGNREGA, cheap rice to BPL families started around 2005-06. The minimum wage has increased and the average daily earning for rural casual labourer increased from Rs. 42.29 in 2004-05 to Rs. 81.00 in 2009-10 for males and from Rs. 29.65 in 2004-05 to Rs. 59.00 for females (Source: NSS). The female/male ratio in the rural workforce also increased from 71.11 per cent to 72.91 per cent between 2004-05 and 2009-10. All this might have contributed to a decline in rural inequality. The Lorenz Curve for rural Odisha is given below and one can see that the Lorenz Curve for 2009-10 lies above the Lorenz curve for 2004-05 signifying a decline in inequality.

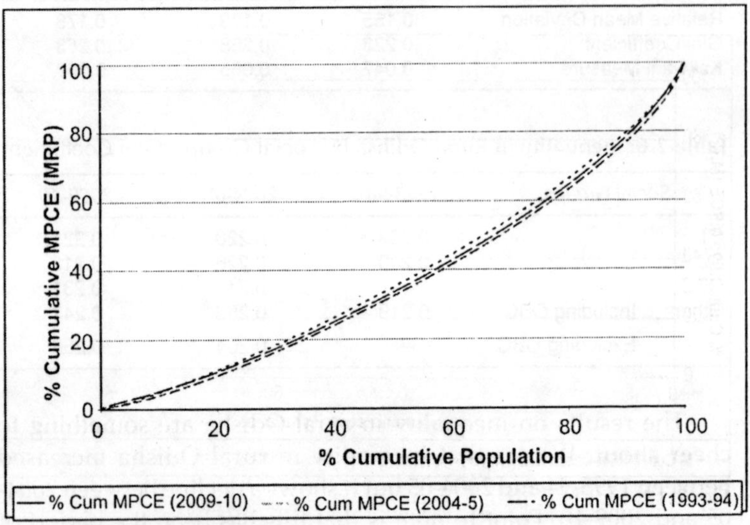

Fig. 2.11: Odisha-Rural (Lorenz Curve)

The results are different when we look at inequality in urban Odisha. Inequality in urban Odisha shows an upward trend all through except for scheduled tribes where there is a marginal fall in inequality between 2004-05 and 2009-10. Results are presented in Tables 2.7 and 2.8 and the Lorenz Curve for urban Odisha is in

Figure 2.12. The Lorenz Curve clearly shows an increase in inequality over the years.

Table 2.7: Inequality in Urban Odisha

Inequality Measures	*1993-94*	*2004-05*	*2009-10*
Relative Mean Deviation	0.213	0.248	0.282
Gini Coefficient	0.294	0.340	0.385
Kakwani Measure	0.077	0.101	0.131

Table 2.8: Inequality in Urban Odisha by Social Groups (Gini Coefficient)

Social Groups		*1993-94*	*2004-05*	*2009-10*
ST		0.279	0.330	0.322
SC		0.233	0.297	0.307
OBC		—	0.318	0.283
Others	Including OBC	0.292	0.329	0.383
	Excluding OBC	—	0.317	0.394

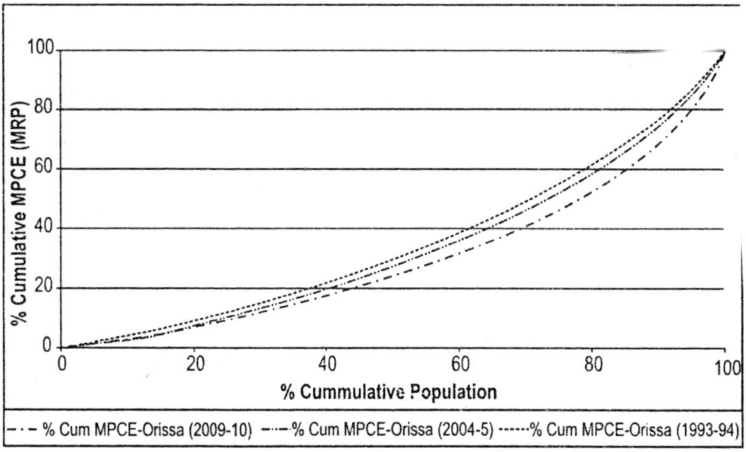

Fig. 2.12: Odisha-Urban (Lorenz Curve)

Poverty

Some Poverty Measures

In poverty measurement literature, several poverty measures have been suggested. We briefly discuss four poverty measures here.

Suppose a society consists of n individuals with consumer expenditure levels $x_1 \ldots x_n$ (arranged in ascending order of magnitude). Let z be the poverty line and let M be the number of individuals with consumer expenditure less than z who are deemed to be poor with reference to the yardstick z.

The simplest measure of poverty is: *Head Count Ratio (HCR)*, which is defined by

$$H = \frac{M}{n}$$

Head Count Ratio is the simplest and most popular measure of poverty but it completely ignores the intensity of poverty. In particular it violates axioms such as Monotonicity and Transfer. To take into account the level of deprivation, a measure called Poverty Gap Ratio was introduced.

It measures an average magnitude of deprivation among the poor and is given by:

$$\text{Poverty Gap Ratio } R = \frac{1}{z} \cdot \frac{1}{M} \sum_{i=1}^{M} (z - x_i)$$

$$= \frac{z - \overline{x}_p}{z}$$

where $\overline{x}_p$ is the mean consumer expenditure of poor individuals.

However, this measure does not take into account income inequality among the poor. Sen's measure of poverty tries to do that by bringing in the Gini coefficient.

$$\text{Sen Index } S = H\,[R + (1 - R)\,G]$$

Where H is HCR, R is poverty gap ratio in G is Gini Coefficient.

FGT Index: Another poverty measure to capture severity of poverty uses Coefficient of Variation among the poor (CVP) and is known as Foster-Greer-Thorebecke (FGT) Index of poverty and is given by

$$FGT = H\,[R^2 + (1 - R^2)\,CVP^2]$$

where H is HCR, R is Poverty Gap Ratio and CVP is the Coefficient of variation among the poor.

Poverty Line: Some Conceptual Issues

As we have seen in the previous subsection, for defining any poverty measure, defining the poverty line is important. The definition of poverty line has changed over time and no matter how we define it; some arbitrariness is bound to be there. While recognizing this, we make a brief review as to how poverty line has been defined.

Earlier definition of poverty line was linked to a calorie norm which was recommended by Lakdawala Committee. It was estimated that if a person per day would procure food items which will provide 2400 calories in rural areas and 2100 calories in urban areas, he or she will not be termed as poor.

This definition of poverty line continued until the next commission, headed by Prof. Suresh Tendulkar, gave its report in 2009. Tendulkar Committee recognized the fact that poverty should not only be linked to food consumption. Along with food, housing, education, health, clothing etc. are also essential components of basic human needs. So they brought in the concept of Poverty Line Basket (PLB) – an individual consuming a basket higher than PLB specification is not poor. They kept the PLB uniform for rural and urban areas but note that the market price of PLB will vary from state to state, between rural and urban areas. So the Planning Commission gives poverty lines for various states and all-India for the year 2004-05 for rural and urban separately and uses Fisher Price Index to extrapolate to other years.

They observe that NSS data is the only source to get consumption expenditure data. We have already observed that NSS data is collected under URP and MRP and that consumption data under MRP is considered more realistic. So, as per Tendulkar Committee recommendations, which are accepted by the Planning Commission we use NSS quinquennial rounds of 1993-94, 2004-05, 2009-10, i.e. 50th, 61st and 66th rounds under MRP to base our poverty estimates.

Poverty in Odisha

In this sub-section we present the poverty estimates for rural and urban Odisha separately.

Table 2.9: Poverty in Rural Odisha

Poverty Measures	*1993-94*	*2004-05*	*2009-10*
Head Count Ratio %	63.16	60.81	39.19
Poverty Gap Ratio %	16.03	17.38	8.99
Sen Index*100	21.760	23.15	12.41
FGT Index*100	5.683	6.638	3.003

Planning Commission Poverty Line for Rural Odisha:

1993-94	:	Rs. 224.20
2004-05	:	Rs. 407.8
2009-10	:	Rs. 567.1

Table 2.10: Poverty in Rural Odisha by Social Groups

Social Groups		*Poverty Measures*	*1993-94*	*2004-05*	*2009-10*
ST		HCR	82.14	84.52	66.03
		Poverty Gap	26.10	30.46	19.58
		Sen Index	33.85	37.98	25.83
		FGT Index	10.50	13.04	7.63
SC		HCR	62.82	67.88	47.11
		Poverty Gap	15.83	19.01	9.16
		Sen Index	21.56	25.48	12.47
		FGT Index	5.67	7.22	2.58
OBC		HCR	—	52.59	25.62
		Poverty Gap	—	12.55	4.64
		Sen Index	—	17.05	6.4
		FGT Index	—	4.18	1.23
Others	Including OBC	HCR	54.78	47.90	25.20
		Poverty Gap	11.60	10.96	4.62
		Sen Index	15.96	14.99	6.45
		FGT Index	3.53	3.56	1.28
	Excluding OBC	HCR	—	37.22	24.54
		Poverty Gap	—	7.35	4.59
		Sen Index	—	10.18	6.51
		FGT Index	—	2.14	1.359

Table 2.11: Poverty in Urban Odisha

Poverty Measures	*1993-94*	*2004-05*	*2009-10*
Head Count Ratio %	34.76	37.58	25.91
Poverty Gap Ratio %	8.35	9.60	5.31
Sen Index*100	11.45	13.15	7.55
FGT Index*100	2.86	3.50	1.70

Planning Commission Poverty Line for Urban Odisha:

1993-94	:	Rs. 279.3
2004-05	:	Rs. 497.31
2009-10	:	Rs. 736.00

Table 2.12: Poverty in Urban Odisha by Social Groups (HCR)

Social Groups		*PL: 279.30 1993-94*	*PL: 497.31 2004-05*	*PL: 736.00 2009-10*
ST		58.05	53.40	34.06
SC		38.96	63.73	47.05
OBC		—	42.36	25.96
Others	Including OBC	30.32	31.11	14.03
	Excluding OBC	—	23.77	18.00

Several observations from these estimates are due. First, we find that the trend in change in poverty is same no matter what poverty measures we use. Therefore, to keep the analysis simple, we use Head Count Ratio figures more than others. Secondly, we find that between 1993-94 and 2004-05, there has been a slight fall in HCR for rural Odisha and a marginal increase in HCR for urban Odisha but between 2004-05 and 2009-10 there has been a significant reduction in poverty, be it rural or urban Odisha. In rural Odisha the decline is nearly 21 percentage points, which is the highest reduction among all states and in urban Odisha, the decline amounts to nearly 12 percentage points. Thirdly, the decline in poverty after 2004-05 cuts across all social groups, be it Scheduled Castes or Scheduled Tribes or OBCs. These estimates cast doubt on the assertion of some authors that growth in Odisha has not been inclusive. Clearly, the benefits of growth, coupled with redistribution mechanism, have benefited the poor. It may be of interest to see how Odisha performed in poverty reduction *vis-à-vis* all India figures. That comparison is given in Table 2.13 below. What we find is that poverty reduction in Odisha between 2004-05 and 2009-10 is much more than all-India figures.

Table 2.13: Poverty Comparison: Odisha and All-India (HCR)

		1993-94	*2004-05*	*2009-10*
Rural	Odisha	63.16	60.81	39.19
	All-India	65.79	41.83	33.81
Urban	Odisha	34.76	37.58	25.91
	All-India	39.09	25.74	20.88

Conclusion

We find that Odisha's economy almost stagnated till 2003-04, the average rate of growth being 3.2 per cent. From 2003-04 onwards, there has been a spurt in growth momentum. The major drivers to this growth story have been agriculture, registered manufacturing and trade, hotels and restaurants. There has been an increase in manufacturing activity since 2003-04 and it seems that the state reaped the benefits of liberalization a bit late. High growth, post 2003-04, has also been associated with a decline in rural inequality and significant reduction in rural and urban poverty. This, in some sense, corroborates the hypothesis that the biggest antidote to poverty is high growth coupled with some government sponsored redistribution measures. The results of this paper annul the view that Odisha's growth has not been inclusive in recent years.

NOTE

1. To estimate this, we used Table 5 of *Handbook of Statistics on Indian Economy* appearing in the website of RBI. This gives Net State Domestic Product at factor cost at constant prices, the base years being 1980-81, 1993-94, 1999-2000 and 2004-05. One can find two entries for the year which becomes the base year for next series. For example, for 1993-94, one can find two entries – one in 1980-81 prices (say, x) and one in 1993-94 prices (say, x_1). Then multiplying by a factor $\frac{x^1}{x}$, one can convert each entry from 1980-81 to 1993-94 to a measure of NSDP at 1993-94 prices. This conversion method is standard practice at CSO and using this technique, we generated NSDP figures from 1980-81 to 2009-10 at 2004-05 prices. This has been used to calculate growth rates in Table 2.1 and regression estimates in Table 2.2.

REFERENCES

Bruno, Michael, Ravallion, Martin and Squire, Lyn (1996). 'Equity and Growth in Developing Countries', *Policy Research Working Paper*. Washington DC: World Bank.

Government of India (2009). *Report of the Expert Group to Review the*

Methodology for Estimation of Poverty (by Suresh D. Tendulkar, R. Radhakrishna and S. Sengupta). New Delhi: Planning Commission.

Panda, Manoj (2008). 'Economic Development in Orissa: Growth without Inclusion?', *IGIDR Working Paper–2008-2025*. Mumbai: Indira Gandhi Institute of Development Research.

Scitovsky, Tibor (1963). 'Equity', in *Papers on Welfare and Growth*. Stanford: Stanford University Press.

Tendulkar, Suresh D., K. Sundaram and L.R. Jain (1993). 'Poverty in India, 1970-71 to 1988-89', *ILO-ARTEP Working Papers*.

3

Economic Inequality and the Kuznets Process: An Indian Recast

Shovan Ray

Introduction

In this paper I show an Indian profile to the set of issues raised by Kuznets in his Presidential lecture of the American Economic Association in 1954 on inequality[1] that set the research agenda on the subject in the following decades. This objective is somewhat different from recent discussions on inequality measures in the wake of economic reforms in India; it is also different, though somewhat related to, the issues raised by the old and fascinating debate on the inverted U-shaped curve. However, it is quite pertinent to the 'post-liberalisation' India scenario in the global context today. In what follows we shall first review some recent observations on poverty and economic inequality in India, and discuss the profiles for a larger view of India's development. In section 2, we refer briefly to the phenomenon underlined by the Kuznets process and note its implications as testable hypotheses. This is important because a large literature has been spawned in validating or otherwise of this presumed implication of economic growth[2]. The empirical scrutiny of the hypotheses underlying the Kuznets process in various contexts and the resultant debates is reviewed briefly in section 3. An important outcome of this scrutiny is lack of robust empirical support for the U-shaped relationship using cross-section data across countries. An alternative empirical regularity with global data which questions the validity of the Kuznets curve has been put forward by Palma (2011); this is discussed in section 4 and its relevance to the Indian scenario is considered. This perspective is then tapped in section 5 to consider the longer term or secular tendencies on inequality in India. The same is then related to the Kuznets process underlined in his defining paper but rarely discussed in the literature. Section 6 concludes the paper with some remarks and caveats. There emerges the possibility of the much sought-after turning point(s) of the inequality relationship, but it may be of the perverse kind.

Let us first look at some empirical trends in poverty and inequality figures presented in Table 3.1. National Sample Survey (NSS) data show that inequality in consumption (using URP data) represented by Gini values increased for both rural and urban areas in the post-reforms period and the rate of increase was higher for urban as compared to rural areas. However, in the immediate pre-reform period from 1983 to 1993-94, there was a decline in Gini values for rural areas. No such pattern was observable for urban areas in the same decade, and it increased only marginally. At the same time it is observable that there have been declines in 'poverty gap' (PG) and 'squared poverty gap' (represented by FGT) for both periods in rural and urban areas. In other words, the distributions of the poor below the official poverty lines have become less unequal as represented by these measures (of PG and FGT) for the entire period from 1980s to the immediate post-reform period. That is, for those that remain below the poverty line the acuteness has declined somewhat in the intervening period. These observations are presented in Table 3.1 (extracted from Dev and Ravi, 2007). What do these imply for assessing inequality in India? In that quest we would like to examine some more measures of poverty and inequality, in both spatial and temporal dimensions.

Some states have high poverty ratios in their total population. In 2004-05, it was over 40 per cent in Odisha and Bihar. Odisha's poverty incidence level (47%) was six times that of Punjab (8%). Bihar, M.P., Odisha and U.P. together had a share of 49.8 per cent of the rural poor in 1983, which increased to 55 per cent in 1993-94 and further on to 61 per cent in 2004-05. The share of seven states (Bihar, Karnataka, M.P., Maharashtra, Rajasthan, Tamil Nadu and U.P.) in urban poor rose from 61.6 per cent in 1983 to 70 per cent in 1993-94 and 76 per cent in 2004-05. Together these reflect a

Table 3.1: Poverty Gap, FGT and Gini (URP)

	Poverty and Inequality			*Changes (%age points per annum)*		*Changes in poverty (per annum changes as %age of base year)*	
	1983	*1993-1994*	*2004-2005*	*1983-1994*	*1993-2005*	*1983-1994*	*1993-2005*
Rural							
Poverty Gap	13.46	8.58	5.9	–0.46	-0.24	–3.45	–2.84
FGT	5.27	2.55	1.47	–0.26	–0.10	–4.93	–3.92
Gini	30.79	28.55	30.45	–0.21	0.17	-0.68	0.60
Urban							
Poverty Gap	11.95	8.37	5.76	–0.34	–0.24	–2.85	–2.87
FGT	4.31	2.61	1.46	–0.16	--0.11	–3.71	–4.21

Source: Dev and Ravi (2007).

major polarisation in poverty incidence in geographic terms, irrespective of how growth in incomes is taking place in rural and urban India. Thus, poverty for the combined population was concentrated in five states, viz. Bihar, M.P., Maharashtra, Odisha and U.P. – together accounting for 65 per cent of the total poor in 2004-05. Thus across states, incidence of poverty is highly unequal and increased over time. This increasing concentration of poverty trends have continued in recent times. Using the MRP method, the figures and trends change somewhat, but nothing that we say here would significantly affect the pursuit of our objective here and hence we shall not enter the important debate on the measurement issues[3].

In the same vein the record on economic inequality show that inequality as measured by Gini coefficient for various states in India either increased or the rate of decline was slower in 13 out of 17 states in the post-reform period. In 10 out of 13 states, inequality increased in rural areas between 1993-94 and 2004-05. Inequality in urban areas increased in 15 states. It may be noted that the levels of inequality are higher for urban areas than rural areas in all the states (Dev and Ravi 2007), a finding that is a stylised fact around the world and treated as a premise in Kuznets (1955) in depicting the Kuznets Process. In stylised language, it may be said that while urban inequality is greater in general than rural India, it has increased with economic growth especially if we consider the post-reforms decade, and this increased inequality has touched both rural and urban India. On the income dimension at least, there has been divergence among regions and states of India; in other words, growth has delivered increased inequality all-around. Combining the observations on poverty and inequality trends, it may be surmised that while the incidence of poverty has decreased somewhat, alongside decreased severity (acuteness) of poverty at the bottom, income inequality as measured by Gini index shows a deterioration over time across India in both rural and urban areas.

Other than what were referred to as PG and FGT for measuring intensity and severity of poverty around and below the benchmark poverty lines, the measurement literature has also considered a category termed as the 'very poor'. The 'very poor' are defined as those below 75 per cent of the respective poverty lines. It is found that their ratio declined from 15.5 per cent in 1993-94 to 10.3 per cent in 2004-05. In other words, we have about 10 per cent of the population who are hard core poor, the 'very poor' – that defines the 1st decile of India's population. The absolute number of total poor in India declined to around 315.5 million (over 28%) in 2004-05 from around 324 million (36%) in 1993-94. The 'very poor' (the bottom 10% of population identified above) in 2004-05 constituted 36.5 per cent of the total poor (over 28% in 2004-05) in India. This is a useful benchmark to which we shall return later in our recast of the post-liberalisation scenario. Before we consider the above processes further let us consider a very rich literature on economic inequality. This may allow us to form some judgement whether inequality has a 'secular' tendency to worsen or improve as per capita income increases. For this we revert to the path-defining Kuznets' (1955) paper on inequality.

The Kuznets Process of Growth and Inequality

The so-called inverted-U curve on inequality and growth (the Kuznets Curve) is well-known but perhaps the Kuznets process which generates this is little known, and may be worth recalling in outline form. An extract from Kuznets (1955) follows. "An invariable accompaniment of growth in developing countries is the shift away from agriculture, a process usually referred to as industrialization and urbanization. The income distribution of the total population, in the simplest model, may, therefore, be viewed as a combination of the income distributions of the rural and the urban population. What little we know of the structures of these two component income distributions reveal that: (a) the average per capita income of the rural population is usually lower than that of the urban; (b) inequality in the percentage shares within the distribution for the rural population is somewhat narrower than in that for the urban population ... Operating with this simple model, what conclusions do we reach? First, all other conditions being equal, the increasing weight of urban population means an increasing share for the more unequal of the two component distributions. Second, the relative difference in per capita income between the rural and urban populations does not necessarily drift downward in the process of economic growth: indeed there is some evidence to suggest that it is stable at best, and tends to widen because per capita productivity in urban pursuits increases more rapidly than in agriculture. If this is so, inequality in the total income distribution should increase" (Kuznets 1955: 7-8).

From the above statement we get some elements of the Kuznets hypothesis: as a country experiences income growth, there is a secular cycle of economic inequality—an inverted u-shaped curve relating per capita income with inequality. Kuznets (1955) asked: "What factors determine the secular level and trends of income inequalities?" it is worth recalling what Kuznets explicitly said about his paper: that it was based on 5 per cent evidence and 95 per cent speculation. It combined limited data available then with certain empirical regularities and a forceful logic. In his exposition he took a somewhat eclectic view of the process, combining economic, political and social factors to explain the observed statistical regularities. But the pre-eminent force spearheading the change is the shift of population from traditional to modern activities, from rural-agricultural pursuits to urban-industrial activities. This underlying model of population shift has been termed as the 'Kuznets process' (Anand and Kanbur, 1993a).

In the above process of population shift, the rural mean income as well as its inequality is lower than that in urban pursuits; so with increasing transfer of the population weight from the first to the second, both the overall mean and inequality of the combined income should increase over time. This is the first component of the growth process. For an inverted-U shape, there has to be a turning point at a critical juncture as the process continues. This is the more challenging part and the source of much controversy on empirical grounds as we shall see.

From the limited data on USA, England, and Germany, Kuznets found long term constancy and reduction in inequality, which is a puzzle – why? First, as Kuznets himself noted, savings were mostly in upper income brackets during that period[4]. For USA all savings were made by the top decile, with two-thirds of that by the top 5 per cent alone. Second, the shift that he underlined was away from agriculture and rural sectors to industrial-urban livelihoods, which gained in weight over time as aggregate per capita income increased. The first (agri-rural) group earns less than the second; its dispersion is also lower than the second. Then a secular shift in shares from primary to secondary (and tertiary) would result in greater inequality in income distribution as growth proceeds. The evidence on inequality trends is quite the contrary (constant and reducing). Taken along with progressive taxes and transfers and the rising per capita income, this implies that lower income groups are enjoying a more favourable disposable income than the average.

Among several factors, Kuznets' prime driver of the process is the inter-sectoral shift from agri-rural to industrial-urban activities as the per capita income increases. He considers two sectors for ease of exposition of his model to conjecture his hypothesis: agriculture (A) and others (B). As growth takes place relative income shares shift from sector A to sector B. Kuznets makes three basic assumptions which are based on the stylised facts of the contemporary world: Per capita income in sector B is higher than in sector A; the share of sector A in the total declines over time; and income inequality in A is less than that in B. Thus if both sectors' (A and B) income distributions get progressively unequal, the outcome would be greater inequality in the aggregate. When sector income distributions remain similar but income share shifts to B, the combined inequality would first increase, and then decline with growth due to intra-sector distribution effects. As the shares change the top quintile income share declines after a critical value and thereafter. This is the moderating effect of a large middle income group emerging in the dynamic economy. This last observation is a huge jump in terms of analytics and is model parameter specific; and we shall return to this issue of turning points of inequality in the next section. There is a vast analytical and empirical literature on this turning point issue.

At this point we quote the central hypothesis of the Kuznets process. "One might thus assume a long swing in the inequality...widening in the early phases...when the transition from the pre-industrial to the industrial civilization was most rapid; becoming stabilized for a while; and then narrowing in the later phases" —Kuznets (1955).

Kuznets (1955) made some rough comparisons between developing countries with developed ones. He found that for India in 1949-50, the inter-quintile distributions were more unequal than for US and UK in the post-war phase. Table 3.2 reflects these observations about India in comparison with developed world in the immediate post-war years. Note that this is cross-country comparison as distinct from the structural-temporal predictions of the hypothesis. Kuznets said this as a rough statistical reflection of a 'fairly common observation relating to income distributions in underdeveloped compared with developed countries. The former have no "middle" classes.' There was no middle income class in India then, only middle quintiles. Where do we figure in this transformational scenario today? The share of agriculture in total GDP is about 16 per cent; the secondary sector share is about a quarter of the total and services account for about 60 per cent. Together what Kuznets termed as 'sector B' is about 84 per cent in India now! With predominantly small holder agriculture in India, both its average income and dispersion among household units are low. Most dynamics occur in industry and services. Examining the above process reflected in Table 3.2, we may ask: Are we still on the upward phase of Kuznets inverted U, if economic growth and the associated per capita income are leading to an increase in economic inequality? Or there is probably some other dynamics at play?

Table 3.2: Economic Inequality: Quintile GDP Shares in 1949-50

Quintile	*India*	*USA*
1.	8	6
2.	9	12
3.	11	16
4.	16	22
5.	55	44

Source: Kuznets (1955).

Empirical Evidence on the Kuznets Process

The original Kuznets model was based solely on a numerical illustration derived from an underlying mathematical relationship. Fields (1979) analysed the Kuznets process by assuming that within-sector inequality remains invariant as the population shifts from the traditional sector to the modern one. Robinson (1976) however tried to investigate the properties of the Kuznets process in the presence of within-sector inequality. He claimed to demonstrate that "the U-hypothesis from a very simple model ... [in which we] assume that the economy can be divided into two sectors with different sectoral income distributions and that there is a monotonic increase in the relative population of one of the sectors over time... The U-hypothesis will be seen to be a necessary implication of the workings of such models" (Robinson, 1976: 437). However, as noted in Anand and Kanbur (1993a: 27), Robinson's analysis is restricted to one specific index of inequality – the variance of the logarithm of income. Other subsequent works have gone on to derive the results under different inequality specifications and indices, and the resultant relationship. This is purely on the theoretical domain, and the empirical tests of the hypothesis are a different set of issues altogether, which is discussed later.

An important early contribution in estimating the parameters and shape of the 'Kuznets curve' with global data was made in a set of papers by Ahluwalia (1976a, 1976b), and Ahluwalia *et al.* (1979), and followed by several estimates elsewhere. The Ahluwalia set of estimates were also influential because they were used by the World Bank and the World Development Reports to estimate turning points of inequality-growth relationships in different countries and regions, and hence about forecasting of poverty maps in developing countries, including India. For the same reason, these studies were in the limelight for further scrutiny by economists[5]. I shall highlight the findings of Anand and Kanbur (1993a, 1993b) in this context as these are quite comprehensive in scope and critique of the issues.

The empirical literature has mostly used cross-section data across countries to estimate the relationship underlying the Kuznets process. To quote Anand and Kanbur (1993a: 29-36): "The focus of this literature has been the cross-country estimation of a relationship between inequality and per capita national income, but it has appealed to the Kuznets process to justify: (i) a turning point in the relationship between inequality and development ..., and (ii) the specific functional form of the inequality-development relationship...". Analysing the 'general properties' of the Kuznets process, they found that under the Kuznets assumptions "the entire Lorenz class of inequality indices increases at the start of the process, but the behaviour of inequality at the end of the process – and hence the existence of a turning point in the inequality-development relation – is ambiguous... In order to derive specific functional forms which can be estimated, we have to specify the inequality index under analysis more closely." They discuss six alternative indices of inequality, and for each index derive the specific functional form and conditions for a turning point in its inequality-development relationship. They estimate the regression equations, and go on to test the hypothesis using these functional forms using data on 60 developing and developed countries derived from the same dataset as used by Ahluwalia (1976b). The six inequality indices for which they present specifications and test the data are Theil T, Theil L, Squared Coefficient of Variation, Decomposable Transform of Atkinson Index, Gini Coefficient, and Variance of Log-income. The first five indices all belong to the Lorenz class of indices. The properties of these indices are discussed in Anand and Kanbur (1993a), and may be found in many others such as Sen (1997), Fields (2001).

Hypothesis testing seriously question the validity of the relationship from the cross-section data as four of the six specifications imply restrictions on one of the coefficients, and three of them are rejected at the 5 per cent level of significance. The exception is the *L* regression. Having tested the basic Kuznets model, Anand and Kanbur (1993a: 43) observe: "Of course it would be quite wrong to conclude from these tests that the Kuznets process is rejected for any individual country... The rejection of this hypothesis still leaves open the possibility that the Kuznets process operates in each country but that each country is on a different inequality-development relationship... Without adequate time series data we cannot hope to resolve these questions." They then consider an extension of the basic model to allow for changes in the mean incomes of the two sectors over time and investigate the implications. They consider some nuanced variations on this extension in line with alternative scenarios. In the cited paper they explicitly test the Theil T inequality index and reject the hypothesis. "*A fortiori* the hypothesis is rejected that [the parameters] are the same across countries and constant over time, i.e. that all countries *mutatis mutandis*...are following the same Kuznets curve" (p. 46). This paper does not, however, consider complete flexibility of the underlying parameters (sectoral means and inequalities) as development proceeds but that complexity is not likely to resurrect the basic model that Kuznets proposed.

Anand and Kanbur (1993b) focus their analysis on the Ahluwalia empirical tests, in view of its pre-eminent position then on the literature on Kuznets curve and policy circles; as they observe (p. 20): "...the centrepiece of this literature consists of the articles by Ahluwalia (1976b) and Ahluwalia *et al.* (1979)... In an influential literature, these have become influential papers." It investigates the robustness of the estimates to variations in functional forms and uses non-nested tests a la Pesaran (1974) and Pesaran and Deaton (1978) to choose the functional form, and find them highly sensitive though the data cannot choose one from another in terms of model-admissibility. It subjects the data to get a more consistent set than what was used by Ahluwalia (1976b) and test the Kuznets hypothesis. It concludes thus (p. 42): "Estimates of the inequality-development relationship for this data set is striking. Not only do the data reject the log-quadratic form in favour of a straight quadratic form, but the preferred form displays a *reversal* of the commonly accepted U-hypothesis."

From the above it is clear that we can no longer work on the basis of the inverted U relationship, though the Kuznets *process* may continue to shed considerable light on inequality in the process of development. However, it should also be noted that the original proposition was based on a structural process for a country-specific situation with its unique set of sectoral distribution parameters which are not being validated or otherwise in the literature that had once acquired the status of an economic law. It must also be noted that at the time Kuznets formulated his famous conjecture, it was by and large believed that there was only a unique path of capitalist or free-market development, and this monolithic belief system permeated both the left and the right of the ideological spectrum. The East Asian, and subsequently the Southeast Asian, experience were to provide very different models of the relationship[6]; and so were the eastern European inequality data which provide a very different inequality-growth experience, so much so that all the empirical literature cited above were constrained to use a socialist model dummy to estimate their regression equations. To our knowledge there is no study that has provided a robust estimate of the Kuznets curve specifically for India using time series data, robust in the sense of parameter estimates that would trace the relationship. We now move to a different set of estimates which by implication assumes the 'end of the Kuznets curve' in the alternate empirical regularity that it establishes.

Palma's Findings on Global Inequality

Palma (2011)[7] provides an interesting alternative set of estimates and a fresh perspective on the global debate on inequality. His estimates relate to 135 countries circa 2005; India figures as a distinct entity among countries and country groups. From this global dataset he estimates that about 80 per cent of the world's population now live in regions whose median country has a Gini value in the neighbourhood of 40. That is, in these vast regions of the world cutting across continents, there is a central tendency of the inequality measure to cluster around the value of 40. In his recasting, the remaining countries that belong to points outside this neighbourhood (cluster)—and where the remaining 20 per cent live—are mostly two clusters of middle-income and rich countries. In the middle-income cluster countries, Latin America and mineral-rich Southern Africa are uniquely unequal, while Eastern Europe follows a distributional path similar to the Nordic countries. Among the other cluster of rich countries there is a large (and growing) distributional diversity.

Palma demonstrates that within a global trend of rising inequality, there are two opposite forces at work. One is 'centrifugal', and leads to an increased diversity in the shares appropriated by the top 10 and bottom 40 per cent. The other is 'centripetal', and leads to a growing uniformity in the income-share appropriated by deciles 5 to 9. He shows that the 50 per cent population located in the middle decile groups D5 to D9 (that is, from the bottom fifth to the second top) seems to have the tendency to appropriate about half the national income of the respective

GDP. Between them, they manage to garner their fair share of the national pie, no matter how this is distributed between them. There are undoubtedly differentiated income shares among deciles and percentiles of population within this middle half, but together they manage to gravitate to their exact half-share of the total across countries. His estimates also show that as these 'outliers' are middle-income and rich countries in the cross-section observations, the 'upwards' side of the Kuznets 'Inverted-U' between inequality and income per capita seem not to exist. Notice that the 'Inverted-U' in the Palma estimate is based on cross-section data across countries, whereas the 'Inverted-U' of Kuznets is actually a structural process[8]. Nevertheless, this is forceful evidence in the debate which, as we have seen, mostly relate to cross-section data.

Palma's estimates lead him to the following observation. Middle (or 'median') classes across the world seem to be able to benefit (as a group) from a distributional safety net — i.e. regardless of the per capita income level of the country, the characteristics of the political regimes, the economic policies implemented, the structure of property rights, or whether or not they belong to countries that managed to get their prices 'right', their institutions 'right', or their social capital 'right', the 50 per cent of the population located in 'D5–D9' income groups seems to have the capacity to appropriate as a group about half the national income.

On the other hand, there is diversity in the shares appropriated by the top 10 and bottom 40 per cent of respective populations. That is, half of national income is up for grabs between the very rich (D10) and the poor. For bottom 40 per cent, characteristics such as the nature of political regimes and institutions, the economic policies implemented etc., can make the difference. In his opinion, globalisation is creating a distributional scenario in which what really matters is the income-share of the rich—because the rest 'follows' (middle classes able to defend their shares, and workers with ever more precarious jobs in ever more 'flexible' labour markets, receive the remaining part). The regional distributional structure suggested by the Gini index only reflects the income disparities of half the world's population—those at the very top and at the bottom of the distribution—but it tells us little about the remarkable distributional homogeneity of the other half. The findings of Palma noted above are presented in Figures 3.1 to 3.5, all of which are extracted from Palma.

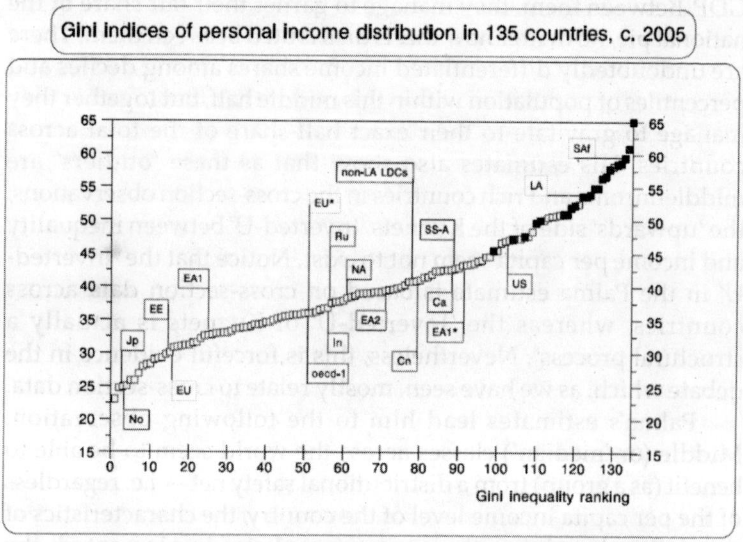

- Median values (multiplied by 100).[9] Latin American and three middle-income Southern African countries (Botswana, Namibia and South Africa) are shown in black (this will also be the case in similar graphs below).[10] The last country in the ranking is Namibia (Gini = 70.7)!
- **Ca** = Caribbean; **Cn**=China; **EA1** = East Asia-1 (Korea and Taiwan); **EA1*** = (Hong Kong and Singapore); **EA2** = East Asia-2; **EE** = Eastern Europe; **EU*** = Mediterranean EU; **EU** = rest of Continental Europe; **In** = India; **Jp** = Japan; **LA** = Latin America; **NA** = North Africa; **No** = Nordic countries; **non-LA LDCs** = non-Latin American developing countries; **OECD-l** = Anglophone OECD (excluding the US, which is shown separately); **Ru** = Russia; **SS-A** = Sub-Saharan Africa (excluding SAf); and **SAf** = middle-income Southern Africa. For the countries in each region, see Appendix 4.

Sources: WB (2010). This will also be the case for the remaining graphs and tables.

Fig. 3.1: (originally figure 1 in Palma)

The Indian Inequality Scenario in Perspective

Much has been commented upon changes in inequality as they appear from one estimate to another over various time segments and across regions in India. In fact a highlight of recent years has been on the changes in inequality measures in the post-liberalization phase in India, including that quoted at the beginning

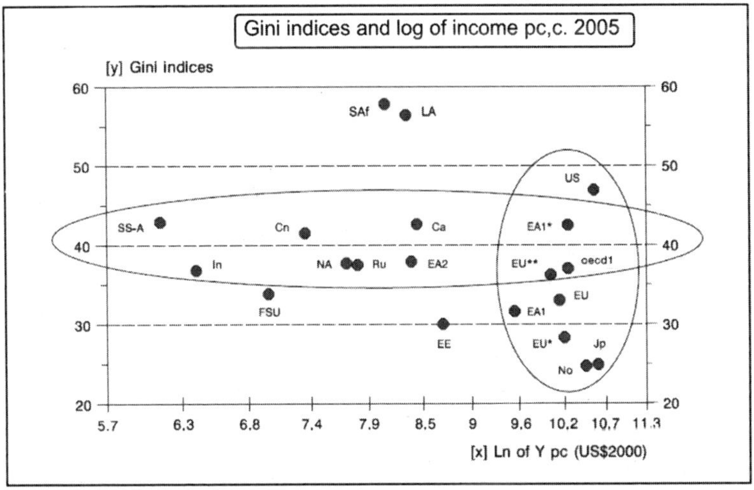

- **[Y]** = vertical axis (Gini indices); and **[X]**=horizontai axis (natural logarithm of income per capita—proxied here by GDP per capita). Regions and countries as Appendix 4. Regional figures are median values. However, in three regions where one country dominates, their data is used instead of the median; this is the case for Brazil in Latin America (Ecuador is the actual median country, Gini = 53.7); South Africa in Southern Africa; and India in South Asia. Also, in the 'Former Soviet Union' the value for Russia and that for the median country (excluding Russia) are highlighted; as it is in the Anglophone OECD vis-a-vis the US. Unless otherwise stated, this will also be the case in figures below. Finally, continental EU is disaggregated between the Mediterranean countries **(EU**)**, Chose with Ginis below 30 (**EU***, Germany and Austria), and the rest **(EU)**.

Fig. 3.2 (originally figure 5 in Palma)

of this paper. There is undoubtedly a lack of tendency towards income convergence in India across regions and population segments, etc. a la Sala-i-Martin (1996) as economic growth has spurted. Commentators have gone on to take various positions on a wide ideological spectrum, which I shall not go into here. A very convenient position is anchored on the inequality-growth relationship attributed to the classic conjectures by Kuznets. As we have seen from a review of surveys above that this position is not quite tenable. Instead, in this paper we look at the changes in inequality from the more secular perspective as originally proposed by Kuznets in the same paper, but not invoke the implied

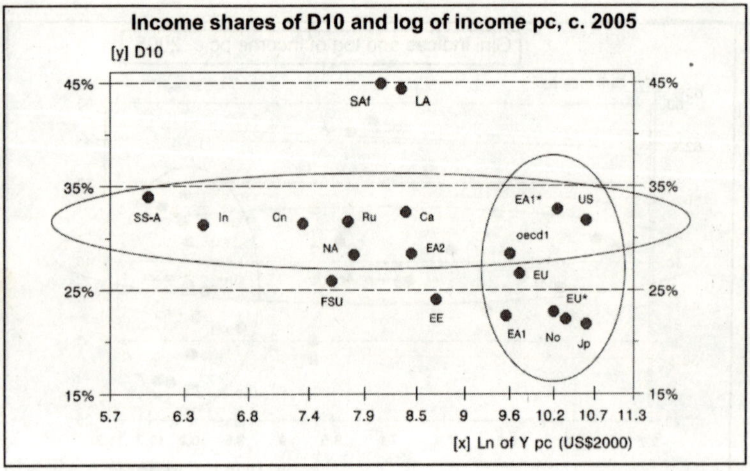

- **[Y]**=vertical axis; and **[X]**=horizontal axis. Regions and countries as Appendix 4, except for **EU***=EU countries with a share below 23 per cent (Austria, Netherlands and Germany); **EU** is the rest of continental Europe. Note that in some regions the median country for D10 is different from that of the Gini in Figure 5.

Fig. 3.3: (originally figure 7 in Palma)

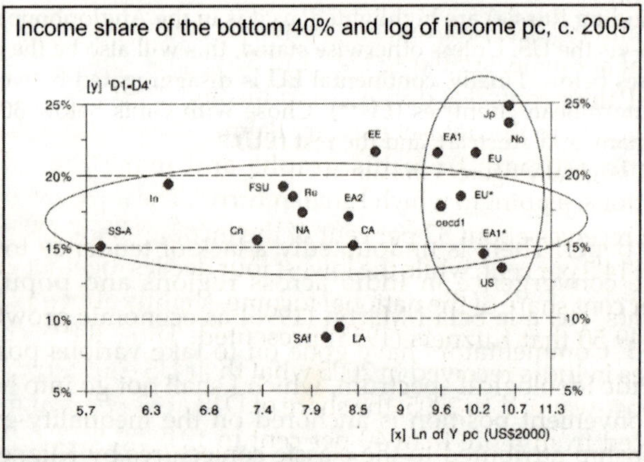

EU* = (Mediterranean EU).

Fig. 3.4: (originally figure 9 in Palma)

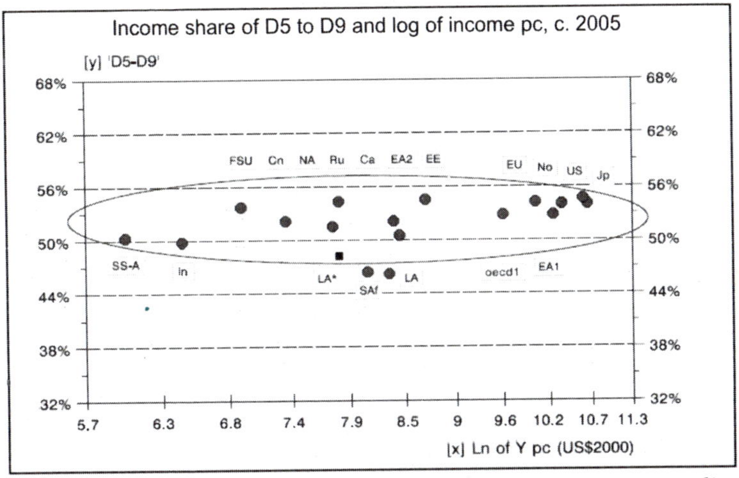

- The black square in the middle of the graph is Latin America's median country (Peru = LA*)

Fig. 3.5: (originally figure 11 in Palma)

shape of the growth-inequality curve, and look at the outcomes of various processes over this long stretch[9]. I shall comment more on the distributional safety net as speculated by Palma and its possible location.

Palma's (2011) estimate of inequality for India shows the Gini ratio at about 36, similar to Dev and Ravi (2007) around the same time. Palma compiles decile group income shares. Since I do not have access to the dataset used by Palma, I have used rough slide rules to estimate from his graphs and make the following assertions, a point to which I shall return[10]. The top decile (D10) in India receives about 32 per cent of the income share. D9 manages about 14.5 per cent, while the lowest four deciles together get about 19 per cent share of the national income, slightly above 17 per cent in 1949-50 that Kuznets (1955) presented. Thus, the bottom four deciles in India received in 2005 what their US counterparts got in the post-war era. In 2005, the share of D10 at 32 per cent may have reduced from more than 40 per cent in 1949-50. In Palma (2011) we find that the D5-D9 groups of middle- and upper-middle income classes c. 2005 claimed roughly 50-51 per cent of the total income in India. That is a robust estimate based on his central hypothesis of the 'homogenous middle' shares around the world.

Worksheet

What follows are some ballpark figures based on interpolations and informed guesses. By interpolation we get the combined share of D5-D8 at 36 per cent, which is similar to the total share of D7-D9 (upper middle groups) estimated in Palma. Thus D5+D6 together get the same as D9, i.e. a share of about 14.5 per cent of the total. Hence D7+D8 together claim about 21 per cent share. From the D10/D1 ratio of 8.6 and D10/D2 ratio of 7.0 and D9/D2 ratio of 3.2, all quoted from Palma, we surmise that D1 and D2 get roughly 3.7 per cent and 4.5 per cent of the total income. Thus D1+D2 in India c. 2005 together had a share of 8.2 per cent, the same as in Kuznets (1955) for 1949-50.

Table 3.3: India: Quintile GDP Shares

Decile	*Circa 2005*	*1949-50*
D1-D4	19	17
D5-D6	14.5	11
D7-D8	21	16
D9-D10	46.5	56

Source: Author's calculations.

D9 and D10 together got about 46 per cent in 2005, down about 10 percentage points from their 55-56 per cent share in 1949-50. This large chunk of income (from growth in GDP) thus got distributed among the newly emerged "middle" class that was seen missing in India in 1949-50. This quintile group (D9+D10) now receives roughly the same as their counterparts in the US in the post-war years quoted in Kuznets (1955).

The bottom three quintiles (i.e. the bottom six deciles D1-D6) in India now get (about 34%), roughly what their counterparts got in post-war years quoted by Kuznets (34% in USA and 36% in UK). It follows that the fourth quintile in India gets a share today (21%) what their US counter-group roughly got in post-war years (22%). Hence the D5-D9 "middle groups" managed to up their share from about 42 per cent at independence to about 51 per cent in c. 2005.

Concluding Remarks

Thus, more than half century of growth and distributional changes in India have resulted in the following picture: While the bottom quintile (20%) has just managed to retain its share at about 8 per cent, other 'middles' have improved their lots. As shown earlier, Dev and Ravi (2007) estimate that about 10 per cent of the population are 'very poor', the hard core including India's tribals (mostly primitive tribal groups or PTGs) and other 'chronic poor', and this D1 group command only about 3.7 per cent of total income with D2 about 4.5 per cent. D1 and D2 were entirely below the official 'poverty line' in 2004-05. Palma's results are consistent with Dev and Ravi (2007) that the 'very poor' group has declined in 2004 05, and there is concentration of poverty near the poverty line – as reflected in the narrowing of PG and FGT values presented in Table 3.1.

Combined with a rising per capita income, the share of the top quintile declined by about 10 percentage points with the major drop in share taken by the top decile. The D1-D4 groups together have gained a little extra share, but it is mostly due to gains accruing to the D3+D4 groups. But a distinct 'middle class' comprising D5-D9 has emerged with roughly half the share of total income, up from about 42 per cent at independence. In the context of India it is perhaps more accurate to state that the 'middle class' is D7-D9 with about 36 per cent income share. As a matter of speculation and breaking away from the Palma (2011) mould, I would hazard the guess that the 'middle' in the new Indian context is the fourth quintile, D7+D8 with a population of 20 per cent and income share of about 21 per cent, which just manages its equal share, as seen in Table 3.3.[11] More detailed data with percentile distributions of income that are available now would reveal the cut-off level where the population begins to enjoy more income than its 'fair share'. My guess is that this would be located at the borderline of the 7-8 decile groups. Hence, it would perhaps be even more accurate to say that this burgeoning 'middleclass' (or upper middle) of India comprises D8+D9 plus about a half of D10. Together this group would comprise a quarter of the population commanding over a third of income in our rough estimate.

Putting together the various estimates that emerge from this discussion certain stylized facts emerge for recent decades: During the reforms period rural and urban income dispersions increased. The Gini increased for rural and urban areas in the post-reform period – the rate being higher for urban than for rural areas. However, if we look at the secular cycle, it is not clear whether income distribution has worsened – using decile group and quintile group income or consumption shares. Gini may not capture this process. Lorenz curves may be crossing at least once for the emerging groups.

Poverty has been concentrated in certain pockets of India and in specific social and occupational groups.[12] There has been greater inequality or divergence of income among states. There has also emerged a middle income class (which was non-existent in India in the immediate post-independence years as explicitly noted by Kuznets) with a share between a third and a half of national income as a result of pruning the share of the top decile. The share of the first and second deciles together is unchanged at 8 per cent. However, their average income has increased with GDP growth, resulting in reduced severity and depth of poverty. But the lowest decile of the 'very poor' has remained stuck in poverty over the decades. The democratic process in India has not put a great deal of power to the lowest two deciles (the first quintile) in relative income terms, and the second quintile (D3+D4) has managed a slightly more comfortable station in life. The third and fourth quintiles have gained considerably over the half century, though the third quintile still gets considerably less (14.5%) than its population share; the fourth quintile garnering more than the race to riches. But it would be interesting to look at more disaggregated data, clearly at the borderline of decile groups 7 and 8 and above, to gain an insight into relative spoils of the gains of the India growth story. As noted earlier, it is perhaps the 25 per cent population segment from 8th decile up that constitutes the upper middle class of India. In the context of Palma's observation it is pertinent to note that in India, it is not so much the prime share of the top that determines the bottom (the heterogeneous tails), but the race is between the top and the middle. Hence, we may need to amend his 'homogeneous middle' to describe the Indian dynamics.

Undoubtedly, there is a lot of dynamism in the movements of population segments as one group gains at the expense of another, and this would be true of regions and states in India. What are the sources of this churning in the country, social, political and economic? The character of the national economy has changed considerably—agriculture now accounts for about 16 per cent of the national output, though employment is considerably higher. The rest is industry and services (Kuznets' sector B)—about 24 per cent for industry and 60 per cent in services? Vast changes in human capability and social and political empowerment have also contributed to changed income shares in the race to economic mobility. Secondly, is the most commonly used Gini measure a good metric of inequality in capturing the Indian dynamic, without doubting its power as a summary measure? Third, it is quite likely that the Kuznets curve (in time dimension that he originally conceived) has 'turned' the corner in India but it may be of the perverse kind. These are issues that I shall leave out of the scope of this paper.

Acknowledgments: I am grateful to Amit Kumar Maurya and Priya Rampal, Ph.D scholars at IGIDR, for research assistance.

NOTES

1. Followed by the publication of his paper, Kuznets (1955).
2. This includes the economic historians' search for the upward sloping phase of the Kuznets curve in historical time that did not figure in the economics literature. See e.g., Van Zanden (1995).
3. An excellent account of many issues on poverty, including measurement debates, is contained in Deaton and Kozel (2005).
4. Recall the Keynes-Kalecki marginal propensity to save for an economy with low per capita income.
5. The list is quite impressive but it is enough to see a select few, e.g. Brenner (1991), Deininger and Squire (1998) and the several citations of Fields.
6. See Stiglitz (1996), and also the related literature on endogenous growth models inspired in part by these experiences not cited here.
7. This is the shorter version of the full-length Cambridge Working paper in Economics cited as Palma. References are made interchangeably to both the versions.
8. Note that the 'evidence' on the inverted-U in Ahluwalia (1976a, 1976b) and Ahluwalia *et al.* (1979) were all based on data across countries which Anand and Kanbur (1993a, 1993b) have seriously questioned, as discussed in sections 2 and 3 above. See also Stiglitz (1996) on lessons from East Asia.

9. I am tempted to go into conjectures on various processes at work, but that will distract our attention from the main focus of this paper – to note the changes that have occurred in the last half century and more. The sources of change in inequality in India is an important subject on which research is underway.
10. NSS data are now available which may be used to verify the assertions made here. This is not done in this paper.
11. Palma's 'middle' of course stubbornly defends its share, leaving the top decile's prime share to determine what is left at the bottom. In the Indian case, both these decile groups get their 'fair' shares, howsoever their incomes may be distributed amongst them. In neither case is this claimed over a time period. My quest here is to locate a segment with narrower band than Palma's middle. The purpose is to locate the cutoff level that is discussed in the following sentence.
12. This has been documented for some time, see e.g., Radhakrishna and Ray (2004-05, 2005).

REFERENCES

Ahluwalia, Montek S. (1976a). 'Income Distribution and Development: Some Stylized Facts', *American Economic Review*, Papers and Proceedings, 66 (2): 128-35.

Ahluwalia, Montek S. (1976b). 'Inequality, Poverty and Development', *Journal of Development Economics*, 3: 307-42.

Ahluwalia, Montek S., N.G. Carter and Hollis B. Chenery (1979). 'Growth and Poverty in Developing Countries', *Journal of Development Economics*, 6: 299-341.

Anand, Sudhir and S.M.R. Kanbur (1993a). 'The Kuznets Process and the Inequality-development Relationship', *Journal of Development Economics*, 40: 25-52.

Anand, Sudhir and S.M.R. Kanbur (1993b). 'Inequality and Development: A Critique', *Journal of Development Economics*, 41: 19-43.

Brenner, Y.S., Hartmut Kaelble and Mark Thomas (1991). *Income Distribution in Historical Perspective*. Cambridge: Cambridge University Press.

Deaton, A.S. and V. Kozel (2005). *The Great Indian Poverty Debate*. Macmillan.

Dev, S.M. and C. Ravi (2007). 'Poverty and Inequality for All India and Major States: 1983 to 2004-05'. Hyderabad: *Centre for Economic and Social Studies*.

Deininger, K. and L. Squire (1998). 'New Ways of Looking at Old Issues: Inequality and Growth'. *Journal of Development Economics*, 57 (2): 259-287.

Fields, Gary S. (1979). 'A Welfare Economic Approach to Growth and Distribution in the dual Economy', *Quarterly Journal of Economics,* XCIII: 325-53.

Fields, Gary S. (1980). *Poverty, Inequality, and Development.* Cambridge: Cambridge University Press.

Fields, Gary S. (2001). *Distribution and Development, A New Look at the Developing World.* Russel Sage Foundation: New York, and The MIT Press, Cambridge, Massachusetts, and London.

Kuznets, Simon (1955). 'Economic Growth and Income Inequality'. *American Economic Review,* 45 (March): 1–28.

Palma, J.G. (Undated). 'Homogeneous Middles vs. Heterogeneous Tails, and the end of the 'Inverted-U': the Share of the Rich is What it's all about', *Cambridge Working Papers in Economics (CWPE)* 1111, (Available at http://www.econ.cam.ac.uk/dae/repec/cam/pdf/cwpe1111.pdf).

Palma, J.G. (2011). 'Homogeneous Middles vs. Heterogeneous Tails, and the end of the 'Inverted-U': It's all about the Share of the Rich', *Development and Change,* 42: 87–153.

Pesaran, M.H. (1974). 'On the General Problem of Model Selection', *Review of Economic Studies,* 41: 153-71.

Pesaran, M.H. and A.S. Deaton (1978). 'Testing Non-nested Non-linear Regression Models', *Econometrica,* 46: 677-94.

Radhakrishna, R. and Shovan Ray (2004-05). 'Poverty in India: Dimensions and Character', chapter 3 in Parikh, Kirit and R. Radhakrishna (eds): *India Development Report 2004-05.* New Delhi: Oxford University Press.

Radhakrishna, R. and Shovan Ray (2005). *Handbook of Poverty in India: Perspectives, Policies, and Programmes.* New Delhi: Oxford University Press.

Robinson, S. (1976). 'A Note on the U-Hypothesis relating Income Inequality and Economic Development', *American Economic Review,* 66(3): 437-40.

Sala-i-Martin, X.X. (1996). 'The Classical Approach to Convergence Analysis', *The Economic Journal,* 106 (July): 1019-36

Sen, Amartya (1997). *On Economic Inequality,* (with Annex by James Foster and Amartya Sen). Oxford: Oxford University Press.

Stiglitz, Joseph E. (1996). 'Some Lessons from the East Asian Miracle', *The World Bank Research Observer,* 11(2): 151–177.

Van Zanden, J.L. (1995). 'Tracing the Beginning of the Kuznets Curve: Western Europe during the Early Modern Period', *The Economic History Review,* 48(4): 643–664.

4
Political Implications of Inequality in Post-Reform India

Prakash Sarangi

'Inequality' is as much a political vocabulary as economic. Volumes have been written by economists on the strategies for reducing poverty and inequality or whether benefits of economic reform have percolated downwards. We will not join this debate. There- seems to be a broad consensus, however, that during the first two decades of economic reform the level of poverty has declined marginally; but inequality has increased. Everyone has benefited somewhat, though the rich and middle class has gained more than others. This paper is an attempt to understand the political implications of this growing inequality. Our analysis will be at two levels: micro-level – unequal access to resources; and at a macro level – regional inequalities leading to tensions in India's federal polity.

Unequal Access to Resources

What worries a student of political science is that about one-third of Indian population is below poverty line, most of them unemployed or underemployed. This number is good enough to make or break a government. It is the good luck of the political elite that the 'poor' in India is not a socially homogeneous category. Its identity has got enmeshed in various other segments based on caste, religion, region or ethnicity.

Let us look at some facts. There seems to be a decline in the headcount of those below poverty line after the commencement of economic reforms. Planning Commission data indicate that the percentage of population below poverty line declined from 45.3 per cent (1993-94) to 37.2 per cent (2004-05). The World Bank estimates this decline to be from 54 per cent (1990) to 42 per cent (2005).

Poverty Estimates

% Below Poverty Line, World Bank ($1.25 a day)	54% (1990)	42% (2005)
% Below Poverty Line, Planning Commission (Rs. 32 a day)	45.3% (1993-94)	37.2% (2004-05)
UN Human Development Index	0.308 (1991)	0.519 (2010)
GDP per person employed ($ 1990 PPP), WB	3531 (1990)	7445 (2009)
Infant Mortality Rate (per 1000 child births), WB	81 (1990)	50 (2009)
% of population undernourished (HDR)	24% (1990)	22% (2006)
Unemployment Rate	7.3% (1991)	10.8% (2010)

'Income-poverty' may not tell us the stoiy of quality of life led by people. Nor can it assess the deprivations suffered by people. For instance, a high income cannot ensure sanitation, safe drinking water or prevention of communicable diseases. Data available in UN Human Development Index and Deprivation Index partly fills the gap. India's position in the Human Development Index has improved from 0.308 (1991) to 0.519 (2010). Percentage of population undernourished has declined from 24 per cent (1990) to 22 per cent (2006). The World Bank data suggest that infant mortality rate (per 1000 child births) has declined from 81 (1990) to 50 (2009).

However, these impressive data on reduction of poverty are not corroborated by other indicators. Normally, reduction of poverty is associated with reduction in unemployment. The rate of unemployment has increased from 7.3 per cent (1991) to 10.8

per cent (2010). The large gap between poverty (about 35%) and unemployment (about 10%) does not tell the full story of economic life. Moreover, there is a high incidence of disguised unemployment: employment in low income activities and in extremely low productivity. The bulk of unemployment is in the rural sector, most of them being landless wage labourers. In 1980, Agriculture contributed 38 per cent to GDP; in 2007, it was only 18 per cent, which is on the expected lines. But still, in 2007, 55 per cent were employed in Agriculture. India has had a jobless growth during the last two decades: only 1.36 per cent growth in jobs in the urban areas and negative (-0.38%) in rural areas. The conventional expectation regarding the transition from agriculture to industry has not happened during the two decades of economic reform.

Even if we accept that the income of the poor has gone up during the last two decades, it is not reflected in their lifestyle. It has been calculated by an economist that an average poor family has 100 kilograms of less food in 2007 compared to 1997 (Sainath, 2009). More farmers are committing suicides due to debt: on an average of 15 per hour. Agrarian distress has increased manifold. While pointing out that in the 1990s the agricultural elites have moved towards a capitalist model of agriculture, Vakulabharanam and Motiram point out that small-holders who constitute a vast majority in the agrarian population "...has now been dragged into the green revolution model that is slowing down even as the state unevenly tampers with its support structures. They come increasingly into the orbit of informal credit markets that further exacerbate their distress" (Vakulabharanam and Motiram, 2011).

The condition of the urban poor does not present a rosy picture either. "[W]hile [the] slum dwellers and young workers express a degree of satisfaction that they are better off as a result of harder work in the present, they point to persistent inequality, insecurity and disparity, and particularly the paucity of present opportunities and the lack of future prospects for themselves, in contrast to the plethora of obvious channels of middle-class upward mobility in India's liberalized economy" (Nandini Gooptu, 2011). In the midst of highly fluid and insecure work, the poor have become 'reluctant entrepreneurs' by informal self-employment, which is due to distress and not because of incentives offered by a new urban economic milieu. They tend to struggle at the lowest rungs of urban economy.

Possible impact of economic reform on inequality may go beyond socio-economic differences. There has been a rise in the rural-urban divide. In the 1990s average per capita consumption expenditure in rural areas rose by 8.7 per cent, whereas it rose by 16.6 per cent in urban areas. Part of an explanation of this trend is the movement of workers from farm to non-farm activities and, therefore, migration from rural to urban areas. There is also an increased migration from the backward states to the urban areas of the forward states in search of lucrative assignments. This has been politically sensitive trend, since parties are known to lose elections if only urban India was shining. Every government takes extra care to ensure that rural areas are looked after well. This has led to another divide: relatively more public funds go to rural areas than to urban areas.

Economic reform has also resulted in other structural inequalities. There has been a decline of certain occupations and rise in others. For instance, sectors like power loom, edible oil, growing of cotton, traditional fishing have declined. But there has been an IT boom. Telecommunication, transport and energy sectors have grown rapidly. Cash crops, floriculture and horticulture have expanded. With the changing occupational patterns, certain types of workers have experienced hidden hardships: seasonal labour migration leading to disruption of family life, spread of HIV-AIDS, irregular school attendance by the children of the migrant labourers, IT workers' work in night shifts and consequent health issues, etc. Also, there is a trend towards informalization of labour market and it has impact on longer working hours, higher insecurity and poorer working conditions. There is also a strong correlation between the highly developed states and gender inequality. There is decline in female-male ratio among the children in the developed states, thanks to easy affordability of neo-natal tests.

In brief, a socio-economic churning has taken place creating new inequalities. It is not enough to say that the rich have become richer and the poor have become poorer. Access to resources has become uneven and unequal. There are new gainers and new losers as a consequence of economic reforms. There has been the emergence of a deprivation syndrome. Now the politics centres around the extent of 'deprivation'. For example, Adivasis are deprived of access to forests, displaced persons are deprived of their land, urban poor is deprived of clean drinking water, rural children are deprived of access to education, women are deprived of safety in the work place, etc. The list could be very long. The crux of the matter is that different segments of population organizing themselves around these deprivations. It is true that there have been legislations to address some of these issues, e.g. NREGA, RTE, RTI, Food Security Bill etc. However, most of the discussions on these measures take note of the 'deprivations' suffered by specific segments. If any segment is left out, it feels deprived. These have become electorally salient issues.

This development has transformed India's political culture. First is the issue of *representation.* There has been an upsurge in participation, especially by the marginalized groups. Political dissents, which were earlier resolved by negotiations, are displayed on the streets. Each deprived segment looks for a space in the political market. These segments clearly understand that the task of politics is to bargain, fight and extract benefits as a right. Unlike the pre-reform period, they would not surrender their votes to a vote bank. Therefore, their political identity is not blindly attached to a political party in search of welfare benefits. Political market today is as competitive as an economic market. A segment's numerical strength and perceived deprivations enhance its bargaining potential. It can shift to any party or coalition based on a calculus of political benefits and costs. Ideological commitments are *passé.* Such realignments are taking place not only at the level of local politics, but also at the national level, where State and regional leaders bargain without any hesitation.

Structure of representation has become fragmented. Deprivations are inherently local and, therefore, raise local voices. No matter where they are located, deprivations make them aware of their own cultural roots. They may be Odia labourers in Surat or Bihari workers in Mumbai or Bangalore's IT workers from North East. These roots are often found at the local level rather than at the national level. People have got sensitized to their own 'imagined world'. Preservation of one's ethnic culture–whether of language, religion or caste – has become a part of political agenda everywhere. Easy dissemination of information has helped them to learn from the world-wide trend of revival of ethnic movements. Further, global communication and global finance has allowed the State and the local authorities to have trans-border contacts. The battle for and against economic reforms have, therefore, been fought at the State and local levels rather than at the national level. Economic reform itself has a regional bias. Political issues and their stakeholders in States with trans-border contacts are different from those which have not been greatly affected by economic reform. Therefore, the policy debates, say in Andhra Pradesh, are different from those in Bihar. The diffused structures of participation and dissent might have low salience in weakening the Indian nation-state. But one can easily discern a pattern: the deprived segments are not keeping quiet on the plea of 'national interest' and are not going to wait till the next elections to resolve the issues.

The second issue is that of *legitimacy*. A democratic government is supposed to govern with the consent of the governed. If the political community is supposed to provide such consent, obtaining it from the Indian political community in the period of economic reform has become problematic, since growing inequality has eroded the autonomy and equality of citizens. There are two issues here: whether the political community is equipped to give its consent and what is an appropriate structure of expressing its consent.

It is easy to secure consent when a political community is located in one territory. Affluence emerging out of economic reforms has created a new division among the citizens. Indians are not only migrating abroad in greater numbers; greater mobility has enabled them to keep in touch with home. Many of them are investing in India and participating in policy debates as well. After all, their remittances help their families to raise their economic status. They are as much participants in the Indian economy as their families are. The same logic is applicable not only to the PIOs, but also to business firms or NGOs investing in India.

Policies in India may be interconnected with policies elsewhere in the world or among different regions within the country. For example, a policy on floriculture is affected by the taste of flowers in Europe. Consent from Indian floriculturists has little relevance for the success of this policy. Consent of the Indian citizens does not matter if the government has committed itself to a specific position because of its agreement with the World Bank or WTO. In fact, the policy of economic reform was initiated in 1991 without consulting Indian voters directly as an election plank or indirectly through the elected representatives.

The consent in a representative democracy is obtained through periodic elections, the winning party's policies getting approval for a period of five years. However, there are many political actors today who are not citizens with a right to vote, e.g. PIOs, international civil society groups, MNCs, etc. Consent from these groups becomes essential for success of many policies. Their consent is obtained indirectly through consultative groups, discussions or even through opinions obtained by the internet. Many international groups are known to lobby for against a policy position in different countries. Expression of dissent through grass-roots movements by deprived groups is often spearheaded by civil society groups who may not have any direct stake in a specific policy. However, if a government succumbs to the pressures from these groups and formulates a policy, what about the citizens who elect that government? This brings us to the next question on *responsiveness*.

The traditional democratic theory suggests that an elected government responds to the needs of its citizens, who have a voice in its reelection. These voices are now dispersed. Political issues as well as governance structures today are sufficiently diffused to be within the capacity of any single government to resolve. For example, if a policy on health-care has to be successful, all levels of government – national, state and local – have to cooperate. Public sector has to join hands with the private sector. Or, inter-group inequalities have to be mediated through civil society groups. A government is helpless when its monetary policy fails because of international compulsions. A message in the social media at a place far away from India could break the trust between government and the people. The capacity of the government to address the issues arising out of inequality seems to have been compromised. The eluding policy consensus is due to the Indian state's sharing of authority at various levels. 'Inclusive growth' has, therefore, remained only a slogan.

Charles Tilly has successfully argued that "this new context threatens the interests of the workers and marginalized groups" (Tilly, 1947). Democratic rights are embedded with sovereign states. Weakening of state sovereignty undermines its capacity to guarantee these rights. The regulatory potential of a state is challenged by the interconnectedness of political, economic and cultural environments. The welfare activities, which were primarily within the domain of the nation-state, are now shared with civil society groups, many with international linkages and with no democratic accountability.

Regional Inequality

There have been many studies analyzing the rising level of regional inequality in the post-reform India (Kurian, 2000; Singh *et al.*, 2003; Shetty, 2003; Bhattacharya and Saktivel, 2004). There is a broad agreement that inequality among States has increased. "While advanced Industrial States tended to leapfrog in the reform years, other states have lagged behind.... Unfortunately, backward States with a higher population growth are not able to attract investment – both public and private – due to a variety of reasons, like poor income and infrastructure and probably also poor governance" (Bhattacharya and Saktivel, *ibid.*). States in the South and in the West have had much rapid rate of development than those in the North and in the East. Moreover, census figures indicate that population growth in the latter has been higher, thus contributing to further inequality.

There has been a great deal of disparity in economic investments. In the 1990s, out of all the investment proposals received, forward States accounted for about two-thirds of the resources, while the backward States accounted for only about 28 per cent. 36.7 per cent of the proposals of investment were meant only for Maharashtra and Gujarat, which is more than that of all the backward states combined (Kurian, *ibid.*). 75 per cent of the foreign direct investment went to only five states in the 1990s. 63 per cent of the disbursements of the all India financial institutions as well as 65 per cent of bank credits went to the developed states. Maharashtra alone got one-fifth of the IFFI assistance. The bank credit share of Tamil Nadu exceeds all the credits to poorer States put together (Bagchi and Kurian, 2005). In general, forward States are better administered and have better infrastructure. The State leadership has successfully marketed the states in India and abroad. Therefore, forward States are able to attract the private sector to invest in their States.

Certain areas and groups have been negatively affected by the economic reforms. These are primarily tribal and forest areas. Private sector has been eager to exploit these areas to acquiring raw materials without corresponding attention to develop these areas. There is a clear trend towards environmental degradation. Uneven development of these areas has led to Maoist violence. The only silver lining in regional inequality is that the rich States could have a demonstration effect on the less developed ones and would strive to be achievers instead of going to New Delhi all the time with a begging bowl.

Federal Market Economy

The regional inequalities have fundamentally altered India's federal structure. The Rudolphs associate the economic reforms in India with the emergence of a federal market economy. They write, "The dawn of liberalization in the early 1990s saw the gradual emergence of a federal market economy, with decision-making powers shared between the Centre and States. A measure of economic sovereignty and decentralization has now placed the onus on state chief ministers to effect economic growth in their respective states. Not only do they need to negotiate a path that avoids undue capitulation to populist pressures; to invite private investment, they must work in consonance with the centre's new role as a regulator and fiscal disciplinarian and deal with the hard budget constraints demanded by the faceless, international credit-rating agencies." The Chief Ministers have become new entrepreneurs trying to attract domestic and foreign investments. Along with decentralization of the market, economic sovereignty is shared between the States and the Centre for economic and financial decision-making.

Each State now plays the role of a viable economic unit. The Centre's contribution to the States' capital formation has declined. By coincidence, during the same time, the regionalization of politics, allowed the States to have their own economic agenda. These economic aspirations could not always be fulfilled by declining public funding. This has provided space to the private investments to contribute to a State's growth. Each State tries to compete with others to attract private investment by bold policy initiatives, imaginative leadership and good governance. Those States which have been able to attract private investments have experienced a higher growth rate than others. In order to compete in this economic race, successful States have given concessions and incentives to business houses as well as provided good work culture with skilled labour force; good infrastructure, especially power, transport and communication; and good governance.

The States have become less dependent on the Centre for formulation and execution of their economic policies. However, "Even as the Centre becomes less able to intervene through its control of public investments, permits, and licences, it assumes a new role as a regulator concerned with market imperfections and State fiscal discipline. As the Centre's role as an interventionist State has faded, its role as regulatory state has grown. The Centre has attempted to impose hard budget constraints on the states. So too have market-oriented international and domestic credit rating agencies." The new-found economic sovereignty by the States is further curtailed by the fiscal discipline imposed by international lenders such as the World Bank, Asian Development Bank, etc.

Nature of Competition Among States

Aseema Sinha suggests that during the pre-reform era there was cooperation among the States and domination by the Centre. There was vertical competition: the States competed with each other for centrally determined resources. The post-reform era is characterized by a horizontal competition: States compete with each other more directly and for resources from a wide variety of actors. Convergence of policy discourses around reform, irrespective of previous ideological differences among parties, generated competition among States. In the race to woo investors, States tried their best to project a good image by highlighting their impressive growth rates or fine credit ratings. They used the media to advertise their industrial policies and achievements. They openly compared themselves to their competitor States. Aggressive marketing and image building became order of the day. Such competition stretched beyond the borders as well. States started to negotiate with foreign governments, multinational corporations and outside investors. "The regional states play an increasing role in bargaining with international actors to attract foreign direct investment and pursue global integration. Direct attraction of foreign investment by states has contributed to *de facto* authority to approve foreign investment projects, establish tax rates for foreign investment firms, and establish rules of the game. Thus state level actors are shaping foreign economic relations." However, while States compete with each other for their share of the market, they all "continue to rely on state-led strategies of reform; there is no 'Washington Consensus' or 'neoliberal' route to reform in India." Each State guided and created its own strategy of reform. Each one of them relied on its inherited past strategies as well as the political and economic resources found in the State. The Centre and States have realized their changing role in economic development. Policy diffusion has helped each unit to assess its own pace of reforms as well as the transformed incentives to the rulers. "India's economic reforms reordered erstwhile Centre-State relations, displacing both power and responsibilities to the regional states. However, institutions of the licence-quota raj–local institutional capacities and pre-existing behaviour patterns–shaped these strategies in diverse ways: change and continuity coexist in post-transition India."

Lawrence Saez argues that the simultaneous impact of two transformations–political party realignment and economic liberalization–has altered the traditional structure of federal relations in India. "Although the diminished significance of the Central Government for a state's development of economic plans could encourage greater opportunities for grassroots local development and increased inter-jurisdictional cooperation, the impact of massive foreign investment inflows will instead push the debates about federalism in a different direction. This incrementally altered trajectory is from inter-governmental cooperation towards inter-jurisdictional competition" (Saez, 2002). He defines inter-jurisdictional competition as 'the rivalrious and contentious relationship for resources among similar tiers of government or among localities within a region.' This competition is reflected in each geographical area—even a city—trying to attract foreign direct investment (FDI), investment by NRIs or providing incentives for industrialization. Economic liberalization has disproportionately benefited middle-income and high-income States, creating a clear divide between what Saez calls as foreign investment magnets and foreign investment laggards. The States which have had a high degree of openness within their jurisdictions have experienced higher rates of growth. At the same time the FDI laggards have tried to compete and improve their economic performance. The influx of foreign investment inflows has gradually diminished the importance of Central Government as a principal source of revenues for some States. The Centre has simultaneously lost its dominant role in cementing cooperation between different units of government. There is a need to create new institutions to manage inter-jurisdictional competition, taking into account the greater importance of powerful States, rather than treating them as equals as per the constitutional arrangements. There is a potential danger, however, that such financial disparities could create new forms of domestic unrest. These shifts in political and socio-economic structure have already generated conflicts based on caste, religion, language or ethnicity.

Conclusion

The goal of formulating economic policies is to provide a 'good life' to the citizens. It is expected that a radical reform in policies would make their lives somewhat better than before. There are several other incidental consequences: higher rate of growth, increasing competition among the firms, integration in the world market, deregulation of industries and above all greater inequality. Any or all of these may not directly contribute to the citizens' (un)happiness. A mere increase in income may not be the sole indicator of the success of a policy. There could be several imponderables. The real benefits are sometimes distorted by poor governance. Some citizens may not have liked when income trickles down to a specific segment of the population.

In a democracy the expectations of people are not confined to only economic benefit. In fact, economic policies are manifestations of a ruling party's strategy to maintain a good equation with the people. Along with the bold economic reforms, governments have experimented with several new policies to bring the benefits of reforms directly to the people or at least to offset the negative aspects of reforms. Some of these examples are: helping to market agricultural products abroad, e-choupal, NREGS, Right to Education, Right to Information, etc. All these efforts are important steps to gain acceptability of reforms among all sections of society irrespective of their political affiliation. The questions, therefore, are: Can the economic reforms reduce the gap between 'India' and 'Bharat'? Can these policies be converted to an ideology that is accepted to all? Given the contextual constraints in India, it is certain that miracles are unlikely to happen. But these roadblocks would add strength to the long-term durability of reform. India may not be able to take the speed of a tiger; but her pace will be the majestic speed of an elephant, slow and steady.

REFERENCES

Bagchi, Amaresh and Kurian, John (2005). "Regional Inequalities in India: Pre- and Post-Reform Trends and Challenges for Policy" in Jos Mooij (ed.), *Politics of Economic Reform in India*. New Delhi: Sage Publications, p. 338.

Bhattacharya, B. B. and Saktivel, S. (2004). 'Regional Growth and Disparity in India: Comparison of Pre- and Post-Reform Decades', *Economic and Political Weekly*, March 6.

Gooptu, Nandini (2011). 'Economic Liberalization, Urban Politics and the Poor' in Sanjay Ruparelia, *et al.*, (eds), *Understanding India's New Political Economy*. London: Routledge, p. 45.

Kurian, N.J. (2000). 'Widening Regional Disparities in India', *Economic and Political Weekly*, February 12.

Saez, Lawrence (2002). *Federalism Without A Centre: The Impact of Political and Economic Reform on India's Federal System*. New Delhi: Sage, pp. 149-50.

Sainath, P. (2009). 'Largest Wave of Suicides in History', *Counterpunch*, February 12.

Shetty, S.L. (2003). 'Growth of SDP and Structural Changes in the State Economies', *Economic and Political Weekly*, December 6.

Singh, Nirvikar; Bhandari, Lavesh; Chen, Aoyu and Khare, Aarti (2003). 'Regional Inequality in India: A Fresh Look', *Economic and Political Weekly*, March 15.

Tilly, Charles (1947). 'Globalization Threatens Labor's Rights', *International Labor and Working Class History*, pp. 1-23.

Vakulabharanam, V. and Motiram, S. (2011). 'Political Economy of Agrarian Distress in India since the 1990s' in Sanjay Ruparelia, *et al.*, (eds), *Understanding India's New Political Economy*. London: Routledge, p. 123.

5

Inequality-Growth Link in the Post-Reform Indian States

Role of Human Capital

Santanu Ray Chaudhuri

Disparities in living standard create a contrast in the growth episodes by generating an abyss between well-off and worse-off – across geographical sub-boundaries and across individuals even within the same political-geographic space. This trepidation has made the social planners much sceptical about the *secluded* growth story in any economy and, therefore, egalitarianism in economic expansion has become hallmark for long. The post-liberalisation Indian growth panorama has shown a similar kind of advances with a lot of inegalitarian components. The present study takes the issue to explore the growth-inequality link in the Indian states in the post-liberalization era through the functional role of human capital.

It might be naive in contemplation if we consider the fact that the interaction between growth and inequality is unidirectional; rather it seems to be bi-directional and mutual in character. Evolution in one would have an underlying effect on the other in an accumulative fashion rather than in a unilateral causality. Thus the growth story of the post-ninety period may have been affected by the inequality trends of the earlier period, while the recent trends in inequality may have contained influences from the growth process of the initial years. Elucidating these issues requires exploring the linkage between growth and inequality–whether one contradicts the other or consolidates it in the long run perspective. These interlinkages and convoluted interactions are sought to be explored in this study.

The present study has taken Indian states within a gross contour of economic and political homogeneity, although heterogeneity perspective is present in the sense that each state has its own democratic government with their own policy agenda. The heterogeneity assumption in the growth models would be logical, particularly when the human capital plays an effective role on distribution. The varying proceeds on education can generate enticement for human capital accumulation. Thus the present research has taken the human capital variables to scrutinize the strait of the inequality-growth link in the Indian states.

Most of the present day mainstream economists have the view that the relationship between growth and income inequality is opposite and income inequality is detrimental to long run economic growth. To explore the link at cross-country level, a vast set of recent works[1] focuses on how imperfect capital market, redistribution policy and other socio-political causes are the reasons behind negative relation between income inequality and growth. Indeed, the works that provide the early feedback of the present study are of Persson and Tabellini (1994) and Alesina and Rodrik (1996).

With Persson and Tabellini (1994), other economists like Alesina and Rodrik (1996), Bénabou (1996a) and Perotti (1996) estimated the relation in cross-country models and obtained negative relation between inequality and growth. But Deininger and Squire (1996) with the two-way link between growth and inequality in land distribution and Robert Barro (1999) by using panel data and country specific fixed effects obtained positive correlation. Barro argued for non-linear relation in that inequality is good for rich economies and bad for low income countries. The study by Ravallion (1998) for China during 1985-1990 showed that the same relation is negative. Forbes (1997) and Li and Zou (1998) have used panel data with country specific fixed effects and obtained a positive relationship.

All the above theoretical approaches largely explain how inequality affects growth. The other side of the analysis is concerned with the impact of growth on income distribution. In his seminal paper Kuznets (1955) argued that inequality would increase at the early stages of growth and would start falling with higher growth rate such that the relationship would be figured like an inverted U-shape. Many economists like Ahluwalia (1976a, 1976b), Williamson (1985), Lindert (1986), Oshima (1970), Robinson (1976), Aghion and Bolton (1997) have argued in favour of Kuznets hypothesis. But the views favouring Kuznets hypothesis have been challenged through different empirical evidences by Anand and Kanbur (1993), Deininger and Squire (1998), Deininger and Olinto (2000), and many others.

In the context of growth-inequality debate, outlay in human capital is vital to the scheme of growth. Augmentation of human capital is linked with the accumulation of knowledge that may dissuade diminishing returns and enhance income growth. Thus government policies to improve these factors would have impacts on the link by improving productivity growth *a la* Romer (1990). Nelson and Phelps (1966) argued that human capital enhancement elevates the capacity of a nation to espouse and implement new knowledge and its propagation. In their studies, Becker (1962, 1964), Uzawa (1965), Rosen (1976) and Schultz (1961) passionately argued about the importance of human capital in economic advancement. Denison (1967) substantiated in favour of labour augmentation by providing education in the context of economic dynamics. Dahan and Tsiddon (1998) studied the perspective through the interactions among fertility, education and income distribution, where in early stages of development both the fertility and inequality increase simultaneously, but with advancement, fertility declines together with increasing investment in human capital and, in effect, inequality would decrease.

Keeping in consideration all the above discussed views, it can be concluded that there are divergent views regarding the relation between inequality and growth, especially on the impact of inequality on growth. For India, most of the literatures concerning the aspect have shown empirically that inequality is of a matter of apprehension, but the link has not been tested expansively for the states in India, especially over a longish time span. From the policy perspective, it is also important to know whether the economy would benefit from a redistributive policy regime or whether inequality would lead to higher income growth which would in turn percolate and reduce inequality. The present study, therefore, aims to fill this gap in existing literature.

In the set up of the paper, Section 2 examines Pre-Reform Backdrop and Economic Reforms in India and Section 3 describes Model framework. Section 4 takes up Regional Growth and Disparity with various subsections including Regression Outcomes. Economic Analysis is taken up in Section 5 and Section 6 sums up the Findings and Conclusions.

Pre-Reform Backdrop and Economic Reforms in India

State patronized industrialization in the framework of highly centralized resource allocation and politically motivated idea of protectionism in the name of *self-reliance* allowed bureaucratic interference that eventually led to economic stagnation during 1970s. The resultant overburden of central borrowing and profligacy of development expenditure resulted in severe budget deficit and consequent balance-of-payments crisis. The whole panorama of fiscal extravagance shoved the government into a serious peril that ultimately played a pivotal role to set off several round of reforms since 1991. The ensuing spurt in growth rate in the following years that put the economy in another cross road of rude reality — that of escalating disparities among and within states.

Thus the history 'awakening giant' in her testimony of economic development is not so impressive for some inherently persuaded constraints which raise impediments in encouraging further growth. The more market-led, private fund endowed strategy, no doubt, has made the economy relatively more competitive in the global arena that led towards an enthusiastic advance in growth rate Economic reforms have generated an endeavour for higher mobility of commodities and factors within and between the states such that efficient allocation and access of both foreign capital and technology could be achieved by the states. But differential in the capabilities and uneven backups and imbalances in the human capital augmentation of the regional governments would heighten inequalities among and within the sub-national boundaries.

Thus the two apparent extremes of economic events are predominantly evident in the post-reform era and largely points out a specific fact that the economic affluence is highly restricted with high distributive injustice.

Works on growth in India have been concentrated mostly in the post-1990 period. Even in the handful of studies researchers have explored mostly the impact of growth on poverty and almost never projected the impact of initial inequality on future growth. In respect of inequality and poverty in India and among states, Deaton and Dreze (2002) have presented a set of poverty and inequality estimates for the periods of 1987-88, 1993-94 and 1999-2000. According to them, poverty estimates have been declined in 1990s, following earlier trends, while at the same time the intra- and inter-regional disparities have increased, especially within urban areas. The study of Banerjee and Piketty (2003) have shown the progress of top incomes and wages in India from 1956 to 2000 using tax returns data and, to them, income inequality as measured by the actual income share of the rich has followed a U-shaped pattern in 1956-2000 period. The Study of Sen and Himanshu (2004) has shown that inequality has increased in India in the post-reform period. They showed that whereas the level of consumption of the top 20 per cent of the rural population went up remarkably during the 1990s, the bottom 80 per cent of the rural population shown the reverse.

Framework

To motivate the empirical analysis the study examines several possible straits linking growth on inequality (measured in terms of Gini coefficient), i.e. the impact of inequality on growth of per capita net state domestic product in both short run and long run through the passage of human capital variables. The whole methodology of study is comprised two basic frameworks. One is set of cross-section models and another is set of pooled and panel fixed effect models with five-year, ten-year and twenty-year growth episodes to explore the link.

For those specific analyses, the study has taken two broadly parallel datasets on income and inequality for a long time period, disaggregated by rural/urban locations for the constituent states in India. The chief sources of the income data at the state level are the Net State Domestic Product which are compiled and annually published by the Central Statistical Office (CSO) under Ministry of Planning and Programme Implementation, Government of India. The study has used up-to-date, comprehensive and comparable dataset published by CSO for the time period 1980-2005.

Additionally, the intra-state living standard disparities have been measured with the help of monthly per capita consumption expenditure (MPCE) data (Large Sample), published by the National Sample Survey Office (NSSO) under Ministry of Planning and Programme Implementation, Government of India. Apart from that the yearly state-wise primary enrolment ratio and per capita education expenditure in the states and at all-India level have been taken from the various issues of supplements from the Data on Education, Education in India, Ministry of Education, Government of India.

The basic frameworks for impacts on income growth of inequality are as follows:

Model 1: $\text{Pcnsdp}_t = \text{Constant} + \alpha_{1t}\ \text{MPCEGINI}_{t,k} + e_t$
Model 2: $\text{Pcnsdp}_t = \text{Constant} + \alpha_{1t}\ \text{MPCEGINI}_{t-1,\ k} + e_t$
Model 3: $\text{Gr\_pcnsdp}_{(t,\ t-1)} = \text{Constant} + \alpha_{1t}\ \text{MPCEGINI}_{t-1,\ k} + e_t$
Model 4: $\text{Gr\_pcnsdp}_{(t,\ t-1)} = \text{Constant} + \alpha_{1t}\ \text{MPCEGINI}_{k,t} + \alpha_{2t}\ \text{lit}_{t-1,k} + \alpha_{3t}\ \text{Prim\_enrl}_{t-1} + \alpha_{4t}\ \text{Pcedu\_exp}_{t-1} + e_t$

Mankiw *et al.* (1992) employ cross-section data to endow with a scheme to incorporate the consequences of regional dynamics on the economic growth. The present study tries to use the similar forms of robust pooled regression by controlling state and time effects as well as panel fixed effect:

Model 1: $\text{Gr\_pcnsdp}_{(t,\ t-1),i} = \Omega_i + \alpha_1\ \text{TotGini}_{t-1,\ i} + \theta\ Z_i + \psi\ \eta_i + e_{t,\ i}$
Model 2: $\text{Gr\_pcnsdp}_{(t,\ t-1),\ i} = \Omega_i + \alpha_1\ \text{TotGini}_{t-1,\ i} + \alpha_2\ \text{Tot\_lit}_{t-1,\ i} + \alpha_3\ \text{Prim\_enrl}_{t-1,\ i} + \alpha_4 \text{Pcedu\_exp}_{t-1,\ i} + \theta\ Z_i + \psi\ \eta_i + e_{t,\ i}$

For scrutinizing the impacts on inequality of growth and human capital, the models are as follows:

Model 1: $\text{MPCEGINI}_{k,\ t} = \text{Constant} + \alpha_{1t}\ \text{lit}_{k,\ t-1} + \alpha_{3t}\ \text{Prim\_enrl}_{t-1} + \alpha_{4t}\ \text{Pcedu\_exp}_{t-1} + e_t$
Model 2: $\text{MPCEGINI}_{k,\ t} = \text{Constant} + \alpha_{1t}\ \text{Gr\_pcnsdp}_{(t,\ t-1)} + \alpha_{2t}\ \text{lit}_{k,\ t-1} + \alpha_{3t}\ \text{Prim\_enrl}_{t-1} + \alpha_{4t}\ \text{Pcedu\_exp}_{t-1} + e_{t,\ i}$

To avoid direct reverse causation, the study takes the inequality measures, i.e. values of Gini coefficients as well as for human capital augmenting variables at the beginning of each growth period. The specifications of the models of the pooled regressions take the growth episodes of five, ten and twenty years respectively.

In the frameworks, '*i*' refers to the state specific variables in consideration and Z is vector of dummies of different states to capture individual state specific heterogeneity and η is time-specific variables, which are ignored in the cross-section analysis. TotGini, Tot_lit, Prim_enrl, and Pceduexp are lagged exogenous regressors and $e_{t,i}$ is the vector of random disturbance term. The framework considers pooled, robust models to control the heteroscedasticity in data-set.

Regional Growth and Disparity

Regional Trends and Fluctuations in Output

The primary focus of the study is to investigate the inequality-growth relationship in Indian states. Thus the study has concentrated equally on the growth perspectives at both the State and all-India level. The Net Domestic Product (NDP), Per Capita NDP (PCNDP), the annual growth rates of NDP and PCNDP of India (at 1993-94 constant prices) and growth rates three-year moving average from 1960-61 to 2004-05 are shown in Table 5.1.

Table 5.1: Level and Growth in NDP and PCNDP and Growth Rates, 1991-2004 (at 1993-94 prices)

Year	*Net Domestic Product*			*Per Capita NDP*		
	Value (Rs. in crore)	*Annual Average Growth Rate (% pa)*	*3-yr moving average Growth Rate (% pa)*	*Value (Rs.)*	*Annual Average Growth Rate (% pa)*	*3-yr moving average Growth Rate (% pa)*
1990-91	704518	0.38	4.09	8230	–1.61	2.02
1995-96	960169	7.31	7.36	10150	5.26	5.28
2000-01	1241240	5.18	5.37	11969	3.35	3.53
2001-02	1292063	4.09	4.35	12155	1.55	2.28
2002-03	1408146	8.98	6.14	13026	7.17	4.04
2003-04	1513435	7.47	6.91	13771	5.72	4.85
2004-05	1722322	13.8	10.21	15433	12.06	8.42

Source: Author's calculations based on CSO data sources.

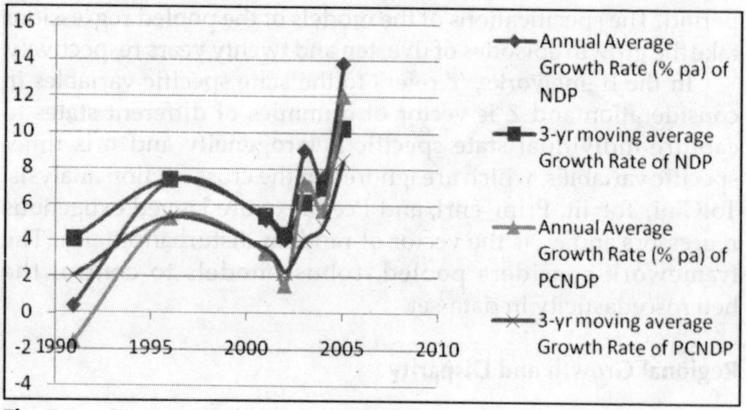

Fig. 5.1: Time Line of NDP and PCNDP Measured at Constant Prices of 1993-94

The value of Net Domestic Product (NDP) of India in 1990-91 at 1993-94 constant prices was Rs.7045.18 billion and was further increased to Rs.12412.40 billion in 2000-01 and to Rs. 17223.22 billion in 2004-05. The Per Capita Net Domestic Product (PCNDP) of India in 1990-91 at constant prices of 1993-94 was Rs. 8230 and increased to Rs. 11969 in 2000-01, and further to Rs. 15433 in 2004-05. In 2004-05, the annual growth rate of PCNDP has reached maximum to 12.06 per cent in which year the annual growth rate of NDP also reached to a maximum of 13.8 per cent, the maximum rates ever since for the whole period between 1960-61 and 2004-05.

Table 5.2: Growth and Variation of PCNSDP Measured at 1993-94 Constant Prices

Period	*Mean Annual Growth of PCNSDP (in %)*	*Standard Deviation of Growth Rates of PCNSDP*
1990-91	1.00	6.60
1995-96	6.26	7.92
2000-01	3.13	4.14
2001-02	4.53	5.33
2002-03	5.84	8.29
2003-04	5.23	2.94
2004-05	5.37	2.89

Source: Author's calculations based on CSO data sources.

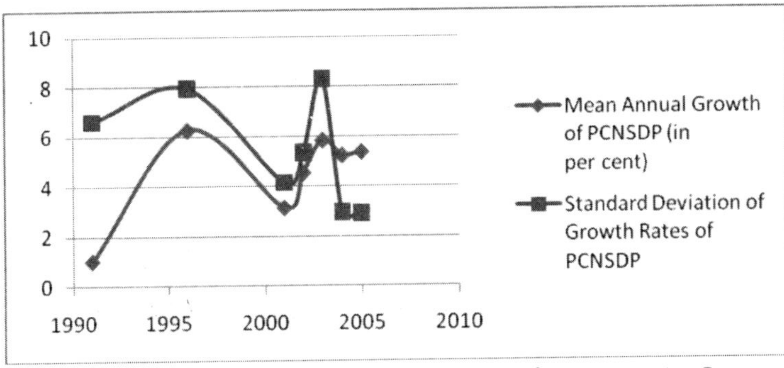

Fig. 5.2: Time Line of PCNSDP and its Standard Deviation (at Constant Prices of 1993-94)

It is evident that the annual growth rate of PCNSDP is a bit uneven, although with relatively stable upward trends for both the rates since 1990s onwards[2]. It is also evident that the standard deviations are seen to be sporadic over time indicating unevenness in the growth rates of PCNSDP, particularly after 1991, and their trends are seemed to be much unstable. This means that although economic reforms help the aggregate economy to grow at a faster pace, but all the states might not be able to internalize the effects of reforms equally. The differences in the political agenda of different state governments coupled with the structural bottlenecks in socio-political facets have led the individual state government not to undertake the whole aspects of reforms. Apart from that, adapted with socialistic prototype of mixed economic culture for a long time, a suspicion towards market oriented reforms has come out with lackadaisical implementation of such policies by a number of state governments which ultimately resulted in the diversities in the growth rates among different states.

Inequality in Living Standards Across States

The inter-state disparity is measured by using the PCNSDP data which is available at 1993-94 prices for the states in a comparable series. Classes of inequality indices are shown in which entropy class of inequality indices by Theil as well as Gini coefficient are determined. Here, E(0) index is called the mean logarithmic deviation, E(1) is called the Theil Index and RE is the class of relative entropy inequality indexes or the relative Theil indices. It is observed that inter-state inequality has been showing an increasing trend for all inequality measures, although there was a small downfall in the years 2002 and 2004 in a fluctuating manner.

Table 5.3: Inter-State Disparity measured in terms of PCNSDP (at 1993-94 Prices)

Year	E(0)	E(1)	RE(1)	E(α = 2)	RE(α = 2)	Gini
1990	0.061199	0.065023	0.02046	0.072109	0.00627	0.203
1993	0.096797	0.097842	0.030031	0.106524	0.008522	0.217
1995	0.076919	0.080159	0.025223	0.089021	0.007741	0.238
2000	0.12594	0.126096	0.038702	0.139421	0.011154	0.264
2005	0.13448	0.132601	0.041195	0.146218	0.012185	0.285

Source: Author's calculations based on CSO data sources.

It has been seen that Gini coefficients and all Theil's indices are rising, although unevenly. This means that spatial inequality in the form of inter-regional disparities is increasing over time. Many economists have different opinions regarding the rise and fall of aggregate Gini values as well as relating to rural-urban disparities. But almost all the studies have agreed to a large extent regarding the post-reform consistent widening up of disparities across the states.

One concern that has been predominantly prevalent in India in recent times is regarding the effects of liberalization of market forces and privatization of public ownership. A common perception of a number of social scientists is that the process would lead to increase disparities in India, although different studies unable to give a clear and unambiguous mandate on it. Economists are having sharp differences in their opinions on whether the inequality in India has been with an increasing trend during the years and also regarding the pattern and relation between income growth and inequality in the Indian states. Bhalla (2003) argued that both urban and rural Ginis based on household consumption expenditure have declined between 1993-94 and 1999-2000. The study by Nirvikar Singh *et al.* (2003) opined in the same way that there is no sign and support of 'overtly dramatic' increase in inequality for the period 1993-94 to 1999-2000.

The National Human Development Report (Government of India, 2001) showed a non-monotonic increase and uneven distribution of the Gini coefficients of the thirty two states and union territories over the years 1983-2000 with the NSS household surveys of 38th, 50th and 55th rounds. The report estimated that Assam, Manipur, Mizoram, Nagaland, Sikkim, Chandigarh, Dadra and Nagar Haveli experienced increase in rural inequality and the bulk of states experienced an increase in urban inequality. The North-Eastern states showed worst evidences where both rural and urban inequalities have increased in the above mentioned time period.

The study concentrates on Gini index for measuring inequality as it is the most widely accepted coefficient that sufficiently and systematically shows the distributional variation among different classes. Several other measures could be used which are shown in Table 5.3, but the study has taken Gini coefficient as inequality measure throughout as using all of them may lead to conflicting outcomes (Partridge, 1997).

Interpersonal Inequality within States

As the dataset on intra-state distribution on income are not available, hence the study takes the expenditure data from NSS Surveys[3] on the distribution of per capita monthly expenditure for calculating Gini coefficient to observe the intra-state inequality of the states. From the point of view of standardization of inequality estimates and its decompositions, calculations should be based on expenditures adjusted for spatial price differentials, particularly for rural and urban areas, rather than calculating them on current expenditures with a general price level at the national level. However, the study has calculated the Gini coefficients separately for rural and urban areas on per capita monthly expenditures across various expenditure classes at constant price level of 1993-94 and then the total inequality is calculated by adjusting with respective population sizes for both rural and urban areas. Interpersonal inequality within the states for both rural and urban sectors are calculated from different large sample NSS Surveys[4] and shown in the following figure.

It is observed from the figure below that the inter-personal inequalities in both rural and urban sectors within the states have also been widened sharply after the reform era in most of the states. Thus the whole analysis underlines the inference that rapid

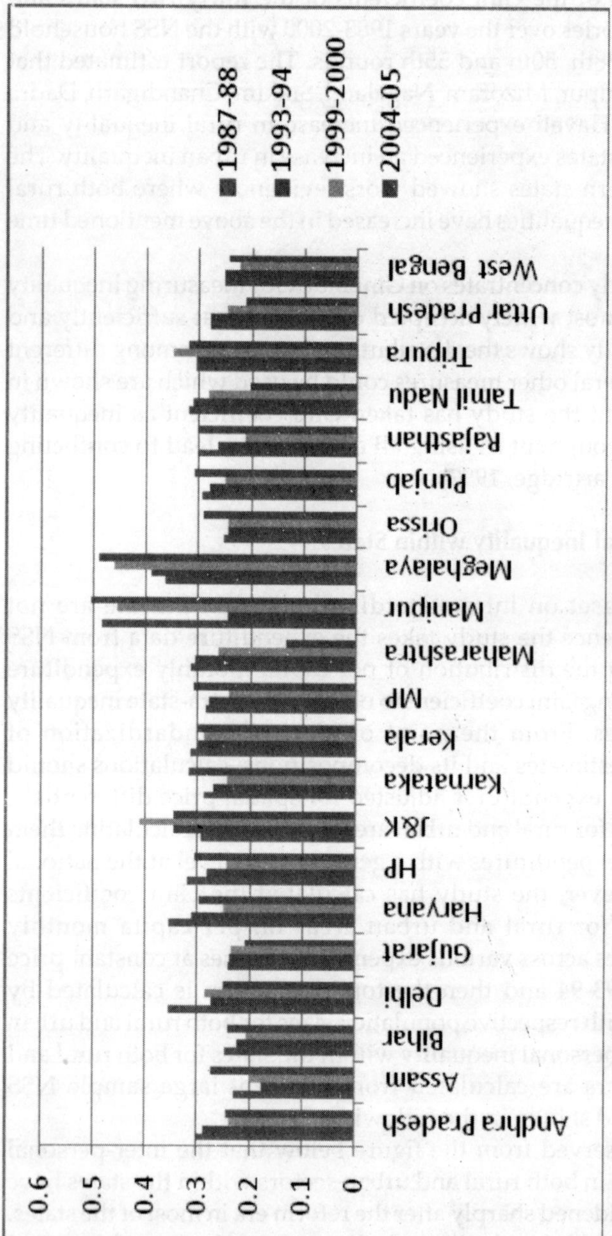

Source: Author's calculations based on NSSO large sample data sources.

Fig. 5.3: Gini Coefficient (Rural) Calculated from MPCE at 1993-94 Prices.

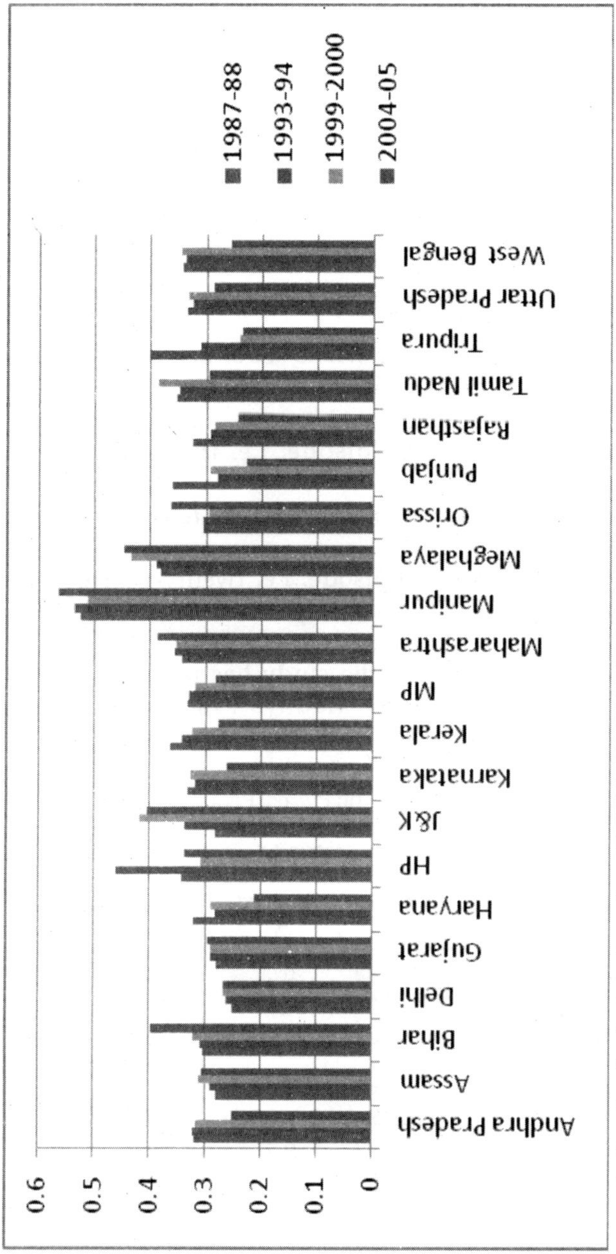

Source: Author's calculations based on NSSO Large Sample Data sources.

Fig. 5.4: Gini Coefficient (Urban) Calculated from MPCE at 1993-94 Prices.

economic growth would not be considered as the 'best bet' for reducing disparities in India as empirical evidences show that rapid economic growth still unable to break the highly skewed distribution of consumption.

Regression Outcomes

In all analyses, *, **, ***, **** denote parameters which are statistically significant respectively at 1 per cent, 5 per cent, 10 per cent and 20 per cent levels, that is, * for $p < 0.01$, ** for $p < 0.05$, *** for $p < 0.1$ and **** for $p < 0.2$.

The growth episodes in the whole set of pooled analysis is structured with three broad divisions of periods:

(a) Short Term Growth Episode, i.e. five-year growth episodes,
(b) Medium Term Growth Episode, i.e. ten-year growth episodes, and
(c) Long Term Growth Episode, i.e. twenty-year growth episodes.

In all regression analyses the study has taken Bihar that includes Jharkhand, similarly Madhya Pradesh including Chhattisgarh and Uttar Pradesh including Uttarakhand.

Table 5.4: Impact of Present Inequality on Present Period Income (PCNSDP)

Year	*Rural Inequality*		*Urban Inequality*		*Aggregate Inequality*	
	Coefficient	*Adjusted R^2*	*Coefficient*	*Adjusted R^2*	*Coefficient*	*Adjusted R^2*
1983	2.8332* (0.03)	0.20	–2.8548 (0.12)	0.08	–1.2731 (0.41)	–0.02
1987	6.0064** (0.00)	0.32	–2.4094 (0.33)	0.00	0.4696 (0.83)	–0.06
1993	4.8032 (0.09)	0.10	–0.5198 (0.85)	–0.05	–0.6507 (0.78)	–0.05
1999	2.2974 (0.27)	0.01	–3.0642 (0.28)	0.01	–4.4458 (0.07)	0.13

Table 5.5: Impact of Previous Period Inequality on Present Period Income (PCNSDP)

Year	Rural Inequality		Urban Inequality		Aggregate Inequality	
	Coefficient	Adjusted R^2	Coefficient	Adjusted R^2	Coefficient	Adjusted R^2
1983	2.7684* (0.03)	0.18	–3.0026 (0.11)	0.09	–0.9023 (0.60)	–0.04
1987	3.4109* (0.05)	0.15	–3.6111* (0.05)	0.15	–1.6748 (0.28)	0.01
1993	4.1910 (0.09)	0.10	–1.0714 (0.65)	–0.04	–0.6387 (0.76)	–0.05
1999	2.4726 (0.24)	0.02	–1.7862 (0.53)	–0.03	–4.6659* (0.04)	0.18
2004	1.7855 (0.40)	–0.01	–3.8038* (0.03)	0.19	–2.2035 (0.49)	–0.03

Table 5.6: Dependent Variable Growth of PCNSDP: Cross-Section

Independent Variables	*Dependent Variable*							
	Gr_pcnsdp_87-83		*Gr_pcnsdp_94-87*		*Gr_pcnsdp_99-94*		*Gr_pcnsdp_04-99*	
	Model 1	*Model 2*	*Model 1*	*Model 2*	*Model 1*	*Model 2*	*Model 1*	*Model 2*
Previous Gini	–0.157	–0.203	–0.506*	–0.572*	–0.217 (–1.110)	–0.301	–0.117	–0.074
Previous Total Literacy		–0.391		–0.046		0.263		0.103
Previous Enrolment Ratio		0.121		0.522**		0.251		0.347****
Previous Education Expenditure		0.032		–0.098		0.234		0.118
Adjusted R^2	0.016	0.57	0.225	0.363	0.009	0.214	0.029	0.032

Table 5.7: Five-Year and Ten-Year Growth Episode for All States: Pooled, Robust Regression-Dependent Variable Growth of PCNSDP

Independent Variables	*Dependent Variable: Gr_pcnsdp*							
	Five Year Growth Episode				*Ten Year Growth Episode*			
	Model 1		*Model 2*		*Model 1*		*Model 2*	
Model	*Pooled, Robust*	*Pooled, Robust*	*Pooled, Robust*	*Pooled, Robust*	*Pooled, Robust*	*Pooled, Robust*	*Pooled, Robust*	*Pooled, Robust*
State Effect	No	No	Yes	Yes	No	No	Yes	Yes
Initial Gini	–0.031	–0.041	–.205***	–0.044	–0.207	–0.394	0.021	0.004
Initial Total Literacy		0.234		0.051***		–0.012		–0.096**
Initial Enrolment Ratio		0.124**		0.067*		0.013		0.041**
Initial Education Expenditure		0.141**		0.003**		0.002****		0.004**
Adjusted R^2	0.191	0.252	0.132	0.302	0.228	0.231	0.282	0.295

Table 5.8: Twenty-Year Growth Episode for All States: Pooled, Robust Regression Dependent Variable Growth of PCNSDP

Independent Variables	*Dependent Variable: Gr_pcnsdp*			
	Ten Year Growth Episode: All States			
	Model 1		*Model 2*	
Model	*Pooled, Robust*	*Pooled, Robust*	*Pooled, Robust*	*Pooled, Robust*
State Effect	No	No	Yes	Yes
Time Effect	No	No	No	No
Initial Gini	0.279***	0.276***	0.161***	0.299**
Initial Total Literacy		0.024		–0.141**
Initial Enrolment Ratio		0.011		0.189***
Initial Education Expenditure		0.005*		0.343**
Adjusted R^2	0.252	0.163	0.153	0.232

Table 5.9: Basic Panel Regression of Growth and Inequality (For All States): Fixed Effects

Variables	*For 5 years growth episodes*		*For 10 years growth episodes*		*For 20 years growth episodes*	
	Model 1	*Model 2*	*Model 1*	*Model 2*	*Model 1*	*Model 2*
Initial Gini	–0.007	–0.415	–0.094*	–0.014**	0.219	0.281**
Initial Total Literacy		0.225***		-0.081**		–0.117
Initial Enrolment Ratio		0.101		0.042		0.089**
Initial Education Expenditure		0.113***		0.015**		0.229**
F	6.87	8.14	7.75	17.57	32.55	34.45
Adjusted R^2	0.141	0.262	0.258	0.375	0.352	0.362

Table 5.10: Impact of Human Capital Variables on Inequality: Rural All States

Year	*Model*	*literacy rural*	*Enrolment ratio*	*Pceduexp*	*Adjusted R^2*
1993	1	0.0043**			0.93
	2	–0.0005	0.0025**	0.0001	0.96
1999	1	0.0039**			0.95
	2	0.0008	0.0015	0.0001	0.96
2004	1	0.0038**			0.97
	2	0.0034**	–0.0001	0.0000	0.97

Table 5.11: Impact of Human Capital Variables on Inequality: Urban All States

Year	*Model*	*literacy rural*	*Enrolment ratio*	*Pceduexp*	*Adjusted R^2*
1993	1	0.0049**			0.96
	2	0.0006	0.0026**	0.0000	0.97
1999	1	0.0046**			0.96
	2	0.0026	0.0017	0.0000	0.96
2004	1	0.0041**			0.95
	2	0.0029*	0.0009	0.0000	0.95

Table 5.12: Impact of Growth in PCNSDP and Human Capital Variables on Inequality – Pooled, Robust

(i) Regression All States – Rural

Time	*Model*	*Coefficients*				*Adjusted R^2*
		Gr_pcnsdp	*Literacy*	*Enrolment ratio*	*Education Expenditure*	
Short	1	0.001*				0.15
Run	2	0.002	0.001**	–0.001	–0.001	0.29
Medium	1	0.001**				0.20
Run	2	0.001	0.001	–0.001	–0.002	0.31
Long	1	0.011				0.15
Run	2	0.009	–0.002	–0.001	0.001	0.32

(ii) Regression All States – Urban

Time	Model	Coefficients				Adjusted R^2
		Gr_pcnsdp	Literacy	Enrolment ratio	Education Expenditure	
Short	1	–0.003**				0.36
Run	2	–0.004*	0.001	0.001**	–0.003**	0.58
Medium	1	–0.005**				0.48
Run	2	–0.006*	0.001	0.001**	0.001	0.63
Long	1	–0.016**				0.34
Run	2	–0.017**	–0.002*	0.001	0.001	0.43

In the above model analyses, the following symbols are used in the equations and they will be represented in the same manners in regression tables in the study.

Gr_pcnsdp = Growth of per capita net state domestic product between periods *t* and *t*-1,

MPCEGINI = Gini coefficient,

Tot_lit = Total literacy rate within a state,

Urblit = Literacy rate for urban areas within a state,

rur_lit = Literacy rate for rural areas within a state,

Prim_enrl = Primary enrolment ratio in the state,

Pceduexp = Per capita state education expenditure.

Economic Analysis of the Results

It is seen that for most of the cross-section points of study the impact of present period's rural Gini coefficients on current per capita NSDP is positive. This means that higher rural inequalities are associated with the higher level of income. During the period of soft liberalization since 1983-84 in India, the relationships are observed significantly positive. But after the implementation of new economic policies of 1991, the relationship has been observed positive but less significant. After 1999-2000, the strength of the positive relation, observed by regression coefficients, has been reduced over time. But the impact of urban inequality on income is observed to be diametrically opposite to the rural case. It has been observed that in most of the cross-section point of time the impacts of urban Gini coefficients are negative on state per capita NSDP. It, therefore, follows that urban inequality is detrimental to growth.

The overall inference is very clear that higher rural inequality leads to higher income, but higher urban inequality is associated with lower growth. Considering that rural and urban income-employment situation and dynamics are completely different, this result is not surprising. The rural sector which is predominantly dependent on agriculture has shown positive link between inequality and income level, but for comparative advanced urban sector the link is negative.

The state promoted structural change in the form of 'package technology' under green revolution not only resulted in increasing surplus, but also helped to develop other non-farm sector in rural areas. The success of the structural change dependent crucially on large farm size and hence was able to raise agricultural output substantially in states with higher rural inequality. The resultant rise in output and income was also concentrated in the hands of few landlords and the surpluses generated have been reinvested for agrarian improvement. This explains largely the positive association between rural inequality and income.

The scenario is totally different in urban sector where the link between income level and urban inequality has been seen negative in almost all cross-sectional points of time which means urban inequality has a negative impact. As most of the urban economy is based on petty entrepreneurship, service sector employment, and trade and commerce, thus greater equality in economic conditions would facilitate higher income in such a backdrop–explaining the negative association between urban inequality and income growth.

The most important and notable part of the cross-section analysis is that of the relation between the growth rate of PCNSDP and Gini coefficient of the initial period of growth successively for the cross-section year results. It has been seen that the growth rate of PCNSDP for a period is significantly negatively related with the previous period aggregate Gini coefficient, and the results do not change when the human capital variables are included in the model.

Hence, the cross-section results as a whole substantiates the Kuznets hypothesis (1955) to a degree in an elaborated manner, but in an opposite causation which robustly adhere the perspectives of endogenous growth characteristics, as the negative relation between economic growth and initial inequality turns up much strongly at the comparatively more developing stages of the Indian states since the period of soft liberalization of late 1980s and in the post-reform era. The results adhere to the perspectives of economic cycle in the sense that after the post-soft-liberalization period of 1980s the Indian economy as a whole has freed largely from the severe industrial slackness of the previous decades. The five-year and ten-year pooled growth regressions have also shown the same trail, but twenty-year episode has shown positive link. This means that although in the long run inequality is beneficial for economic growth, but impact in short run is detrimental for growth, at least in the present situation.

The human capital variables have the potential to augment income in both short and long runs. While in the initial period literacy is important, in long run enrolment to be the more important factor indicating the importance of universalization of elementary education in achieving economic growth in India.

At the theoretical level expansion of human capital is expected to reduce inequality. However, that happens only if the human capital formation itself is equal across the population. If, on the other hand, attainment of education and other human capital are themselves unequal, then increase in average human capital will be associated with increased inequality. It is observed that for all periods of study, educational attainment is linked with higher inequality, both rural and urban (Tables 5.10 and 5.11). While by itself higher literacy level is associated with higher inequality, enrolment ratios seem to be more important in affecting inequality levels. It thus appears that human capital formation effects in India have been mostly inegalitarian. Higher educational levels in the states lead to higher earning capacity among selected few, leading to rising inequality. Therefore, the egalitarian impact of human capital formation is still not operational in India.

Thus, we have seen that though inequality may hinder growth in the short run, in the long run inequality appears to augment income growth. The results may spur us to embark on an inegalitarian drive with the hope of achieving higher growth in the long run, but the opportunity of such a path is questionable on social grounds. If the growth itself is inegalitarian then today's inequality led growth will lead to a still higher disparity tomorrow and create associated problems of social tension and unrest. Only if the growth process is itself egalitarian can we think of an inequality led growth today, expecting that this growth will usher in a more equal society in near future. For that we must examine the short run and long run impact of economic growth on inequality.

It is observed from Table 5.12 that for rural areas growth in income increases inequality in all three time spans, though in the short and medium run the growth-inequality trade-off seems rather weak. However, in the long run, growth-inequality association is quite strong. Literacy too has an increasing impact on inequality, especially in the long run. Enrolment ratio and state expenditure on education have a negative impact on inequality in the short and medium terms, but increases inequality in the long run.

For urban areas, growth has a negative association with inequality for all the three time spans, indicating that growth indeed leads to an egalitarian effect in the urban areas, benefiting various sections of the society. The same is true for state expenditure on education. For literacy and enrolment ratio, the association is positive in the short run but significantly negative in the long run.

Findings and Conclusions

What do the outcomes imply in the broader perspective of Indian economy? Theoretical premise, *a la* Kuznets, hypothesized that in initial levels of development higher income growth would create several processes in the economy that would widen the gap between socio-economic groups. In the later stages of development trickle down effects would be powerful which would benefit all sections and thereby inequality would come down.

The findings obtained in the present study are slackly conventional to this theoretical premise, albeit revealed the unique characteristics of Indian scenario. It appears that the process of growth is more favourable to the urban sector as compared to the rural sector, thus shown clearly the dualistic nature of the Indian economy with sharp rural-urban divide in the post-reform era also. The process of economic growth and the human capital augmenting process have benefited the urban sector by and large, and so high growth or better human capital situation is associated with lower economic inequality. The widening of gaps evident in the short run vanishes in the long run when the entire process supports high growth-low inequality thesis.

In the rural segment resultants of economic and human capital expansion have not benefited equally every section of rural mass, and, thus, high growth or higher educational attainment levels are associated with higher rural inequality. Therefore, whole scenario of the present study indicates that Kuznets type trickledown effect is operative in, but limited to, the urban areas in the post-reform era too—proves the symbiotic coexistence of loosely integrated two broad and distinct subeconomies, rural and urban, but yet retaining their own characteristics.

Coming back to the unique issue with which we started–do we support inegalitarian policies to enhance growth? It appears that the answer should be negative. Indian experience shows that high income growth is associated with higher resultant rural inequality, though urban inequality does come down with growth. India is still largely a rural sector based economy, thus any process that creates further disparity in rural areas cannot be taken for granted.

Instead, the other major ingredient of growth, viz. human capital variables should be the focus of policies for its dual role in enhancing growth on one hand and reducing inequality on the other. Therefore, better, comprehensive and broad-based improvement and use of human capital as well as adequate importance on agricultural rural sector in terms of productivity growth may lead to higher income levels and growth in a more egalitarian way. It is important particularly after structural adjustment of the economy where market-based profit oriented goal should be contained within the broader societal goal of equity and welfare.

Acknowledgements: The author is greatly indebted to Rajarshi Majumder and Sugata Marjit for many useful suggestions and to the Indian Statistical Institute, Kolkata, NSSO, Kolkata and IEG, New Delhi, for giving the opportunities to obtain valuable dataset to get the perspective of present study. The general disclaimer applies. The author is fully responsible for results and observations used in the present paper.

NOTES

1. Bertola (1993), Perotti (1993), Persson and Tabellini (1994), Alesina and Rodrik (1994), Krussel, Quadrini and Rios-Rull (1997), Acemoglu

and Robinson (1996), Bénabou (1996a, 1996b), Rodriguez (1999b), Bourguignon and Verdier (1996), Benhabib and Rustichini (1996), Kim and Grossman (1996), Bannerjee and Newman (1991), Aghion and Bolton (1992) and Galor and Zeira (1993), Ferreira (1995) and many others.

2. A number of possible explanations for this rise in productivity/ growth include that Keynesian type demand-led expansion in the 1980s and liberalization in different sectors in 1990s as well as attitudinal changes in the governments is the basic factors. See Rodrik and Subramanian (2004).
3. During the period between 1972-73 and 2004-05, the NSSO has conducted seven large quinquennial surveys on distribution of household consumption expenditure for the years 1972-73, 1977-78, 1987-88, 1993-94, 1999-2000 and 2004-05.
4. During the period between 1972-73 and 2004-05, the NSSO has conducted seven large quinquennial surveys on distribution of household consumption expenditure for the years 1972-73, 1977-78, 1987-88, 1993-94, 1999-2000 and 2004-05.

REFERENCES

Aghion, P. and P. Bolton (1997). 'A Trickle-Down Theory of Growth and Development with Debt Overhang,' *Review of Economic Studies*, 64(2): 151-72.

Alesina, Alberto and Dani Rodrik (1994). 'Redistributive Politics and Economic Growth,' *Quarterly Journal of Economics*, 436: 465-90.

Alesina, Alberto and Roberto Perotti (1996). 'Income Distribution, Political Instability, and Investment,' *NBER Working Paper* 4486.

Anand S. and S.M. Kanbur (1993). 'The Kuznets Process and the Inequality-Development Relationship,' *Journal of Development Economics*, 40: 25-72.

Barro, Robert J. (1991). 'Economic Growth in a Cross Section of Countries', *Quarterly Journal of Economics*, 106, pp. 407-444.

Barro, Robert J. (2000). 'Inequality and Growth in a Panel of Countries', *Journal of Economic Growth*, 5: 5-32.

Becker, G.S. (1962). 'Investment in Human Capital: A Theoretical Analysis', *Journal of Political Economy*, 70: 9–49 (supplement).

Cashin, P. and R. Sahay (1996). 'Internal Migration, Centre State Grants and Economic Growth in the States in India', *IMF Staff Papers*, 43(1): 123-171.

Dahan, M. and D. Tsiddon (1998). 'Demographic Transition, Income Distribution and Economic Growth', *Journal of Economic Growth*, 3: 29-52.

Datt, Gaurav and Martin Ravallion (2002). 'Is India's Economic Growth Leaving the Poor Behind?', *Journal of Economic Perspectives,* 16(3): 89-108.

Deininger, K. and L. Squire (1996). 'A New Data Set Measuring Income Inequality', *World Bank Economic Review,* 10: 565–91.

Dreze, Jean and J. Loh (1995). 'Literacy in India and China', *Economic and Political Weekly,* 30(45): 2868-78.

Jha, Raghbendra (2000). 'Growth, Inequality and Poverty in India: Spatial and Temporal Characteristics', *Economic and Political Weekly,* 35(11): 921-28.

Mankiw, N.G., P. Romer, D.N. Weil (1992). 'Contribution to the Empirics of Economic Growth'. *Quarterly Journal of Economics,* 107: 407–37.

Ojha, V.P. and B.K. Pradhan (2006). *Human Capital Formation and Economic Growth in India: A CGE Analysis.* New Delhi: National Council of Applied Economic Research (NCAER).

Persson, T. and G. Tabellini (1994). 'Is Inequality Harmful for Growth?' *American Economic Review,* 84: 600-21.

Sen, Abhijit and Himanshu (2004). 'Poverty and inequality in India–I: Getting closer to the Truth', *Economic and Political Weekly,* 39 (38): 4247-63.

Sen, Abhijit and Himanshu (2004). Poverty and Inequality in India–II: Widening Disparities during the 1990s', *Economic and Political Weekly,* 39(39): 4361-75.

Singh, Nirvikar, L. Bhandari, A. Chen and A. Khare (2003). 'Regional Inequality in India: A Fresh Look', *Economic and Political Weekly,* 38(11): 1069-73.

Sylwester, K. (2000). 'Income inequality, education expenditures, and growth', *Journal of Development Economics,* 63: 379-98.

6
Regional Inequalities in Human Development in India

Madhusudan Ghosh

Redressing regional disparities has been one of the primary objectives of the Indian planning. The concerns for regional disparities in development in general and in the standard of living in particular have been expressed in government's policies and programmes. It is recognised that growth should be 'more inclusive' in terms of the benefits of growth accruing to those sections of population, which have been bypassed by the high rates of growth achieved in recent years. It has also been perceived that regional disparities have been increasing and the gains of the rapid growth have not reached all parts of the country in an equitable manner. For growth to be 'more inclusive', the benefits of growth should be shared by different sections of the population and by all the regions of the country. Since the regional inequality in per capita income may not necessarily reflect the same degree of regional disparity in human development, special attention has been focused on the issue of regional disparity in human development.

This paper evaluates the relative performance of 15 major Indian states on human development with special reference to education and health. Since human development is defined as a process of enlarging people's choices to lead a long and healthy life, to acquire knowledge and be educated and to have access to resources needed for a decent level of living, it discusses the attainment of the major states on education, health and human development. It examines the inter-state variations in various dimensions of human development, and their association with per capita income and per capita expenditure on social services. Since human development is measured in terms of HDI (Human Development Index) involving three dimensions of human well-being, viz. (i) education and knowledge, (ii) health and longevity, and (iii) a decent standard of living, the regional disparities in HDI as well as in its three components are examined. While the first component of HDI is represented by the literacy rate (LR), and the second one by the life expectancy at birth (LEB), the third is represented by per capita real income (PCI) measured in terms of per capita net state domestic product (SDP) at constant (1980-81) prices. Since the degree of regional inequality in the human development indicators (HDI, LR and ELB) may not necessarily be the same as in the economic growth indicator (PCI), the outcomes of the human development indicators are compared with those of the economic growth indicator. The analysis covers 15 major states, viz. Andhra Pradesh (AP), Assam, Bihar, Gujarat, Haryana, Karnataka, Kerala, Madhya Pradesh (MP), Maharashtra, Odisha, Punjab, Rajasthan, Tamil Nadu, Uttar Pradesh (UP) and West Bengal (WB).

Human Development

Table 6.1 shows that at the all-India level, human development improved significantly during the two decades from 1981-2001, as the estimated HDI increased from 0.302 in 1981 to 0.472 in 2001. Both the rural and urban India experienced higher level of human development in 1991 relative to 1981. The HDI in rural area increased from 0.263 in 1981 to 0.340 in 1991 and from 0.442 to 0.511 in urban area.

Regional Variations in HDI

In order to evaluate the relative performance of the states on human development, and to examine which states achieved sustained improvement in human development and which ones fell back over time, the states were ranked on the basis of their performance on human development at different time points. Table 6.1 reports the achievement of the states in HDI at different time points. Kerala

Table 6.1: Human Development Index (HDI)

States	1981				1991				2001
	Combined	Rural	Urban	Rural/ Urban	Combined	Rural	Urban	Rural/ Urban	Combined
Andhra Pradesh	0.298 (9)	0.262	0.425	0.62	0.377 (9)	0.344	0.473	0.73	0.416 (10)
Assam	0.272 (10)	0.261	0.380	0.69	0.348 (10)	0.326	0.555	0.59	0.386 (14)
Bihar	0.237 (15)	0.220	0.378	0.58	0.308 (15)	0.286	0.460	0.62	0.367 (15)
Gujarat	0.360 (4)	0.315	0.458	0.69	0.431 (6)	0.380	0.532	0.71	0.479 (6)
Haryana	0.360 (5)	0.332	0.465	0.71	0.443 (5)	0.409	0.562	0.73	0.509 (5)
Karnataka	0.346 (6)	0.295	0.489	0.60	0.412 (7)	0.367	0.523	0.70	0.478 (7)
Kerala	0.500 (1)	0.491	0.544	0.90	0.591 (1)	0.576	0.628	0.92	0.638 (1)
Madhya Pradesh	0.245 (14)	0.209	0.395	0.53	0.328 (13)	0.282	0.491	0.57	0.394 (12)
Maharashtra	0.363 (3)	0.306	0.489	0.63	0.452 (4)	0.403	0.548	0.74	0.523 (4)
Odisha	0.267 (11)	0.252	0.368	0.68	0.345 (12)	0.328	0.469	0.70	0.404 (11)
Punjab	0.411 (2)	0.386	0.494	0.78	0.475 (2)	0.447	0.566	0.79	0.537 (2)
Rajasthan	0.256 (12)	0.216	0.386	0.56	0.347 (11)	0.298	0.492	0.61	0.424 (9)
Tamil Nadu	0.343 (7)	0.289	0.445	0.65	0.466 (3)	0.421	0.560	0.75	0.531 (3)
Uttar Pradesh	0.255 (13)	0.227	0.398	0.57	0.314 (14)	0.284	0.444	0.64	0.388 (13)
West Bengal	0.305 (8)	0.264	0.427	0.62	0.404 (8)	0.370	0.511	0.72	0.472 (8)
India	0.302	0.263	0.442	0.60	0.381	0.340	0.511	0.67	0.472
CV (%)	22.50	25.70	12.10	14.59	19.02	21.22	9.62	12.56	16.29

Notes: Figures in parentheses are ranks of the states. CV is the coefficient of variation among the states.
Source: Planning Commission (2002).

has been the best performing state, and Bihar the worst performing one in all the years. There have been wide inter-state variations in HDI – from 0.237 to 0.50 in 1981, from 0.308 to 0.591 in 1991, and from 0.367 to 0.638 in 2001. The better-off states, viz. Kerala, Punjab, Tamil Nadu, Maharashtra and Haryana had an HDI of above 0.50, while the worse-off states like Bihar, Assam, UP and MP had an HDI of less than 0.40 in 2001. Though seven states (Bihar, Haryana, Kerala, Odisha, Punjab, UP and WB) could manage to maintain their relative positions in HDI, and three states (MP, Rajasthan, and TN) to improve, the remaining five states (AP, Assam, Gujarat, Karnataka, and Maharashtra) experienced deterioration in 2001 relative to 1981. However, the performance of all the states on HDI improved during 1981-2001, and the poorer states have made strides in improving their relative position in human development. Human development improved in both rural and urban areas in all the states during 1981-1991. The rural-urban disparity in HDI has declined in India, as the ratio of rural to urban HDI increased from 0.60 in 1981 to 0.67 in 1991. The rural-urban disparity in HDI has also declined in all the states except Assam. The inter-state variation in the rural-urban gap in HDI has declined, as the CV in the rural-urban ratio in HDI declined from 14.59 per cent in 1981 to 12.56 per cent in 1991.

Convergence in HDI

The trend in regional inequality in human development is also studied by examining σ-convergence and absolute β-convergence. σ–convergence human development is concerned with cross-sectional dispersion in human development, and it holds if the dispersion in human development across regions decreases over time. The simplest way to test for σ–convergence is to estimate the trend in some measure of dispersion in the indicators of human development. Absolute β-convergence is concerned with the question of mobility of different regions in terms of human development over time, and it holds if initially poorer regions perform better than initially richer ones.

The existence of σ-convergence is examined by estimating the coefficient of variation (CV) of HDI across states. The estimated CVs of HDI have consistently declined over time, indicating that there has been σ-convergence in human development across the states (Fig. 6.1). The regional disparities in HDI have declined over the period, suggesting that the poor states have managed to catch up the rich states in terms of human well-being. The convergence has also taken place in rural and urban areas, as the CV in HDI across the states declined in both the areas between 1981 and 1991 (Fig. 1).

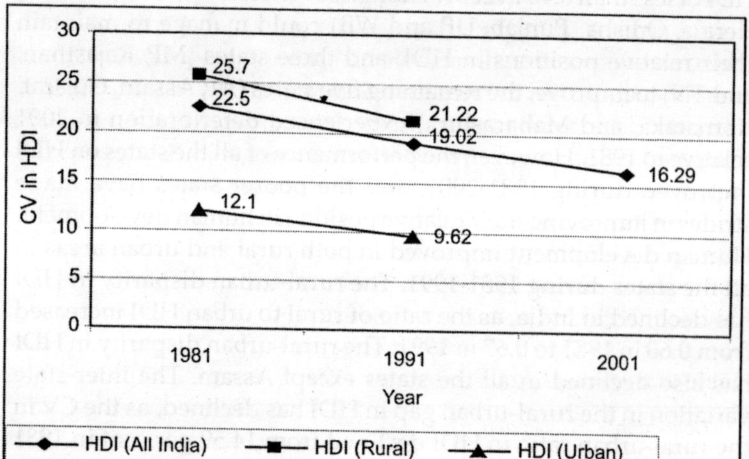

Fig. 6.1: σ-Convergence in HDI

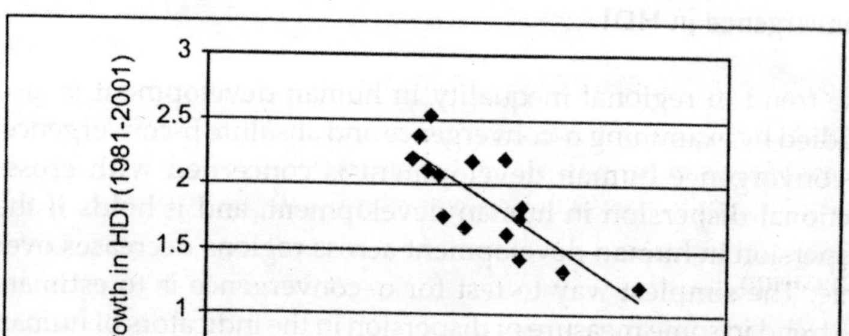

Fig. 6.2: Absolute Convergence in HDI (1981-2001)

The absolute β-convergence in human development is examined to see whether the initially poor regions performed better than the rich ones. This is carried out by plotting the annual average growth rates of HDI against initial levels of HDI. Figure 6.2 shows a negative relationship between the two, suggesting that there has been absolute convergence in human development across the states during 1981–2001. This is also performed by estimating a β-convergence equation in which the annual average growth rate in HDI is regressed on initial level of HDI. The ordinary least squares (OLS) estimates of the convergence equation (Table 6.2) show that the coefficients on initial level of HDI are negative and statistically significant in all the periods, indicating that absolute convergence has happened in human development. However, a comparative study of the results between the pre- and post-reform periods reveals that the rate of convergence in HDI declined marginally from 1.65 per cent in the 1980s to 1.48 per cent in the 1990s. Thus, the HDI exhibited significant convergence and the gap between the rich and poor states in human development has declined over time.

Table 6.2: Absolute β-convergence in HDI

Dependent Variable	*Period*	*Constant*	*Coefficient on initial Level*	R^2
Growth in HDI	1981-1991	0.0042 (0.115)	–0.0165* (–3.347)	0.463
Growth in HDI	1991-2001	0.0007 (0.170)	–0.0148* (–3.507)	0.486
Growth in HDI	1981-2001	0.0018 (0.525)	–0.0146* (–4.921)	0.649

Notes: Figures in parenthesis are *t*-statistics.
* denotes significance at the 1 per cent levels. $N = 15$.

Education

The government has accorded special importance to education, which has been an integral part of economic planning. Expenditure on education has been regarded as an investment in human capital that plays an important role in economic growth. The major objectives of education planning in India have been to achieve equity in education by gender, caste, and socio-economic group, and to reduce regional disparity in educational development

(Tilak, 2006). A large volume of literature on educational planning and achievements in India is available in Tilak (1987; 1999; 2006). This section evaluates the progress achieved in education, particularly in literacy and elementary education (primary and upper primary) with a focus on regional and gender disparities.

Literacy Rate

Literacy rate is the most commonly used indicator of educational development. The Indian government aims at achieving 100 per cent literacy, for which it has adopted various policies and programmes. A review of progress achieved in literacy reveals that the literacy rate of the population in the age group of 7 years and above increased from 43.57 per cent in 1981 to 52.21 per cent in 1991 and further to 65.2 per cent in 2001 (Table 6.3). The increase

Table 6.3: Progress in Literacy in India

	Literacy Rate (Per cent)			*Improvement (Points)*	
	1981	*1991*	*2001*	*1981 – 1991*	*1991 – 2001*
Rural					
Male	49.59	57.87	71.18	8.28	13.31
Female	21.70	30.62	46.58	8.92	15.96
Total	36.01	44.69	59.21	8.68	14.52
GPI	0.438	0.529	0.654	0.091	0.125
Urban					
Male	76.8	81.0	86.4	4.2	5.4
Female	56.4	63.9	73.0	7.5	9.1
Total	67.3	73.1	80.1	5.8	7.0
GPI	0.734	0.789	0.845	0.055	0.056
Combined					
Male	56.38	64.13	75.64	7.75	11.51
Female	29.76	39.29	54.03	9.53	14.74
Total	43.57	52.21	65.20	8.64	12.99
GPI	0.528	0.613	0.714	0.085	0.101
Rural-Urban Disparity (Rural literacy ÷ Urban literacy)					
Male	0.646	0.714	0.824	0.068	0.110
Female	0.385	0.479	0.638	0.094	0.159
Total	0.535	0.611	0.739	0.076	0.128
GPI	0.597	0.670	0.916	0.073	0.246

Notes: GPI = Gender Parity Index (Female literacy ÷ Male literacy).
Sources: Planning Commission (2002), Tilak (2006).

of 13 percentage points in the literacy rate during the period 1991-2001 indicates the fastest decadal growth since Independence. Despite this progress in literacy, the literacy rate in 2001 is far below the Eleventh Plan's proposed literacy rate of 85 per cent in 2011-12 and the Millennium Development Goals (MDG) of 100 per cent by 2015.

The literacy rate for males and females has improved over the census years in both the rural and urban areas (Table 6.3). The rate of improvement in literacy was faster during the decade 1991-2001 than during the preceding decade of 1981-91. The male literacy rate increased from 56.38 per cent in 1981 to 75.64 per cent in 2001 – signifying an increase of 19.26 percentage points. On the other hand, the female literacy rate increased from a very low level of 29.76 per cent in 1981 to 54.03 per cent in 2001, showing an increase of 24.28 percentage points. Thus, the female literacy rate increased at a faster rate because of which the male-female literacy gap declined from 26.62 percentage points in 1981 to 21.61 percentage points in 2001. As a result, the gender parity index (GPI) improved over the census years, and the rate of improvement was faster in the 1990s than in the 1980s. The gender disparity in literacy, even though showing a decline over time, appears to be quite high in 2001, which is more than double the Eleventh Plan's targeted gender gap in literacy of 10 percentage points in 2011-12. There has also been a substantial rural–urban gap in the literacy rate for both the males and females. Even though the rural–urban gap declined over the years, the gap in female literacy was wider than that in male literacy.

Inter-State Variations in Literacy

There have been wide inter-state variations in literacy, even though the variations have declined over the years. Table 6.4 shows that in 1981, eight of the 15 major states had literacy rates higher than the national average; Kerala had the highest literacy rate (81.56%) and Rajasthan had the lowest rate of 30.11 per cent – a gap of 51.45 percentage points. In 1991, the literacy rate improved in all the states, but the inter-state variations in literacy were prevailing, as Kerala had the highest literacy rate of 89.81 per cent and Bihar had the lowest rate of 38.48 per cent. Although the literacy rate improved further in all the states in 2001, it varied from the highest

Table 6.4: Literacy Rate of the Population in the Age Group 7 Years and Above: Major States

(Per cent)

States	1981			1991			2001		
	Combined	Rural	Urban	Combined	Rural	Urban	Combined	Rural	Urban
Andhra Pradesh	35.66	27.85	61.00	44.09	35.74	66.35	61.11	55.33	76.39
Assam	42.05	34.39	75.09	52.89	49.32	79.39	64.28	60.92	85.76
Bihar	32.05	27.70	61.77	38.48	33.83	67.89	47.53	44.42	72.71
Gujarat	52.21	43.57	71.00	61.29	53.09	76.54	66.43	58.53	79.24
Haryana	43.88	37.26	66.83	55.85	49.85	73.66	68.59	63.82	79.89
Karnataka	46.21	37.63	66.91	56.04	47.69	74.20	67.04	59.68	81.05
Kerala	81.56	80.31	86.91	89.81	88.92	92.25	90.92	90.05	93.38
Madhya Pradesh	36.63	29.33	64.55	44.20	35.87	70.81	64.08	58.10	79.67
Maharashtra	55.83	45.65	74.29	64.87	55.52	79.20	77.27	70.84	85.76
Odisha	40.97	37.77	64.81	49.09	45.46	71.99	63.61	60.44	80.95
Punjab	48.17	41.73	64.96	58.51	52.77	72.08	69.95	65.16	79.13
Rajasthan	30.11	22.47	58.05	38.55	30.37	65.33	61.03	55.92	76.89
Tamil Nadu	54.39	45.00	73.25	62.66	54.59	77.99	75.47	66.66	82.07
Uttar Pradesh	33.35	28.53	54.87	41.60	36.66	61.00	57.36	53.68	70.61
West Bengal	48.65	40.18	70.68	57.7	50.50	75.27	69.22	64.06	81.63
India	43.57	36.01	67.30	52.21	44.69	73.10	65.2	59.21	80.06
CV (%)	28.35	35.08	11.73	24.18	29.34	10.07	14.59	16.17	6.80

Notes: Literacy rates of Meghalaya are used for Assam for 1981. CV is the coefficient of variation among the states.
Sources: Planning Commission (2002), Tilak (2006).

rate of 90.92 per cent in Kerala to 47.53 per cent in Bihar, keeping the difference between the highest and lowest literacy rate at 43.39 percentage points.

Convergence in Literacy

The literacy rate appears to have converged across the states, as the CV in the literacy rate declined from 28.35 per cent in 1981 to 24.18 per cent in 1991 and further to 14.59 per cent in 2001 (σ-convergence). This convergence is also observed in the rural and urban areas, as the CV in the rural and urban literacy rates across the states declined consistently over the period (Fig. 6.3). There has been absolute convergence in literacy rate. Figure 6.4 displays that the annual average growth rate of LR is inversely related to initial level of LR during 1981-2001. The OLS estimates of the absolute β-convergence equation (Table 6.5) show that absolute convergence across the states has occurred in literacy, as the coefficient on initial level of LR is negative and statistically significant in all the cases. The estimated annual rate of convergence in literacy increased significantly from 1.25 per cent in the 1980s to 4.23 per cent during the 1990s.

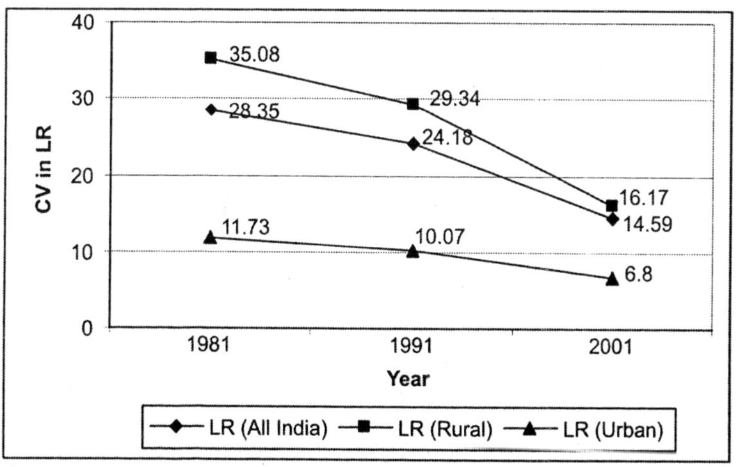

Fig. 6.3: σ-Convergence in Literacy Rate (LR)

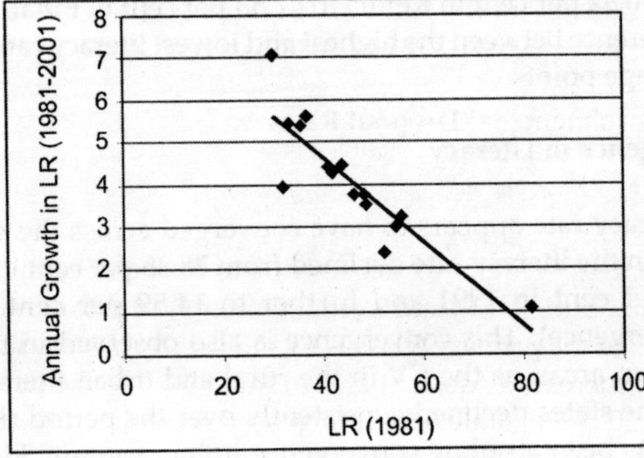

Fig. 6.4: Absolute Convergence in LR (1981-2001)

Table 6.5: Absolute β-convergence in Literacy

Dependent Variable	*Period*	*Constant*	*Coefficient on initial Level*	R^2
Growth in LR	1981-1991	0.066 (6.739)	–0.0125* (–4.842)	0.643
Growth in LR	1991-2001	0.190 (6.761)	–0.0423* (–5.984)	0.734
Growth in LR	1981-2001	0.115 (9.013)	–0.0251* (–7.433)	0.809

Notes: Figures in parentheses are *t*-statistics.
* denote significance at the 1 per cent level. *N* = 15.

Rural-Urban Disparity

The literacy rate was uneven not only among the states but also between rural and urban areas. Table 6.4 shows that the rural-urban disparity in literacy has been quite large in most of the states, even though it has declined over the years. In 1981, while Rajasthan had the highest rural-urban gap in literacy, as rural literacy constituted only 39 per cent of urban literacy; Kerala had the lowest gap with rural literacy constituting 92 per cent of urban literacy. However, in 2001, Bihar had the highest rural-urban gap in literacy, with rural literacy constituting 61 per cent of urban literacy and Kerala had the lowest corresponding gap, with rural literacy constituting 96 per cent of urban literacy. The inter-state variations in the rural-urban disparity in literacy declined over the census years, as the CV in the rural-urban ratio in literacy rate declined from 22.62 per cent in 1981 to 10.08 per cent in 2001.

Gross Enrolment and Dropout Rates

All-India

The progress in literacy has been due to the progress in the gross enrolment ratio (GER) and a reduction in the dropout rate (DOR). The GER at the primary (class I–V) and upper primary level (class VI–VIII) increased substantially in India during the period from 1981 to 2005-06 (Table 6.6). It increased from 47.2 per cent at the primary level and 50.0 per cent at the upper primary level in 1981 to 109.4 per cent and 71.15 per cent, respectively in 2005-06 (The GER exceeds 100 due to enrolment of children in the classes beyond the specified age group). The improvement in GER is observed

Table 6.6: Gross Enrolment Ratio and Dropout Rate: All-India

(Percentage)

Category/ Year	*Classes I-V (6-11 years) (Primary)*				*Classes VI-VIII (11-14 years) (Upper Primary)*			
	Boys	*Girls*	*Total*	*GPI*	*Boys*	*Girls*	*Total*	*GPI*
A. Gross Enrolment Ratio								
1981	55.3	38.5	47.2	0.696	62.0	36.7	50.0	0.592
1991	56.6	45.4	51.2	0.802	71.1	52.2	62.1	0.734
2005-06	112.69	105.87	109.40	0.939	75.41	66.50	71.15	0.881
B. Dropout Rate	Classes I-V (6-11 years)				Classes I-VIII (6-14 years)			
1981-82	51.1	57.3	53.5	1.121	68.5	77.7	72.1	1.134
1992-93	43.8	46.7	45.0	1.066	58.2	65.2	61.1	1.120
2005-06	28.53	21.54	25.47	0.755	48.49	48.98	48.71	1.010

Notes: Age-specific Enrolment Ratio = (Estimated enrolment in an age group ÷ Estimated child population in that age group)×100. The ratio may exceed 100 due to enrolment of children in the classes beyond the specified age group.
GPI = Gender Parity Index (= Girls ÷ Boys)

Sources: For 1981 and 1991: Census data as reported in Planning Commission (2002); For 2005-06: Selected Educational Statistics 2005-06, Ministry of Human Resource Development (Government of India) as reported in Planning Commission (2008).

for both boys and girls at both the levels. Moreover, the GPI in GER improved significantly from 0.696 at the primary level and 0.592 at the upper primary level in 1981 to 0.939 and 0.881, respectively in 2005-06.

The improvement in GER has been accompanied by a substantial drop in the dropout rates at the primary and upper primary levels. Table 6.6 shows that, at the all-India level, the dropout rate at the primary level declined from 53.5 per cent in 1981-82 to 25.47 per cent 2005-06. At the upper primary level, it declined from 72.1 per cent in 1981-82 to 48.71 per cent in 2005-06. The reduction in the dropout rate is evident in the case of both boys and girls. The GPI in the dropout rate also improved during the period, as the GPI declined from 1.121 at the primary level and 1.134 at the upper primary level in 1981-82 to 0.755 and 1.01, respectively, in 2005-06. Nevertheless, the dropout rates achieved in 2005-06 are quite above the Eleventh Plan's proposed dropout rate of 20 per cent at the elementary education in 2011-12.

Inter-State Variations in GER

The state-wise data reported in Table 6.7 reveal that while the GER at the primary level increased in all the states, the same at the upper primary level increased in all the states except Bihar during the period from 1981 to 2005-06. The inter-state variations in GER at the primary level declined substantially, as the CV in GER declined from 30.68 per cent in 1981 to 16.77 per cent in 2005-06. However, the variations at the upper primary level increased marginally, as the CV in GER increased from 23.85 per cent in 1981 to 24.76 per cent in 2005-06.

Table 6.8 shows that the dropout rate at the primary level has declined significantly in all the states except Rajasthan. Two states, viz. Kerala and Tamil Nadu experienced zero dropout rates in 2005-06. The dropout rate at the upper primary level has also declined substantially in all the states. Kerala experienced zero dropout rates in 2005-06. There are, however, large variations in the dropout rate at the primary and upper primary levels across the states, and the variations have increased over time. The CV in the dropout rate at the primary level increased from 32.85 per cent in 1981-82 to 83.82 per cent in 2005-06; the same at the upper

Table 6.7: Gross Enrolment Ratio: Major States

(Percentage)

States	Classes I-V (6-11 years) (Primary)			Classes VI-VIII (11-14 years) (Upper Primary)		
	1981	1991	2005-06	1981	1991	2005-06
Andhra Pradesh	46.3	53.0	94.87	39.9	55.9	73.91
Assam	—	46.0	107.11	—	63.4	72.83
Bihar	33.6	34.3	87.20	42.1	51.1	34.27
Gujarat	56.5	62.3	119.44	59.6	68.1	74.24
Haryana	50.0	62.2	79.61	53.8	73.1	74.83
Karnataka	51.7	61.9	106.19	46.3	63.2	84.64
Kerala	89.7	91.2	93.85	84.0	93.1	97.94
Madhya Pradesh	37.4	47.4	143.67	40.9	57.3	91.67
Maharashtra	63.4	69.1	112.34	60.7	75.7	100.64
Odisha	48.7	54.3	118.15	41.7	56.7	64.55
Punjab	64.4	65.9	77.46	61.2	73.4	67.53
Rajasthan	33.7	38.9	121.69	40.2	52.2	74.12
Tamil Nadu	67.4	77.4	120.07	52.8	72.1	106.81
Uttar Pradesh	33.9	36.7	110.57	43.8	51.3	53.02
West Bengal	45.9	45.9	119.89	52.8	61.1	66.71
India	47.2	51.2	109.40	50.0	62.1	71.15
CV (%)	30.68	28.02	16.77	23.85	17.93	24.76

Notes: Age-specific Enrolment Ratio = (Estimated enrolment in an age group ÷ Estimated child population in that age group)×100. The ratio may exceed 100 due to enrolment of children in the classes beyond the specified age group.

Sources: For 1981 and 1991: Census data as reported in Planning Commission (2002); For 2005-06: Selected Educational Statistics 2005-06, Ministry of Human Resource Development (Government of India) as reported in Planning Commission (2008a).

primary level increased from 23.23 per cent in 1981-82 to 51.22 per cent in 2005-06.

The review of the achievements in education reveals that though there has been a significant improvement in education with respect to inter-state, rural-urban and gender disparities, the inequalities have been persisting, and the quantitative expansion of education achieved have been unsatisfactory. The achievements in some of the dimensions of education are below the targets set by the Eleventh Plan and the MDG concerned.

Table 6.8: Drop-out Rate: Major States

States	*Classes I-V*			*Classes I-VIII*		
	1981-82	*1992-93*	*2005-06*	*1981-82*	*1992-93*	*2005-06*
Andhra Pradesh	60.3	54.96	24.75	76.5	75.94	59.07
Assam	62.5	55.37	47.78	82.5	69.22	73.48
Bihar	69.6	62.52	46.55	80.4	78.61	73.37
Gujarat	54.6	41.37	31.58	67.2	58.36	46.61
Haryana	21.8	17.95	5.40	44.9	35.56	10.63
Karnataka	60.8	41.0	15.50	75.1	61.09	44.83
Kerala	10.1	–2.35	0.0	23.0	2.40	0.0
Madhya Pradesh	52.6	34.34	0.29	68.0	53.52	41.25
Maharashtra	54.9	30.33	5.14	70.6	51.21	23.50
Odisha	63.4	50.63	41.20	82.9	69.24	62.63
Punjab	60.1	31.42	23.66	59.7	45.37	32.98
Rajasthan	48.8	74.68	52.84	70.1	81.88	59.47
Tamil Nadu	34.2	18.27	0.0	65.2	38.85	22.11
Uttar Pradesh	44.5	33.77	9.76	77.3	48.39	41.25
West Bengal	60.1	57.75	38.67	73.8	74.29	62.45
India	53.5	45.01	25.47	72.1	61.10	48.71
CV (%)	32.85	49.79	83.82	23.23	37.03	51.22

Sources: For 1981-82 and 1992-93: Planning Commission (2002); For 2005-06: Selected Educational Statistics 2005-06, Ministry of Human Resource Development (Government of India) as reported in Planning Commission (2008a).

Health

The health status of a population, which is a reflection of the socio-economic development of an economy, is shaped by a variety of factors. It is argued that the poor health status of low-income countries is due to inadequate nutrition, and lack of housing, sanitation, water supply, and healthcare delivery services. Moreover, attainments on other dimensions of human well-being, viz. education and income reinforce the achievement of better health and longevity (Nanda and Ali, 2006). A higher per capita income can help in attaining nutritional adequacy and food security for the poor. This, in association with the public provisioning of basic amenities including education, water, sanitation, housing, etc., can ensure a significant improvement in the health status of the population. The health status is measured in terms of some broad indicators, and the attainments on the health status are assessed by examining the temporal and regional variations in the indicators, viz. expectation of life at birth and infant mortality rate.

Expectation of Life at Birth

At the all-India level, the expectation of life at birth (ELB) improved from 55.5 years in 1981-85 to 62.5 years in 1998-2002, and further to 63.5 years in 2002-06. India's life expectancy of 63.5 years is, however, well below the life expectancy of around 80 years in the industrialized countries and 72 years in China.

Convergence in Life Expectancy

Table 6.9 shows that ELB has improved in all the major states and the inter-state variations in ELB have been low and declining over the years, as the CV in ELB declined from 8.84 per cent in 1981-85 to 7.78 per cent in 1991-95 and further to 6.95 per cent in 1998-2002. The ELB has improved in both rural and urban areas in all the states. The inter-state variations in ELB in rural and urban areas have been low and declining consistently, as the CV in ELB across the states for rural and urban areas declined between 1981-85 and 1998-2002 (Table 6.9 and Figure 6.5). There is, however, rural-urban disparity in ELB to some extent, which appears to have declined in all the states except Kerala, Maharashtra and Odisha. The regional variations in rural-urban disparity in ELB have also declined, as the CV in rural-urban ratio in ELB declined from 5.22 per cent in 1981-85 to 3.77 per cent in 1998-2002 (Table 6.12).

In order to see whether absolute β-convergence has occurred in ELB, the annual average growth in ELB has been plotted against initial level of ELB. It can be seen from Figure 6.6 that annual average growth rate in ELB is inversely related to initial level of ELB, indicating that absolute convergence has happened in ELB across the states. The OLS estimates of the convergence equation (Table 6.10) show that the coefficients on initial level of ELB are negative and statistically significant in all the cases, indicating absolute β-convergence in life expectancy across the states. The rate of convergence, however, declined from 1.64 per cent during the 1980s to 1.47 per cent during the 1990s.

Table 6.9: Expectation of Life at Birth (ELB)

(Years)

States	1981-85			1991-95			1998-2002		
	Combined	*Rural*	*Urban*	*Combined*	*Rural*	*Urban*	*Combined*	*Rural*	*Urban*
Andhra Pradesh	58.4	57.1	63.8	61.8	60.7	65.1	63.5	62.4	67.0
Assam	51.9	51.2	60.2	55.7	55.1	64.1	57.9	57.1	66.6
Bihar	52.9	52.1	61.0	59.3	58.5	65.8	60.8	59.9	66.8
Gujarat	57.6	56.2	60.7	61.0	60.1	63.2	63.4	62.1	65.6
Haryana	60.3	58.9	66.0	63.4	62.6	67.4	65.2	64.4	68.6
Karnataka	60.7	58.7	67.1	62.5	60.9	66.6	64.5	62.8	68.9
Kerala	68.4	68.5	67.6	72.9	73.0	73.6	73.5	73.4	74.1
Madhya Pradesh	51.6	50.0	60.3	54.7	53.2	62.8	56.9	55.6	64.3
Maharashtra	60.7	59.0	64.0	64.8	62.5	69.1	66.2	64.4	70.3
Odisha	53.0	52.4	59.6	56.5	55.7	64.4	58.5	57.8	65.6
Punjab	63.1	61.7	68.1	67.2	66.5	70.1	68.5	67.7	71.0
Rajasthan	53.5	52.0	61.1	59.1	57.0	64.2	61.1	59.7	66.1
Tamil Nadu	56.9	54.6	62.5	63.3	61.7	67.1	65.2	63.8	68.9
Uttar Pradesh	50.0	48.7	57.8	56.8	56.0	61.2	59.1	58.2	63.1
West Bengal	57.4	55.1	64.9	62.1	60.6	67.6	63.9	62.5	69.0
India	55.5	53.7	62.8	60.3	58.9	65.9	62.5	61.2	67.9
CV (%)	8.84	9.26	5.11	7.78	8.22	4.80	6.95	7.26	4.15

Sources: Planning Commission (2002); Registrar General (2003).

Table 6.10: Absolute β-convergence in ELB

Dependent Variable	Period	Constant	Coefficient on initial Level	R^2
Growth in ELB	1981/85-1991/95	0.0735 (2.518)	–0.0164** (–2.267)	0.283
Growth in ELB	1991/95-1998/2002	0.0648 (7.87)	–0.0147* (–7.36)	0.806
Growth in ELB	1981/85-1998/2002	0.0648 (4.30)	–0.0145* (–3.90)	0.539

Notes: Figures in parenthesis are *t*-statistics. * and ** denote significance at 1 per cent and 5 per cent levels, respectively. N = 15.

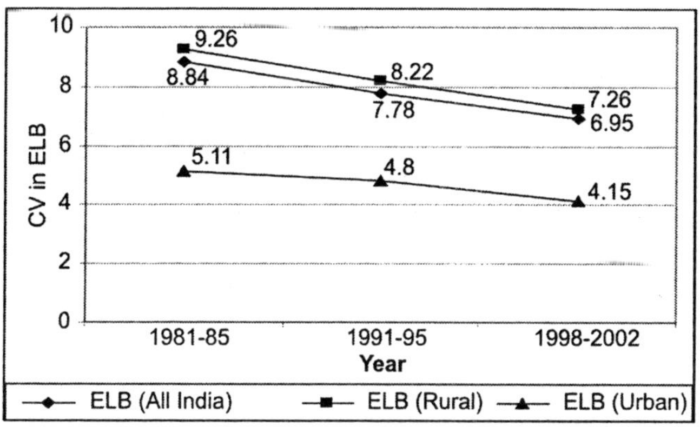

Fig. 6.5: σ-Convergence in Expectation of Life at Birth (ELB)

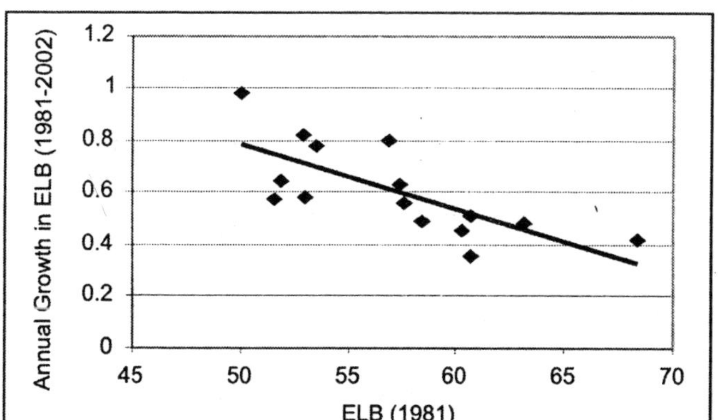

Fig. 6.6: Absolute Convergence in ELB (1981-2002)

Infant Mortality

The improvement in ELB has been accompanied by a substantial reduction in infant mortality. Table 6.11 shows that the infant mortality rate (IMR) at the all-India level declined remarkably from 115 per 1000 live births in 1981 to 53 in 2008, signifying a drop of 62 in 28 years. The achievement, however, appears to be unsatisfactory, in comparison with the Eleventh Plan's targeted IMR of 28 per 1000 live births in 2011-12. Moreover, infant mortality rate in India is much higher than that in East Asian countries.

Regional Disparities in IMR

Even though the IMR declined in the rural and urban areas of all the states during the period from 1981 to 2008, there have been wide variations in IMR across states. In 1981, it varied from 54 in Kerala to 163 in Odisha. In 2008, it varied from the lowest figure of 12 in Kerala to the highest of 70 in MP. The inter-state variations in IMR are observed in both rural and urban areas. The variations have also increased over the years, as the CV in IMR increased from 25.72 per cent in 1981 to 33.7 per cent in 2008. Similarly, the CV in IMR for rural and urban areas increased from 25.62 per cent (rural) and 24.27 per cent (urban) in 1981 to 32.28 per cent and 29.55 per cent, respectively, in 2008. Moreover, the rural-urban disparity in IMR has been quite high. At the all India level, the IMR in rural area was 1.84 times higher than that in urban area in 1981; it was 1.61 times higher in 2008 (Table 6.12). The rural-urban disparity in IMR has been large in all the states and the disparity has increased in all the states except Bihar, Haryana, Maharashtra, Odisha, Tamil Nadu, Uttar Pradesh and West Bengal. The inter-State variation in the rural-urban ratio in IMR increased significantly during the period 1981–2001, as the CV in the ratio increased from 13.57 per cent in 1981 to 23.63 per cent in 2001; it, however, declined to 14.71 per cent in 2008.

Per Capita Income

The regional convergence in the human development indicators (HDI, LR and ELB) has happened, despite regional divergence in per capita income (PCI). Table 6.13 and Figure 6.7 show that the

Table 6.11: Infant Mortality Rate (Number of death by age 1 per 1000 live births)

States	*1981*			*1991*			*2001*			*2008*		
	C	*R*	*U*	*C*	*R*	*U*	*C*	*R*	*U*	*C*	*R*	*U*
Andhra Pradesh	91	95	72	55	58	42	66	74	39	52	58	36
Assam	—	—	—	92	94	48	73	76	33	64	66	39
Bihar	94	98	62	75	77	50	62	63	52	56	57	42
Gujarat	115	129	85	78	83	64	60	67	42	50	58	35
Haryana	126	132	94	52	56	37	65	68	54	54	58	43
Karnataka	81	87	62	74	84	45	58	69	27	45	50	33
Kerala	54	56	49	42	45	42	11	12	9	12	12	10
Madhya Pradesh	150	158	105	133	142	84	86	92	53	70	75	48
Maharashtra	119	131	67	74	85	47	45	55	27	33	40	23
Odisha	163	171	111	125	130	72	90	94	60	69	71	49
Punjab	127	135	104	74	81	56	51	55	37	41	45	33
Rajasthan	141	153	97	87	93	55	79	83	57	63	69	38
Tamil Nadu	104	116	78	54	62	40	49	54	35	31	34	28
Uttar Pradesh	130	139	81	99	104	76	82	86	62	67	70	49
West Bengal	95	103	59	62	66	41	51	53	38	35	37	29
India	115	123	67	77	84	51	66	72	42	53	58	36
CV (%)	25.72	25.62	24.27	32.94	31.67	27.15	32.08	30.49	35.31	33.70	32.28	29.55

Notes: *C* = Combined; *R* = Rural; *U* = Urban.
Sources: Planning Commission (2002); Registrar General (2002, 2009).

Table 6.12: Rural-Urban Disparity in Some Indicators of Education and Health: Major States

States	*Rural-Urban Ratio in Literacy Rate*				*Rural-Urban Ratio in Expectation of Life at Birth*			*Rural-Urban Ratio in Infant Mortality Rate*			
	1981	*1991*	*2001*	*2011*	*1981-85*	*1991-95*	*1998-2002*	*1981*	*1991*	*2001*	*2008*
Andhra Pradesh	0.46	0.54	0.72	0.75	0.89	0.93	0.93	1.32	1.38	1.90	1.54
Assam	0.46	0.62	0.71	0.79	0.85	0.86	0.86	1.32	1.96	2.30	1.73
Bihar	0.45	0.50	0.61	0.78	0.85	0.89	0.90	1.58	1.54	1.21	1.33
Gujarat	0.61	0.69	0.74	0.83	0.93	0.95	0.95	1.52	1.30	1.60	1.67
Haryana	0.56	0.68	0.80	0.87	0.89	0.93	0.94	1.40	1.51	1.26	1.32
Karnataka	0.56	0.64	0.74	0.80	0.87	0.91	0.91	1.40	1.87	2.56	1.52
Kerala	0.92	0.96	0.96	0.98	1.01	0.99	0.99	1.14	1.07	1.33	1.09
Madhya Pradesh	0.45	0.51	0.73	0.77	0.83	0.85	0.86	1.50	1.69	1.74	1.60
Maharashtra	0.61	0.70	0.83	0.86	0.92	0.90	0.92	1.96	1.81	2.04	1.68
Odisha	0.58	0.63	0.75	0.83	0.88	0.86	0.88	1.54	1.81	1.57	1.48
Punjab	0.64	0.73	0.82	0.86	0.91	0.95	0.95	1.30	1.45	1.49	1.35
Rajasthan	0.39	0.46	0.73	0.77	0.85	0.89	0.90	1.58	1.69	1.46	1.86
Tamil Nadu	0.61	0.70	0.81	0.85	0.87	0.92	0.93	1.49	1.55	1.54	1.15
Uttar Pradesh	0.52	0.60	0.76	0.88	0.84	0.92	0.92	1.72	1.37	1.39	1.40
West Bengal	0.57	0.67	0.78	0.85	0.85	0.90	0.91	1.75	1.61	1.39	1.26
India	0.54	0.61	0.74	0.81	0.86	0.89	0.90	1.84	1.65	1.71	1.62
CV (%)	22.62	18.89	10.08	6.95	5.22	4.21	3.77	13.57	15.20	23.63	14.71

Notes: An increase in the rural-urban ratio in Literacy Rate and Expectation of Life at Birth implies an improvement of relative performance in favour of rural area (that is, lower rural-urban disparity). However, an increase in the rural-urban ratio in Infant Mortality Rate indicates the opposite. The value of the ratio equal to unity implies perfect rural-urban parity

Sources: Estimated from data in Tables 6.4, 6.9 and 6.11.

CV of PCI has increased over time. Thus, while there has been σ-convergence in human development, there has been σ-divergence in per capita income across the states, implying that while the regional disparities in HDI, LR and ELB have been consistently declining, there has been an increasing trend in the regional disparities in PCI. There has also been absolute β-divergence in PCI. The annual average growth rate of PCI is found to be positively related to initial level of PCI during 1980-81–2006-07, the estimated line representing the relationship between the two being upward sloping (Fig. 6.8).

Table 6.14 shows that the coefficient on initial level of PCI is significantly positive in all the periods, indicating absolute divergence of PCI across states. Moreover, a comparison between the pre- and post-reform periods shows that the rate of divergence in PCI has increased from 1.2 per cent during the 1980s to 1.81 per cent during 1991-92 – 2006-07. Thus, while the human development indicators exhibited significant convergence, PCI experienced significant divergence across the states. This indicates that the gap between the rich and poor states observed in PCI has been reduced for human development. This suggests that the poor states, which failed to catch up with the rich ones in terms of per capita income, have managed to catch up in terms of human well-being. Despite significant divergence in PCI, the convergence in LR and ELB made it possible to achieve significant reductions in the regional disparities in HDI.

Income, Public Expenditure and Human Development

This section examines the effects of per capita income and per capita social sector expenditure on human development. A higher per capita income is likely to raise the ability of households to spend a larger amount of income on food and non-food items, which may lead to an improvement in human well-being. Evidence shows that higher per capita income is associated with lower poverty incidence (Ahluwalia 1978; Ghosh 2008, 2009), and expenditure on human development-related items is influenced by the rate of poverty reduction. Evidence also indicates that expenditure on child schooling and healthcare are significantly related to household income. Moreover, an increase in government spending on human development-related activities leads to an

Table 6.13: Per Capita Real State Domestic Product at Constant (1980-81) Prices

(in Rupees)

States	*1980-81*	*1990-91*	*2000-01*	*2006-07*
Andhra Pradesh	1380	2060	2994	4137
Assam	1284	1544	1635	2051
Bihar	917	1197	1205	1577
Gujarat	1940	2641	3905	6938
Haryana	2370	3509	4385	6539
Karnataka	1520	2039	3564	4709
Kerala	1508	1815	2673	3692
Madhya Pradesh	1358	1693	1965	2278
Maharashtra	2435	3483	5026	7304
Odisha	1314	1383	1778	2704
Punjab	2674	3730	4788	5682
Rajasthan	1222	1942	2233	2669
Tamil Nadu	1498	2237	3597	4791
Uttar Pradesh	1278	1652	1796	2147
West Bengal	1773	2145	3524	4774
India	1630	2223	3234	4540
CV (%)	31.09	36.0	40.55	45.69

Sources: Chandhok and the Policy Group (1990), Government of India (2003, 2008), and EPW Research Foundation (1998).

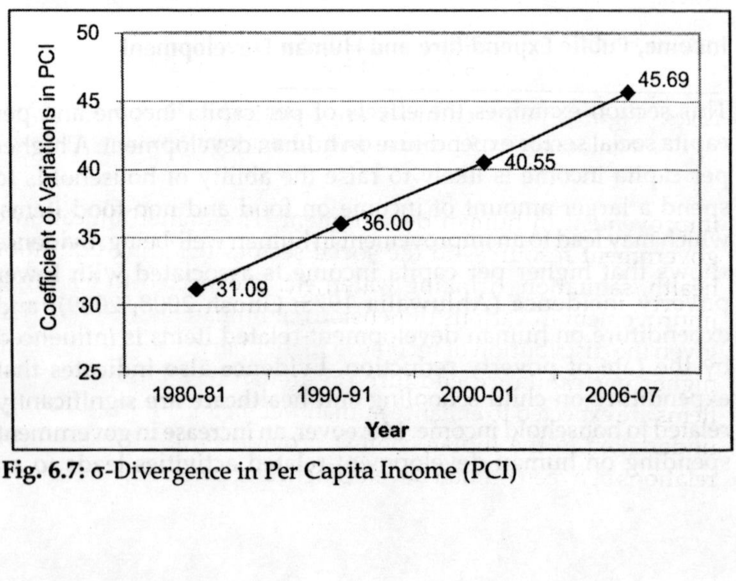

Fig. 6.7: σ-Divergence in Per Capita Income (PCI)

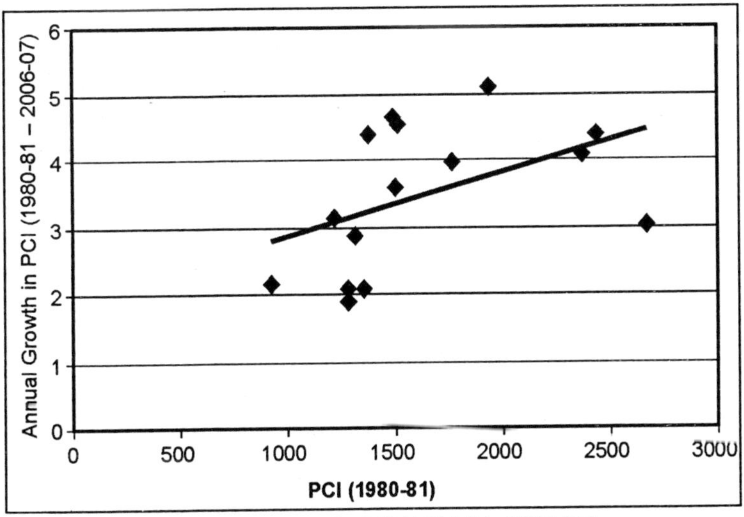

Fig. 6.8: Absolute β-Divergence in PCI (1980/81–2006/07)

Table 6.14: Absolute β-convergence in Per Capita Income (PCI)

Dependent Variable	*Period*	*Constant*	*Coefficient on initial Level*	R^2
Growth in PCI	1980-81– 1990-91	–0.061 (–1.087)	0.012*** (1.552)	0.156
Growth in PCI	1991-92– 2006-07	–0.102 (–1.19)	0.0181*** (1.61)	0.166
Growth in PCI	1980-81– 2006-07	–0.101 (1.64)	0.0182** (2.18)	0.267

Notes: Figures in parentheses are t-statistics. ** and *** denote significance at 5 per cent and 10 per cent levels, respectively. N = 15.

improvement in human development. The higher allocation of government resources to the social sector, including education, health, sanitation, drinking water, etc. is expected to lead to an improvement in various dimensions of human well-being. Thus, given the distribution of income, a higher per capita income and a higher per capita expenditure on human development-related items are expected to enhance human well-being. Empirical studies undertaken in the Indian context provide evidence for positive relations between human development and per capita income and expenditure (Dholakia 2003, 2009; Ghosh 2006, 2008, 2011; Kurian 2000; Tilak 2002).

The effects of per capita income and per capita social sector expenditure on human development are examined by estimating correlation between the human development indicators and per capita income and per capita government expenditure on human development-related items. The estimated correlation coefficients are reported in Table 6.15. The correlation of per capita income and per capita social sector expenditure (PCSSE) with the human development indicators like HDI, LR, GER and ELB are positive; their correlations with IMR are negative. These indicate that higher per capita income and per capita social sector expenditure (PCSSE) have improved human well-being by raising HDI, LR, GER and ELB, and lowering IMR. The states with higher per capita incomes, which were able to spend a higher per capita amount on social services, performed better in achieving improvements in human development.

Table 6.15: Correlation between Human Development and Income and Expenditure

Human Development Indicator	*Correlation Coefficient Between Human Development Indicator and Income and Expenditure*	
	PCI	*PCSSE*
HDI	0.6966	0.3910
LR	0.5566	0.4725
GER	0.4179	0.4476
ELB	0.6421	0.3764
IMR	–0.4774	–0.4436

Notes: The correlation coefficients are estimated by using cross-sectional data for 15 states at three time points. Number of observations = 45. PCI = Per capita income; PCSSE = Per capita social sector expenditure.

Summary and Conclusions

The paper has evaluated the performance of 15 major Indian states on education, health and human development. It has examined the regional variations in human development and their association with per capita income and per capita expenditure in the social sector. While the regional disparity in human development has declined, the same in terms of per capita income has increased, suggesting that the poor states, which failed to catch up with the rich ones in terms of per capita income, have, however, managed to catch up in terms of human development. Higher per capita income and per capita social sector expenditure have improved human well-being by raising HDI, LR, GER and ELB, and lowering IMR. The states with higher per capita incomes are able to spend a higher per capita amount on social services, performed better in improving human development. This suggests that improvements in human well-being and reductions in regional disparities in various dimensions of human development require increasing public investment in the social sector activities, including education, health, water supply, sanitation, housing, social security and welfare of the weaker sections of the population.

REFERENCES

Ahluwalia, M.S. (1978). 'Rural Poverty and Agricultural Performance in India', *Journal of Development Studies*, 14(3): 298-323.

Chandhok, H.L. and the Policy Group (1990). *India Database: The Economy*, Vol. 1. New Delhi: Living Media India Ltd.

Dholakia, R.H. (2003). 'Regional Disparity in Economic and Human Development in India', *Economic and Political Weekly*, 38(39): 4166-72.

Dholakia, R.H. (2009). 'Trends in Regional Disparity in Human and Social Development in India', *Indian Journal of Human Development*, 3(1): 5-26.

EPW Research Foundation (1998). *National Accounts Statistics of India 1950/51 to 1996-97* (Third Edition). Mumbai: Sameeksha Trust.

Ghosh, M. (2006). 'Economic Growth and Human Development in Indian States', *Economic and Political Weekly*, 41(30): 3321-29.

Ghosh, M. (2008). *Economic Reforms and Indian Economic Development—Selected Essays*. New Delhi: Bookwell.

Ghosh, M. (2009). 'Dynamics of Agricultural Development and Rural Poverty in Indian States', *Margin—The Journal of Applied Economic Research*, 3(3): 265-95.

Ghosh, M. (2011). 'Regional Disparities in Education, Health and Human Development in India', *Indian Journal of Human Development*, 5(1): 5-28.

Government of India (2003). *National Accounts Statistics*, National Accounts Division, Central Statistical Organization, Ministry of

Statistics and Programme Implementation, New Delhi, Available at: *http://www.mospi.nic.in.*

Government of India (2008). *State Domestic Product (State Series)*, National Accounts Division, Central Statistical Organization, Ministry of Statistics and Programme Implementation, New Delhi, Available at: *http://www.mospi.nic.in*, Accessed on 28 February, 2008.

Kurian, N.J. (2000). 'Widening Regional Disparities in India: Some Indicators', *Economic and Political Weekly*, 35(7): 538-50.

Nanda, A.R. and A. Ali (2006). 'Health Sector—Issues and Challenges', in *India Social Development Report*, pp. 18-32. New Delhi: Council for Social Development and Oxford University Press.

Planning Commission (2002). *National Human Development Report 2001*. New Delhi: Government of India.

Planning Commission (2008). 'Data for Use of Deputy Chairman, Planning Commission', Government of India, New Delhi, Available at: http://planningcommission.gov.in, Accessed on 20 December 2008.

Registrar General of India (2002). *Sample Registration System Bulletin*, 36(2): October. New Delhi: Vital Statistics Division, Ministry of Home Affairs, Government of India.

Registrar General of India (2003). *SRS Based Abridged Life Table 1998-2002*. New Delhi: Vital Statistics Division, Ministry of Home Affairs, Government of India.

Registrar General of India (2009). *Sample Registration System Bulletin*, 44(1): October. New Delhi: Vital Statistics Division, Ministry of Home Affairs, Government of India.

Tilak, J.B.G. (1987). *Economics of Inequality in Education*. New Delhi: Sage Publications.

Tilak, J.B.G. (1999). 'Investment in Human Capital in India: An Inter-State Analysis of Stock and Flow of Human Capital', *Journal of Indian School of Political Economy*, 11(1): 39-75.

Tilak, J.B.G. (2002). 'Education Poverty in India', *Review of Development and Change*, 7(1): 1-44.

Tilak, J.B.G. (2006) 'Education—A Saga of Spectacular Achievements and Conspicuous Failures', in *India Social Development Report*, pp. 33-49. New Delhi: Council for Social Development and Oxford University Press.

7

Post-Reform Economic Growth and Regional Inequality in India

Shibalal Meher

India has made significant economic progress after the reform initiated in the early 1990s and rapidly emerged as a major economic force. The overall economic growth has continued at an impressive rate. This growth is all the more impressive, even though the significant obstacles like high rate of poverty and income inequality inherent in the Indian economy remains to be overcome. Because of the specific localization of the nascent economic growth, the benefits have been realized by a selective minority, while hundreds of millions continue to live in abject poverty. This could result in income inequality, a situation that may have significant repercussions.

Economists have put significant efforts to the study of income inequality. However, the topic has lost its importance over the years, with many academicians and policy experts choosing to focus more on absolute poverty than overall income distribution. Income inequality is important because of the implications for social and political development. It is widely understood that income equality can provide stability for a nation, which can only help in fostering long term economic growth. More directly, income equality enables many more individuals to participate in the economy. Therefore, it is necessary to understand the income distribution efforts in India during the post-reform period.

After going through a brief review of earlier studies concerning economic growth, income inequality, and convergence/divergence, the paper presents the methodological aspects for measuring the growth and income inequality adopted in the present study. Then the empirical findings of the study are presented. Finally, conclusions of the results are discussed.

Review of Literature

The relationship between growth and inequality has been debated extensively in the literature. Starting with the classical economists, Ricardo's two sector model which mainly concentrated on growth and distribution within agriculture and industry addressed the shares of rent and profits and growth process eventually approaching the steady state of zero growth due to diminishing returns in agriculture (Boyer, 1996). Karl Marx also believed that capitalist development would inherently result in uneven distribution of wealth and capitalist have an incentive for pushing wages to the subsistence level (Martin and Sunley, 1998; Dunford and Smith, 2000). The neo-classical growth models for closed economies (Solow, 1956, 1957 & 1970; Cass, 1965; Koopmans, 1965) state that per capita growth rate tends to be inversely related to the starting level of output/income per head and if economies are similar in respect of preferences and technologies, then poor economies grow faster than rich ones. The neo-classicalists, however, were more optimistic about market forces and postulated that regional inequality is a passing phase and that market forces would ensure that the returns to all factors of production would approach their marginal products (Smith, 1975). Neo-Keynesians such as Kalechi (1954, 1971), Steindl (1952), Kaldor (1955-56, 1960) and Pasinetti (1962, 1977 & 1981) have explained the inter-relationship between income distribution and economic growth. By and large, Neo-Keynesian growth models have concluded that reduction in concentration raises the real wage and provides a redistribution of income which leads to higher capacity utilization and higher rate of economic growth.

The link between inequality and average well-being for two sector economy is known as Kuznet's hypothesis (1955, 1963) which maintains that given a two-sector economy with not too distinct degrees of sectoral mean incomes, a perennial shift of population from one sector to another will initially raise aggregate inequality and it will decrease at later stage. This formulation has been labelled as the "Inverted U" (I-U) hypothesis or Kuznets cycle (Branlke, 1983). Regional concentration/diversification has also been examined through 'convergence hypothesis' which has primarily emerged due to seminal theoretical contributions on endogenous growth models by Romer (1986, 1987, 1990, 1992, 1993) and Lucas (1988). The hypothesis asserts that differences in contemporaneous per capita income between any pair of regions will be transitory so long as the two regions contain identical technologies, preferences and population growth (Bernard and Durlauf, 1966). The bulk of the new theoretical literature on growth and inequality has focused on models which generate divergence across nations. The theoretical as well as empirical presentation by Barro, Robert, J. (1990, 1991, 1999), Borro, Robert, J. and Jong-Wha Lee (1994), Barro, Robert, J., N. Gregory Mankiw, and Xavier Sala-i-Martin (1991, 1992a, 1992b, 1992c, 1997, 2007), Baumol (1986), Cashin (1995), Cashin and Sahay (1996), Delong (1988), Dowrick and Nguyen (1989), Easterlin (1960a, 1960b), Quah (1993, 1995, 1996a, 1996b) etc. deal with process of convergence/ divergence at national as well as international level.

In India, inter-state/region inequality has been one of the major concerns before policymakers and planners. After independence, reduction in inter-state/regional disparities has been emphasized during the successive five year plans. Apart from that the issue has been examined in depth by the scholars. The number of studies on convergence or divergence among the Indian States has mushroomed in the past few years (Aiyar, 2001; Bajpai and Sachs, 1996; Cashin and Sahay, 1996; Marjit and Mitra, 1996; Marjit and Ghosh, 2000; Nagaraj, Varoudakis and Veganzones, 1998; Rao, Shand and Kalirajan, 1999; Rao and Sen, 1997; and others). This interest has been driven by the general resurgence of growth theory and done within the framework of neoclassical growth models. These models demonstrate that in closed economies with no differences in technology and preferences, the growth rate in per capita incomes tends to be inversely related to the initial levels of per capita incomes.

The earlier studies mostly support in favour of absolute divergence among the Indian States in the past three decades, with the rate of increasing in the 1990s (Rao and Singh, 2001). The evidence on conditional convergence is less decisive, but even if one accepts conditional convergence as descriptive of Indian States, the conclusion remains that the States may be converging to very different steady states (*ibid.*). The differences in infrastructure and institutions that seem to explain inter-State differences have been persistent, and neither the Finance Commission transfer or Planning Commission transfer, nor centrally sponsored schemes have made a substantial dent in regional inequalities in India.

Methodology

The present study uses statistical techniques:

(1) to estimate the growth rates of income of states,
(2) to test the change in the structure of income in the later part of the reform period, and
(3) to measure the regional inequality in income in India.

(1) Estimation of Growth Rates

The growth rate of per capita income of 17 major non-specific states in India during the post-reform period has been estimated to compare the performance of poorer states with the richer states. It is studied to see whether the direction of divergence has changed and become forces for convergence during post-reform period. The growth rate has been estimated by using semi-log model, viz.

$$Y = \alpha\beta^t$$

i.e. $\log Y = \log \alpha + \log \beta t$

where Y = Per capita NSDP

t = Time period

The Growth rate is given by

$$[\text{Anti log } (\log \beta) - 1] * 100.$$

(2) Test of Structural Change

To test the change in structure of the income, the dummy variable technique has been used. The objective is to see whether there is a significant change in the intercept and slope of the income in 2001-10 from 1993-2001. To test this, the following semi-log model along with the dummy variable technique has been used.

$$\log Y = \log \alpha + \log \beta_t + \lambda_1 D + \lambda_2 Dt + \varepsilon_t$$

where

Y = per capita income

t = time period

D = dummy variable

= {0, for the period 1993-2001, and 1, for the period 2001-10}

λ_1 = differential intercept or change in intercept

λ_2 = differential slope or change in slope

(3) Measurement of Inequality

The present study measures inequality by testing the convergence/ divergence of the per capita income of the States by using both the measures of beta (β) convergence and sigma (σ) convergence.

β *Convergence*

The study uses a panel data to estimate β convergence coefficient from the following regression model.

$$\ln(Y_{i,t}) - \ln(Y_{i,t-1}) = \alpha_i - \beta \ln(Y_{i,t-1}) + u_{i,t}\,,\ 0 < \beta$$

where $Y_{i,t}$ is the per capita income of the ith State at time period t. According to this equation, the annual growth rate of per capita income, ln $(Y_{i,t})$ – ln $(Y_{i,t-1})$, should be negatively related to the previous level of income, ln $(Y_{i,\,t-1})$, if neoclassical convergence dynamics are present. This would suggest that not only poorer regions grow faster than richer regions, but also that they all converge to the same level of per capita income.

In the β convergence measure, the speed of convergence is measured by β. A negative value of β indicates convergence while β assuming a positive value indicates divergence. The absolute value of β, however, shows the intensity with which convergence/ divergence takes place.

σ *Convergence*

The study uses a related but alternate measure of convergence, called σ convergence, which measures cross-sectional dispersion of per capita incomes across states. This is measured here as the coefficient of variation of the logarithm of per capita incomes.

Thus, while β convergence is measured here as the speed at which the poorer regions/States catch up with richer ones, σ convergence measures inter-regional inequality in per capita incomes at a given point of time. These two notions of convergence that are used extensively in empirical works are used here to examine the inter-State disparities and the speed of convergence.

Findings

Growth in Per Capita Income

It can be seen from Table 7.1 that the variation in per capita income (at 2004-05 prices) of State governments has increased overtime even though the share of State with lowest per capita income to the State with highest per capita income has declined from 23.62 per cent in 1993-94 to 20.12 per cent in 2009-10. The coefficient of variation has increased from 32.56 per cent in 1993-94 to 40.48 per cent in 2009-10. The distance of per capita income continues to remain significantly high across various income category States. The real per capita income varied within a range of Rs. 11,558 in the case of Bihar (the lowest income State) to Rs. 57,458 in the case of Maharashtra (the highest income State) in the year 2009-10.

Table 7.1: Inter-State Comparison of Real Per Capita Income

Sl. No.	*States*	*1993-94*	*2001-02*	*2009-10*
1.	Andhra Pradesh	15364	21833	36345
2.	Bihar	**6134**	**6868**	**11558**
3.	Jharkhand	13535	15034	22780
4.	Gujarat	19060	24963	49030
5.	Haryana	23838	**31613**	55214
6.	Karnataka	16947	23458	37464
7.	Kerala	18897	26209	46511
8.	Madhya Pradesh	12687	15035	19736
9.	Chhattisgarh	14989	16095	25835
10.	Maharashtra	24807	30049	**57458**
11.	Odisha	11826	13967	24098
12.	Punjab	**25974**	30689	43539
13.	Rajasthan	12255	17351	23669
14.	Tamil Nadu	18741	25877	46823
15.	Uttar Pradesh	10723	11917	16182
16.	Uttarakhand	16277	19469	41126
17.	West Bengal	13472	20148	30504
	CV (%)	32.56	34.35	40.48
% share of lowest income to highest income		23.62	21.72	20.12

Table 7.2 shows the growth rates in 17 states for the period 1993-2010 and the two sub-periods, viz. 1993-2001 (1990s) and 2001-10 (2000s). The higher level increases in the growth of per capita income during 2001-10 over 1993-2001 were posted by Uttarakhand (9.25%), Chhattisgarh (6.41%), Maharashtra (6.1%), Gujarat (5.61%) and Odisha (5.56%). Also, Bihar with growth rate of 4.57 percentage points and Haryana with 4.36 percentage points were not far behind. The most laggards were West Bengal (0.24%), Rajasthan (0.72%), Madhya Pradesh (1.19%) and Karnataka (1.47%).

Table 7.2: Annual Growth Rates of per capita NSDP of States during Post-Reform Period

(%)

Sl. No.	States	1993-94 to 2000-01	2001-02 to 2009-10	1993-94 to 2009-10
1.	Andhra Pradesh	4.23	7.4	5.68
2.	Bihar	2.09	6.66	3.75
3.	Jharkhand	2.8	5.44	2.8
4.	Gujarat	3.28	8.89	5.2
5.	Haryana	3.04	7.4	5.44
6.	Karnataka	5.44	6.91	4.95
7.	Kerala	3.99	7.65	5.68
8.	Madhya Pradesh	2.8	3.99	2.33
9.	Chhattisgarh	0	6.41	3.28
10.	Maharashtra	3.04	9.14	5.2
11.	Odisha	2.09	7.65	4.71
12.	Punjab	2.57	4.71	3.04
13	Rajasthan	4.23	4.95	3.51
14.	Tamil Nadu	4.71	8.64	5.44
15.	Uttar Pradesh	1.62	3.99	2.33
16.	Uttarakhand	1.16	10.41	5.93
17.	West Bengal	5.2	5.44	4.95
	CV (%)	47.34	27.47	28.74

Figure 7.1 plots the per capita NSDP growth rate of these 17 states for two time periods, 1993-2001 (on the horizontal axis) and 2001-10 (on the vertical axis). The figure shows that seven states, viz. Uttarakhand, Chhattisgarh, Odisha, Bihar, Maharashtra, Gujarat, and Haryana lie above the 45-degree line, showing substantially higher growth in the 2000s than in the 1990s.

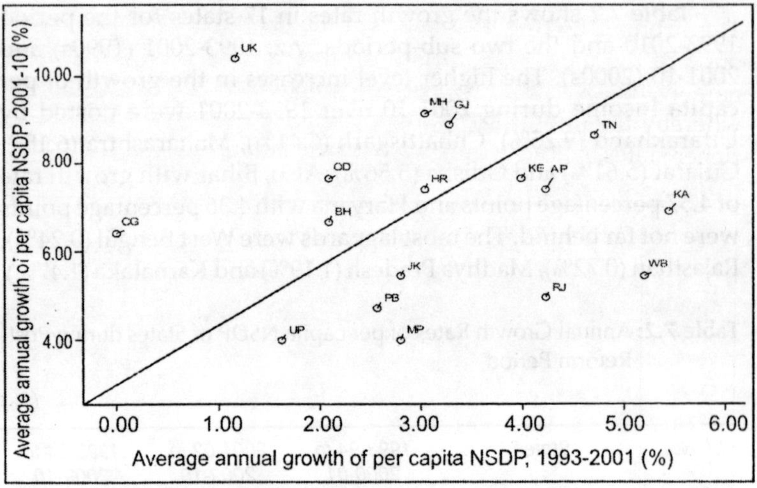

Note: 1. Straight line is a 45-degree line.

2. NSDP = Net State Domestic Product, AP = Andhra Pradesh, BH = Bihar, JK=Jharkhand, GJ = Gujarat, HR = Haryana, KA = Karnataka, KE = Kerala, MP = Madhya Pradesh, CG = Chhattisgarh, MH = Maharashtra, OD = Odisha, PB = Punjab, RJ = Rajasthan, TN = Tamil Nadu, UP = Uttar Pradesh, UK = Uttarakhand, WB = West Bengal.

Source: Central Statistical Office and author's calculations.

Fig. 7.1: Average Annual Growth of Per Capita NSDP, 1993-2001 and 2001-2010

A remarkable feature of growth performance during the 2000s was the strong performance of hitherto laggard states. Uttarakhand, Chhattisgarh, Odisha and Bihar recorded some improvements during the period 2001-10 as compared to the previous period, i.e. 1993-2001. It is, therefore, necessary, to see whether the direction of divergence has changed and become forces for convergence during the 2000s.

Figure 7.2 provides initial evidence on this. It plots the growth rate of the states for the period 2001-10 against the per capita NSDP in 2001-02. If there is convergence with the income level of the richer states, the relationship should be downward sloping. That means the income of the richer states should grow at a slower rate. But, as Figure 7.2 shows, richer states on average grew faster so that the inequality across states is actually increasing. We find that far from changing directions the forces of divergence continue.

The strong growth performance of the laggard states should not obscure the more general pattern that across the Indian states, namely, that we still do not see the phenomenon of convergence, whereby the poorer states, by virtue of growing faster than the richer states, start catching up with the latter's level of income.

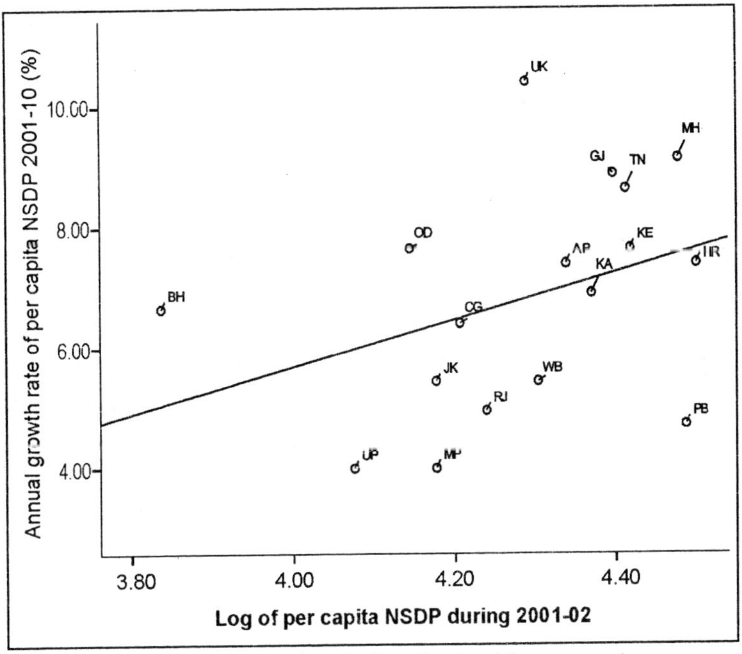

Note: 1. Line shown is the fitted plot obtained by regressing average annual growth rate of per capita NSDP during 2001-10 on the ln of per capita NSDP in 2001-02.

2. NSDP = Net State Domestic Product, AP = Andhra Pradesh, BH=Bihar, JK = Jharkhand, GJ = Gujarat, HR = Haryana, KA=Karnataka, KE = Kerala, MP = Madhya Pradesh, CG = Chhattisgarh, MH = Maharashtra, OD = Odisha, PB = Punjab, RJ = Rajasthan, TN = Tamil Nadu, UP = Uttar Pradesh, UK = Uttarakhand, WB = West Bengal.

Source: Central Statistical Office and author's calculations.

Fig. 7.2: Per capita NSDP during 2001-02 and annual growth during 2001-10

Now we consider the total time period under study (i.e. 1993-2010) to see if there is convergence over a longer period of time. That means whether the richer states grow at a slower rate during the post reform period. Figure 7.3 shows that states with a higher per capita income in 1993-94 grew faster over the next seventeen years. In other words, we do not find any evidence of convergence over a shorter or a longer period.

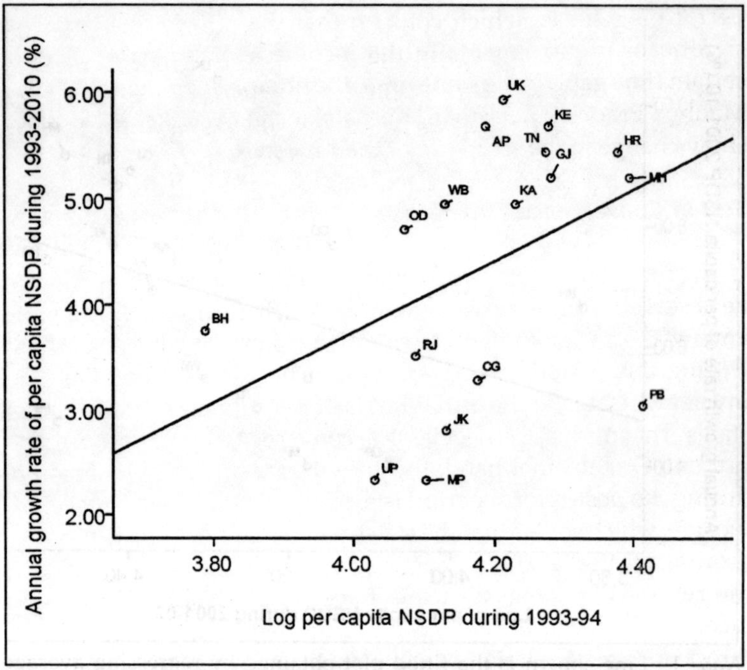

Note: 1. Line shown is the fitted plot obtained by regressing average annual growth rate of per capita NSDP during 2001-10 on the ln of per capita NSDP in 2001-02.

2. NSDP = Net State Domestic Product, AP = Andhra Pradesh, BH = Bihar, JK = Jharkhand, GJ = Gujarat, HR = Haryana, KA = Karnataka, KE = Kerala, MP = Madhya Pradesh, CG = Chhattisgarh, MH = Maharashtra, OD = Odisha, PB = Punjab, RJ = Rajasthan, TN = Tamil Nadu, UP = Uttar Pradesh, UK = Uttarakhand, WB = West Bengal.

Source: Central Statistical Office and author's calculations.

Fig. 7.3: Per capita NSDP during 1993-94 and growth rate during 1993-2010

Structural Change

Improvement in the growth of per capita income of better performing states has been verified from the structural change in income of the states from 1993-2001 to 2001-10. Table 7.3 shows that there is significant change in the structure of the better performing states, which confirm that the reform has brought significant improvements in the income of these states after a certain time gap. At the same time, the non-performing states like Madhya Pradesh, Rajasthan, Karnataka and West Bengal do not show change in the structure of their income.

Test of Convergence/Divergence

Using the β convergence/divergence measure of inequality, it can be observed from Table 7.4 that there is no convergence of income among the major Indian states during the post-reform period. During this period the growth rate of per capita income is not inversely related to the initial levels of per capita income of these states. That means, the neoclassical convergence dynamics are not present. On the other hand, the growth rate of per capita income during the post-reform period is directly related to initial level of income, which shows that the states with higher per capita income grow at a faster rate in the post-reform period. This indicates that the reform has intensified the disparity in the distribution of income. However, in the initial period there was no significant direct or inverse relation of the growth rate with initial income. But with the gathering momentum of reform, the richer states show faster growth of income, which can be seen from the significant direct relation of growth rate with initial income in the later part of reform period under study.

The trend in the dispersion of per capita income across states over the period 1993-2010 as measured by the coefficient of variation of log per capita income is presented in Figure 7.4. It is seen that there is an increasing trend in the dispersion of income during the post-reform period. This shows that inter-state inequality in per capita income has been growing over the post-reform period. Or, we can say that the divergence of income of the states has been observed through the measure of σ convergence.

Table 7.3: Structural change of per capita income of major non-special category states

Sl. No.	States	Intercept	t	d	dt	R^2
1	Andhra Pradesh	4.165* (449.338)	0.018* (9.984)	–0.120* (–5.349)	0.012* (5.176)	0.99
2	Bihar	3.769* (157.737)	0.009*** (1.959)	–0.204* (–3.546)	0.019* (3.049)	0.90
3	Jharkhand	4.120* (152.400)	0.012** (2.199)	–0.163** (–2.496)	0.011 (1.641)	0.82
4	Gujarat	4.314* (217.000)	0.014* (3.539)	–0.245* (–5.099)	0.023* (4.458)	0.96
5	Haryana	4.365 (761.480)	0.013 (11.844)	–0.153* (–11.087)	0.018* (11.835)	0.99
6	Karnataka	4.199* (376.809)	0.023* (10.517)	–0.103* (–3.816)	0.006 (1.923)	0.99
7	Kerala	4.267* (925.557)	0.017* (18.578)	–0.138* (–12.406)	0.015* (12.279)	0.99
8	Madhya Pradesh	4.086* (316.326)	0.012* (4.792)	–0.090** (–2.872)	0.005 (1.370)	0.93
9	Chhattisgarh	4.178* (315.397)	0.000 (.079)	–0.236* (–7.396)	0.027* (7.911)	0.97
10	Maharashtra	4.381* (438.649)	0.013* (6.820)	–0.260* (–10.796)	0.024* (9.490)	0.99
11	Odisha	4.062* (330.359)	0.009* (3.707)	–0.222* (–7.487)	0.023* (7.322)	0.98
12	Punjab	4.397* (585.871)	0.011* (7.654)	–0.113* (–6.216)	0.009* (4.596)	0.98
13	Rajasthan	4.106* (180.876)	0.018* (3.955)	–0.085 (–1.548)	0.003 (0.575)	0.89
14	Tamil Nadu	4.264* (377.423)	0.020* (9.121)	–0.204* (–7.498)	0.016* (5.428)	0.99
15	Uttar Pradesh	4.031* (544.591)	0.007* (4.473)	–0.122* (–6.821)	0.011* (5.583)	0.97
16	Uttarakhand	4.216* (424.891)	0.005** (2.794)	–0.326* (–13.622)	0.037* (14.595)	0.99
17	West Bengal	4.108* (852.434)	0.022* (23.427)	–0.023 (–2.016)	0.001 (0.513)	0.99

Note: (1) Figures in the parentheses indicate *t* value
(2) * indicates significant at 1 per cent level
** indicates significant at 5 per cent level

Table 7.4: Absolute β Convergence/Divergence in Panel Regression

	β Coefficient	*Adjusted R^2*	*F*
1993 - 2010	0.020* (2.601)	0.021	6.767
1993 - 2001	-0.006 (–.395)	–0.007	0.156
2001 - 2010	0.020** (2.124)	0.023	4.511

Note: Figures in parentheses indicate t-values.
* denote significant at 1 per cent level
** denote significant at 5 per cent level.

Source: Author's calculations.

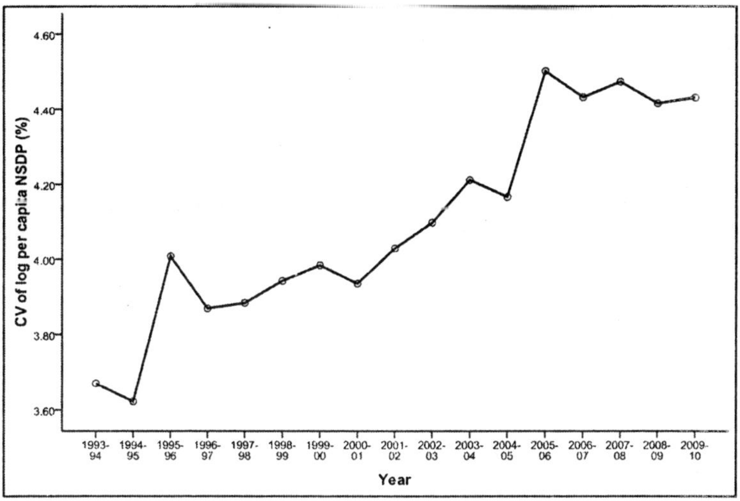

Fig. 7.4: Inter-state Dispersion in per capita NSDP

From the above it can be concluded that there is divergence of income during the post reform period, whether the measure of β convergence or the measure of σ convergence is taken into consideration. This indicates that inter-state inequality in per capita income has increased in the post-reform period. The increase in the divergence or inequality in income across various states implies that the fiscal transfer to states has not been able to redress the inter-state disparities in India, which is the result of disparities in the investment in infrastructure among states.

Conclusion

The growth of per capita income has increased in almost all the major states in India during 2001-10 compared to 1993-2001. The structure of per capita income of these states has also changed significantly in the later part of the reform period. However, in contrast to our hypothesis, the study has found divergence of income or rising inequality across states during the post reform period. This indicates that the economic reform in India initiated in the early 1990s has accentuated the disparities across states, even though there is growth everywhere. Since the inter-state disparities in India is the result of disparities in the investment in infrastructure, it is suggested that the system of fiscal transfer to states, which is regressive (Meher, 2008), should be altered suitably to redress the inter-state disparities in India.

REFERENCES

Aiyar (2001). 'Growth Theory and Convergence across Indian States: A Panel Study', Chapter 8 in Tim Callen, Patrica Reynolds and Christopher Towe (eds.), *India at the Crossroads: Sustaining Growth and Reducing Poverty*. Washington DC: International Monetary Fund.

Bajpai, Nirupam and Jeffrey Sachs (1996). 'Trends in Inter-State Inequalities of Income in India', *Development Discussion Paper* No. 528, Harvard Institute for International Development.

Barro, Robert J. (1990). 'Government Spending in a Simple Model of Endogenous Growth', *Journal of Political Economy*, 98, October, Part-II: S103- S125.

Barro, Robert J. (1991). 'Economic Growth in a Cross Section of Countries', *Quarterly Journal of Economics*, 106, May: 407-43.

Barro, Robert J. (1999). 'Lisbon Meets Ramsey in the Neo-classical Growth Model', *Quarterly Journal of Economics*, 114, November, 1125-52.

Barro, Rovert J. and Xavier Sala-i-Martin (1991). 'Convergence across States and Regions', *Brookings Paper on Economic Activity*, pp. 107-182.

Barro, Robert J. and Xavier Sala-i-Martin (1992a). 'Convergence', *Journal of Political Economy*, 100, April: 223-51.

Barro, Robert J. and Xavier Sala-i-Martin (1992b). 'Regional Growth and Migration: A Japan-United States Comparison', *Journal of Japanese and International Economies*, 6, December: 312-46.

Barro, Robert J. and Xavier Sala-i-Martin (1992c). 'Public Finance in Models of Economic Growth', *Review of Economic Studies*, 59, October: 645-61.

Barro, Robert and Xavier Sala-i-Martin (1997). 'Technological Diffusion, Convergence, and Growth', *Journal of Economic Growth*, 2, March: 1-26.

Barro, Robert J. and Xavier Sala-i-Martin (2007). *Economic Growth*. New Delhi: Prentice-Hall of India, Pvt. Ltd. (2nd ed.).

Barro, Robert J., and Jong-Wha Lee (1994). 'Sources of Economic Growth', *Carnegie-Rochester Conference Series on Public Policy*.

Baunol, William J. (1986). 'Productivity Growth Convergence and Welfare: What the Long-run Data Show', *American Economic Review*, Vol. 76(5): 1072-85.

Boyer, R. (1996). 'The Convergence Hypothesis is Revisited: Globalisation but still a century of Nations?' in S. Gerger and R. Dore (eds.) *National Diversity and Global Capitalism*. London: Cornell University Press.

Brankle, Micheal (1983). 'A Note on Kuznet's U', *The Review of Economics and Statistics:* 135-39.

Cashin, Paul A. (1995). 'Economic Growth and Convergence Across the Seven Colonies of Australia: 1861-1991', *Economic Record*, Vol. 71, June: 132-44.

Cashin, Paul A. and Ratan Sahay (1996). 'Internal Migration, Centre-State of India', *IMF Staff Papers*, Vol. 43, No. 1 March: 123-71.

Cass, David (1965). 'Optimum Growth in an Aggregative Model of Capital Accumulation', *Review of Economic Studies*, 32: 233-40.

DeLong, J. Brodford (1988). 'Productivity Growth Convergence and Welfare: Comment', *American Economic Review*, Vol. 78(5):1138-54.

Dowrick-Steve and Dcu Tho Nguyen (1989). 'OECD Comparative Economic Growth 1950-1980: Catch up and Convergence', *American Economic Review*, Vol. 79: 1010-30.

Dunford, M. and A. Smith (2000). 'Catching up or Falling Behind? Economic Performance and Regional Trajectories in the New Europe', *Economic Geography*, 76(2): 169-95.

Easterlin, Richard A. (1960a). 'Regional Growth Income: Long Term Tendencies', in Simon Kuznets, Ratner Miller and Richared A. Easterlin (eds.) *Population Redistribution and Economic Growth: United States, 1870-1950*, Vol. II. Philadelphia: American Philosophical Society, pp. 141-203.

Easterlin, Richard A. (1960b), 'Inter-regional differences in Per Capita Income, Population and Total Income, 1840-1950: Trends in the American Economy in the Nineteenth Century', Vol. 24, NBER Studies in Income and Wealth, NBER: 73-140.

Kaldor, Nicholas (1955-56). 'Alternative Theories of Distribution', *Review of Economic Studies*, 23(2): 81-100.

Kaldor, Nicholas (1960). *Essays on Economic Stability and Growth*. London: Duckworth.

Kalecki, Michal (1954). *Theory of Economic Dynamics*. London: Allen and Unwin.

Kalecki, Michal (1971). *Selected Essays on the Dynamics of the Capitalist Economy 1933-70*. Cambridge: Cambridge University Press.

Koopmans, T.C. (1965). 'On the Concept of Optimal Economic Growth', *The Econometric Approach to Developmental Planning*. Amsterdam: North Holland.

Kuznets, Simon (1955). 'Economic Growth and Income Inequality', *American Economic Review*, 45: 1-28.

Lucas, Robert E. Jr. (1988). 'On the Mechanic of Economic Development', *Journal of Monetary Economics*, 22, July: 3-42.

Marjit, Sugata and Buddhadeb Ghosh (2000). 'Economic Growth and Regional Divergence in India, 1970-1996'. Calcutta: Centre for Studies in Social Sciences.

Marjit, Sugata and S. Mitra (1996). 'Convergence in Regional Growth Rates: Indian Research Agenda', *Economic and Political Weekly*, Vol. 31(33).

Martin, R. and Sunley, P. (1998). 'Slow Convergence? The New Endogenous Growth Theory and Regional Development', *Economic Geography*, 73: 201-27.

Nagaraj, Rayaprolu, Aristomene Varoudakis and Marie-Ange Veganzones (1998). 'Long-Run Growth Trends and Convergence across Indian States', *OECD Technical Paper* No. 131.

Pasinetti, Luigi (1962). 'The Rate of Profit and Income Distribution in Relation to the Rate of Economic Growth', *Review of Economic Studies*, 29: 267-79.

Pasinetti, Luigi (1977). *Lectures on the Theory of Production*. London: Macmillan.

Pasinetti, Luigi (1981). *Structural Change and Economic Growth*. Cambridge: Cambridge University Press.

Quah, D.T. (1993). 'Empirical Cross-section Dynamics in Economic Growth', *European Economic Review*, Vol. 37, April: 426-34.

Quah, D.T. (1995). 'Galton's Fallacy and Tests of the Convergence Hypothesis', *The Scandinavian Journal of Economics*, Vol. 95(4): 427-43.

Quah, D.T. (1996a). 'Convergence Empirics with Capital Mobility', *Journal of Economic Growth*, Vol. 1(1) March: 95-124.

Quah, D.T. (1996b). 'Twin Peaks: Growth and Convergence in Models of Distribution Dynamics', *The Economics Journal*, Vol. 106, July: 1045-55.

Rao, M. Govinda and Kunal Sen (1997). 'Internal Migration, Centre State Grants and Economic Growth in the States of India: A Comment on Cashin and Ratna Sahay', *IMF Staff Papers*, Vol. 44(2): 283-88.

Rao, M. Govinda, Ric Shand and K.P. Kalirajan (1999). 'Convergence of Incomes across Indian States: A Divergent View', *Economic and Political Weekly*, 27 March-2 April.

Romer, Paul M. (1986). 'Increasing Returns and Long-Run Growth', *Journal of Political Economy*, 94, October: 1002-37.

Romer, Paul M. (1987), 'Growth Based on Increasing Returns Due to Specialization', *American Economic Review*, 77, May: 56-62.

Romer, Paul M. (1990). 'Endogenous Technological Change', *Journal of Political Economy*, 98, October, Part-II: S71-S102.

Romer, Paul M. (1992). 'Two Strategies for Economic Development: Using Ideas and Producing Ideas', in World Bank, Annual Conference on Economic Development, Washington D.C.

Romer, Paul M. (1993). 'Idea Gaps and object Gaps in Economic Development', *Journal of Monetary Economics*, 32, December: 543-73.

Smith, D. (1975). 'Neoclassical Growth Models and Regional Growth in the US', *Journal of Regional Science*, Vol. 15, 165-81.

Solow, R.M. (1956). "A Contribution to the Theory of Economic Growth", *Quarterly Journal of Economics*, 65-94.

Solow, R.M. (1957). 'Technical Change and the Aggregate Production Function', *Review of Economics and Statistics*, 312-20.

Solow, R.M. (1970). *Growth Theory: An Exposition*. Oxford University Press: Oxford.

Steindl, Josef (1952). *Maturity and Stagnation in American Capitalism.* Oxford: Basil Blackwell.

8

Health Inequality in India

A Measure for Its Mitigation

Bimal K. Mohanty

India initiated a major policy shift in mid-July 1991. It has pursued an economic model, which is featured by liberalisation of the market and phase-wise withdrawal of the government from many sectors and activities. Since then India's achievements in almost all fronts and in all sectors have been perceptible. The sectors which were near collapse in the pre-reforms period were revitalised and have continued to generate magnificent outcomes beyond expectations of both advocates and adversaries of reforms. The overall achievements of India in the post-reforms period have grabbed the attention of the world of nations including that of the economic super powers. Because of the tremendous success, India is recognised world over as one of the emerging economies. In spite of the fabulous economic gains, however, in the opinions of a segment of researchers and policy evaluators, India has not been able to achieve distributional efficiency in the post-reforms period. The opponents of reforms herald one more step further and claim that the policy shift has rather aggravated the extent of inequality in the distribution of income and policy outcomes across the regions, across the states and among the households in India. In their respective studies Bhaduri (2008), Dev (2007) and Sarkar and Mehta (2010), to refer to a few only, have examined the reforms impact on inequality in its some form or other and have concluded that reforms of the Indian economy could not have been successful in mitigating the extent of inequality existed in the pre-reforms period. The sector in which India has fared the best is in the domains of GDP and per capita income. The conservative annual average growth rate of GDP by 3.56 per cent during 1950-51–1979-80 has been displaced by a massive growth rate of 6.04 per cent during 1980-81–2007-08 and further by 7.83 per cent during 2008-09–2010-11. But similar is not the fact with other sectors of the Indian economy. The health sector reforms that were initiated in India along with overall programmes for reforms and thereafter have not yet responded to the national objective of meeting equity in healthcare, which is one of the most cherished goals of a welfare society.

Link between Individual Health and Aggregate Inequality

Economic growth and health are two-way related. Economic growth causes improvement in health related parameters like infant mortality rate (IMR), life expectancy at birth (LEB), maternal mortality rate (MMR) and crude death rate (CDR). An improvement in overall health status of any population is measured particularly in terms of increase in life expectancy at birth. The improvement in this parameter is capable of seizing disability adjusted life years (DALY). By definition, one DALY approximates one year of healthy life lost. DALY being saved with improvement in healthcare indices would inevitably cause economic gain of one year's per capita income. This favourable link between increase in overall health and per capita income gain is said to be vitiated if inequitable distribution in personal income organises along with increase in per capita income. This brings forth an inverse relationship between socio-economic status (SES) and health (Smith, 2004). Increase in SES is expected to increase health status of the population provided the former reduces the socio-economic inequality or at least does not cause the existing income distribution to be more regressive. If on the contrary, increase in SES increases income inequality, though there is increase in income, it would adversely affect the overall health status of the people predominantly of those who belong to lower socio-economic strata. Once income inequality persists, it causes health inequality to get widened over time. People's ability to purchase healthcare depends on their paying capacity which is normally defined by their income. If income distribution is regressive, so also is the affordability of healthcare as a commodity. Reforms packages introduced in India formally with the declaration of the New Economic Policy in mid-1991 have brought about huge gain in per capita income terms not only for the country as a whole but also for its constituent states. In spite of this, health inequality across the states is strongly exhibited (Table 8.1).

Table 8.1: Selected Health related Parameters of the Indian States

Parameters→	*IMR*		*LEB*		*MMR*		*CDR*	
Year→ / *States↓*	*1991*	*2010*	*1991-1995*	*2011*	*1997-1998*	*2007-2009*	*1991*	*2010*
Andhra Pradesh	73	46	61.8	64.4	197	134	9.7	7.6
Bihar	69	48	59.3	61.6	531	261	9.8	6.8
Chhattisgarh	94 (1998)	51	54.9	58.0	441	335 (2004-06)	13.8	8.1 (2007)
Gujarat	69	44	61.0	64.1	160	148	8.5	6.7
Haryana	68	48	63.4	66.2	176	153	8.2	6.6
Jharkhand	62 (1998)	42	59.3	62.6	531	269	9.8	8.0
Karnataka	77	38	62.5	65.3	245	178	9.0	7.1
Kerala	16	13	72.9	74.0	150	81	6.0	7.0
Madhya Pradesh	117	62	54.9	58.0	441	269	13.8	8.3
Maharashtra	60	28	64.8	67.2	166	104	8.2	6.5
Odisha	124	61	56.5	59.6	346	258	12.8	8.6
Punjab	53	34	67.2	69.4	280	172	7.8	7.0
Rajasthan	79	55	59.1	62.0	508	318	10.1	6.7
Tamil Nadu	57	24	63.3	66.2	131	97	8.8.	7.6
Uttar Pradesh	97	61	56.8	60.0	606	359	11.3	8.1
West Bengal	71	31	62.1	64.9	303	145	8.3	6.0
All India	80	47	60.3	63.5	398	212	9.8	7.2

Sources: 1. SRS Bulletin, Vol. 46, No. 1, December 2011.
2. Economic Survey, Government of India 1998-99 and 2011-12.
3. Family Welfare Statistics in India 2011, Ministry of H&FW, Government of India.
4. Human Development Report, UNDP India, 2011.

However, it is clear that the health related parameters after reforms for all the non-special category major states of India have moved favourably with time but these movements are neither uniform nor near uniform in the cross-section thus confirming the continuation of inequality in overall health.

Income inequality could itself be the source of health hazards (Wilkinson, 1996). This is based on the hypothesis that the probability of mortality would be high among the people living in a more unequal society. Wilkinson's views have not gone uncontested. Overall inequality might be one of the causes of high mortality among the residents but not the only cause. There may be several other factors to cause higher probability of mortality. In spite of this, the hypothesis undeniably draws a relationship between aggregate inequality and overall health of the individuals. Given this hypothesis, it is thus conceivable how aggregate inequality in income distribution causes aggregate health inequality. In this current piece of work it is needed, as a passing reference, to forge a link between aggregate inequality and individual health. This needs to bring the concept of relative income into the picture (Deaton, 2003; Leigh *et al.*, 2009; Wilkinson 1997). Individual health is affected by individual income relative to the mean income of the reference cohort to which he/she belongs. Thus the inequality in the distribution of group income causes inequality in individual health. Though health inequality like income inequality is always undesirable, the former is considered more offensive than the latter. One can learn to tolerate the pinch of income inequality and continue to live with it, but falling prey to health inequality is one way of losing right to life which may be considered to be more than a fundamental right of a man in a democratic society. Though one causes the other, beyond this simple bilateral causality, something more is seen to have contributed to health inequality at individual level. While income inequality has no genetical factors behind, health inequality at individual level is some time exhibited to congenital and hereditary factors. Thus health inequality is beset by several issues. Accordingly, in the agenda for alleviation of inequality in all its forms and shapes, it is needed to assign priority to the elimination of health inequality. Having felt its need, national governments and international bodies (from Alma Ata Declaration 1978 to Millennium Development Goals 2005) all have assigned priority to the overall development of the health sector with the principal aim to contain inequality in overall health. The Government of India, in the National Health Policy (2002), has committed to eliminate all forms of health inequities through promoting universal accessibility to health care provisions. In Alma Ata Declaration 1978, all the member nations of the World Health Organisation (WHO) expressed their common concern for the existing gross inequality in health and promised for action. The member states of the United Nations (UN) in 2005 adopted Millennium Development Goals to overcome poverty, exclusion and environmental problems of which three are health related goals (Goals 4, 5 and 6). The spirit of all these charters and policies is in favour of state action for amelioration of health inequality. UNDP (2010) has drawn a negative relationship between inequality in any form and human development for all categories of countries irrespective of their economic standard. It has recognised fiscal policy as a 'vital lever' to reduce inequality. In this respect, public spending would be one of the most befitting instruments to counter the problems of health inequality in any population.

Conceptualising Health Inequality

Health inequality, in its narrow sense may be defined as the difference in individual health in a cross-section. This definition rules out the scope for policy intervention in health inequality at individual level for the reason that it presents an obvious phenomenon. No two individuals will be having the same health standard even if both of them are from the same parents. Each individual is born with a given physiological stock which is affected by antenatal factors, genetic factors, hereditary factors and environmental factors. In some cases, health inequality among the individuals emanates out of inter-generational factors. The physical and/or mental deficiency in parents may be transmitted to their offspring and accordingly, inequalities in health are passed from the present generation to the next. These factors of health inequality at individual level being non-modifiable do not qualify for public action. To give a wider coverage, health inequality may be defined as systematic difference in health between different socio-economic groups while each socio-economic group is differently positioned in the society which is called the 'gradient measurement' of health inequality. Health inequality thus is a scalar numerical representation of interpersonal differences (Cowell, 1995) in health within a given population. Socio-economic groups occupying higher position on the socio-economic rating scale[1] (Batista-Foguet *et al.*, 2004) exhibit flattening gradient[2] among the households, while socio-economic groups occupying lower position encounter steepening gradient. The difference in gradient measurements across socio-economic classes is the measure of health inequality in its wider connotation. Addressing health inequality necessitates flattening the gradient relating to lower socio-economic classes. This is beyond the own capacity of the socio-economic groups positioned on the steepening segment of the socio-economic rating scale who are under the shackles of perennial state of socio-economic inequality. They can be pushed to the flattening segment of the socio-economic rating scale only on the intervention of the state by uplifting their employment, education and income status and reducing the burden of morbidity and mortality on these low positioned socio-economic groups. State policy and state action together are necessary to break the vicious link between overall inequality and health inequality by shifting the gradient relating to the low positioned socio-economic classes to the level of the 'natural rate of subjective inequality'[3] (Lambert *et al.,* 2003). The natural rate of subjective inequality is that level of inequality among the socio-economic groups which is of the minimum tolerance and all sections are equally least averse to this level of inequality. It would have been the best to live in a society without any inequality in any form, but such a society is hopelessly impossible. Accordingly, that society is the best which is attuned with the minimum tolerable level of inequality which may be referred to as the 'natural rate of subjective inequality'. Though the natural rate of inequality is a subjective phenomenon, it has to be empirically weak, but it exists for all countries and at all times.

For the mitigation of health inequalities, life expectancy at birth (LEB) and infant mortality rate (IMR) are considered to be at the nucleus of the target areas. These two are the leading parameters used to measure the extent of inequalities in health status (WHO, 2007) among the socio-economic groups. Table 8.2 exhibits LEB among social and economic classes in India. As Table 8.2 reads, on an average, poor irrespective of their caste, sex, creed and religion are likely to die earlier than a non-poor in India, which further leads to the inference of a poor being susceptible to be in ill health and under control of morbidity for longer period during his/her life time than a non-poor. Table 8.3 displays IMR and Under-5 Mortality Rate (U5MR) among the social groups in India. The social group termed as 'Others' that excludes the vulnerable sections like SCs, STs and OBCs has exhibited the least mortality rates measured in terms of both IMR and U5MR throughout. Accordingly, SCs,

STs and OBCs fair far worse in terms of both IMR and U5MR than 'Others'. The contents of Tables 8.2 and 8.3 summarise into the fact that India is in the grips of menacing inequalities in health status in the post-reforms period which needs public action for their mitigation. Of course, putting these two parameters for judging the extent of health inequalities among the economic and social groups is not enough. They produce a rough estimation of the whole incident of health inequality. Several parameters contribute to the phenomenon. LEB as a measure of health inequality has its own limitations. Improving LEB is not essentially a factor in reducing health inequality. Mexico illustrates the best. Mexico's healthcare system has been very carefully designed. It is not only impressive but in some cases, it is seen to have been excellent. In spite of this, there are major inequities in health and healthcare particularly in terms of healthcare accessibility (Barraza-Llorens *et al.*, 2002). Non-availability of data on other parameters of health has forced to admit LEB and IMR for locating health inequalities among socio-economic groups in India.

Table 8.2: LEB among Social and Economic Groups in India 2005-06

(In Years)

Economic Groups	*Hindus*	*Muslims*	*Christians*	*SCs*	*STs*	*OBCs*
Poor	61.5	65.5	64.4	63.0	56.9	62.7
Non-Poor	67.8	68.4	72.0	66.0	64.1	67.2

Source: Mohanty, S.K. and F. Ram (2010).

Table 8.3: IMR and U5MR by Social Groups in India (1992-93 – 2005-06)

Parameters	*Social Groups*	*NFHS-1: 1992-93*	*NFHS-2: 1998-99*	*NFHS-3: 2005-06*
IMR	SCs	107.3	83.0	71.0
	STs	90.5	84.2	63.9
	OBCs	NA	76.2	61.1
	Others	82.2	61.8	55.7
U5MR	SCs	149.1	119.3	94.7
	STs	135.2	126.6	99.8
	OBCs	NA	103.1	78.7
	Others	111.5	82.6	68.2

Sources: Reports of the National Family Health Survey-1, 2, 3.
NA: Not Available.

Mitigating Health Inequality: A Case for Public Expenditure

Economic inequality which is normally equated with income inequality and health inequality move together. Since there is bi-directional causal relationship between these two, the mitigation in the former (income inequality) may cause mitigation in the latter (health inequality). This is a mere logical deduction supporting alleviation of income inequality as a corrective measure for health inequality. This inference is not practically tenable. Correcting health inequality by correcting income inequality, if at all any merit is there in this measure, seems to be a long-run solution and hence illusory. No society can afford to wait for that long-run which would ultimately bring permanent easing to health inequality along with income inequality. Income inequality is an unsolved problem for the countries irrespective of their level of human development and economic prosperity. Moreover, in spite of all efforts by the national governments, the countries have not been able to solve the problems of income inequality. The Kuznets inverted-U curve is no more universally valid. Though the empirical evidence on the legitimacy of the shape of the curve is mixed (Acemoglu and Robinson, 2002), the weight of rejection falls more heavily. If Kuznets was right, he was more or less right, but only for his life time, says a critic. In one of its publications, the OECD (2011) has listed 10 industrialised developed countries that have experienced the worst income inequality indexed on the basis of Gini coefficient, in spite of their honest and sustained efforts to alleviate inequality. Moreover, the healthcare systems of these countries (Table 8.4) are known for their distinctiveness in some sense or the other. Countries like United States, Portugal and New Zealand dominate the rest of the world's countries in terms of healthcare expenditure as a percentage of GDP. Australia is unique in providing equity and access to life saving treatment. Israel has built a high quality healthcare system and it is considered to be one of the best in the world.

Gini coefficient varies between 0 and 1. If zero, it is a state of perfect equality. If unity, it is a case of absolute inequality implying all income gains are being grabbed by a single individual. On this basis, the countries in Table 8.4 have been arranged in ascending order of the magnitudes of income inequality. Some of these developed countries having worst income inequality also exhibit

Table 8.4: List of Developed Countries with Worst Income Inequality

Sl. No.	*Countries*	*Health Expenditure as % of GDP (2007-11)*	*Gini Coefficient*
1.	New Zealand	10.1	0.33
2.	Australia	8.7	0.34
3.	Italy	9.5	0.34
4.	United Kingdom	9.6	0.34
5.	Portugal	11.0	0.36
6.	Israel	7.6	0.37
7.	United States	17.9	0.38
8.	Turkey	6.7	0.41
9.	Mexico	6.3	0.48
10.	Chile	8.0	0.50

Sources: OECD (2011). World Bank (2012).

one of the best healthcare systems. On the basis of WHO's criteria[4] for healthcare ranking, from among these 10 countries listed in Table 8.4, Italy, Portugal and United Kingdom are evaluated to have excellent healthcare systems. Each one of them has a healthcare system guaranteeing universal accessibility and utilisation, and thus each has achieved equity in healthcare. It is thus evident that countries in the presence of income inequality could also achieve equity in healthcare.

Achieving equity in health is not necessarily pre-conditioned by achieving equity in income distribution, as the empirical evidence shows. A country having healthcare inequality may go for some solutions other than waiting for complete alleviation of income inequality. Among these solutions, one may consist of increasing per capita expenditure on health by the government. This is the reason as to why several international charters and national policies on health have emphasised increase in budgetary outlays by the national governments to the health sector of their respective countries. Among the international declarations, United Nations Millennium Declaration 2000 adopted eight development goals of which three (Goals 4, 5 and 6)[5] relate to public health. Achievement of these goals necessitates strengthening primary healthcare and targeting people living in inaccessible regions. Health is a public service and thus a public good. Each should have equal access to healthcare facilities irrespective of his/her socio-economic conditions. This requires the state to continue to be the lead actor which directly points to the relevance of state sector expenditure on health. The National Health Policy 2002 (India) has firmly emphasised increases in the share of health in Central grants to states on the one hand and state sector health expenditure for the fulfilment of the goals on the other. The argument in favour of increasing health expenditure per capita for achieving equity in healthcare is also disputed. World Health Organisation (2000) while ranking 191 member nations on the basis of the quality of their healthcare systems has brought into the fact that among all the industrialised nations, the US leads the list in terms of healthcare spending but secures 37th position in healthcare standard, while France has one of the best healthcare systems but ranks 6th in spending. Thus increasing health expenditure might not be a cause for mitigating health inequality. This deduction from the work of WHO could not be a refuting argument for India. On the one hand, India is not an industrialised nation and it has yet to go for universal health insurance. And on the other, for developing countries like India where common men's capacity for out-of-pocket expenditure is limited by their poor economic conditions, public provision of public health is one of the immediate solutions to increase healthcare accessibility and utilisation. This draws a case for public expenditure as one of the mitigating factors of health inequality in India.

Health Expenditure of the States in India—An Overview

In the current context, health expenditure means the expenditure borne by the state governments out of their budgetary provisions on 'medical and public health' both on revenue and capital accounts. It excludes private healthcare expenditure. Government intervention in public health makes a difference. The National Health Policy 2002 has reiterated several time-bound goals for the achievement of the objective of providing acceptable standard of good health to the people. One such goal relates to the state sector expenditure on public health. This goal affirms that states should increase their expenditure on health to 5.5-7.0 per cent of the budget size by 2005 and further to 8 per cent by 2008.

Table 8.5 shows that all the states of India are lagging much behind the national objective. Between the groups of high income and middle and low income states, on an average, the latter is allocating a larger percentage of the budget size to health sector.

Table 8.5: State-wise Public Expenditure on Health as a Percentage of GSDP and Per Capita Health Expenditure 2009-10

Sl. No.	States	Health Expenditure as a % of GSDP	Health Expenditure as a % of Budget	Per Capita Health Expenditure (Rs.)
High Income States				
1	Andhra Pradesh	0.66	3.18	388.13
2	Gujarat	0.40	2.94	289.93
3	Haryana	0.43	2.94	390.55
4	Karnataka	0.60	3.40	349.59
5	Kerala	0.64	4.10	446.88
6	Maharashtra	0.35	2.63	288.46
7	Punjab	0.51	2.85	407.04
8	Tamil Nadu	0.61	3.89	408.97
9	West Bengal	0.69	3.23	313.32
Middle and Low Income States				
10	Bihar	0.87	3.27	156.14
11	Chhattisgarh	0.88	3.83	356.11
12	Jharkhand	1.08	4.52	328.59
13	Madhya Pradesh	0.64	3.00	208.92
14	Odisha	0.74	3.70	296.64
15	Rajasthan	0.82	4.36	332.05
16	Uttar Pradesh	1.02	4.39	277.17

Sources: Handbook of Statistics on State Government Finances, Reserve Bank of India, 2010.
Economic Survey 2010-11, Government of India.
Odisha Budget 2012-2013 at a Glance, Government of Odisha.

Similar inference is drawn in respect of public health expenditure as a percentage of GSDP of the states. In India, no state policy has recommended the minimum level of government expenditure on health as a percentage of GSDP/GDP. But the UPA government at the centre, in its 'National Common Minimum Programme 2004' has declared to increase the public spending on health to at least 2-3 per cent of GDP. Since healthcare is in the 'State List', such declaration would materialise only when all states increase their expenditure on healthcare. State governments in India face the trouble of meeting high expectations of the people with limited revenue raising capacity. Given the revenue raising capacity and expenditure obligations at the state level, and the present trend of health expenditure as a percentage of GSDP (Table 8.5), the norm of '2-3 per cent of GSDP' seems quite ambitious. Table 8.5 presents three important indicators (health expenditure as a percentage of

GSDP, health expenditure as a percentage of budget size, and per capita health expenditure) of state level performance in respect of public health during 2009-10. Among these three, per capita health expenditure having measured distributional impact of public expenditure on healthcare is considered to be more an ideal indicator of the performance of a state in respect of its healthcare sector. On an average, per capita government expenditure on healthcare for the high income states is seen to have been much above the one for the middle and low income states. Thus the high income states in India have achieved better distributional impacts from health expenditure than the middle and low income states.

Table 8.6: Growth Rates of Public Expenditure on Health State-wise during 1991-92 – 2009-10

Sl. No.	*States*	*Annual Average Percentage Growth Rates*	
		At Current Prices	*At 2004-05 Base*
High Income States			
1	Andhra Pradesh	11.90	23.80
2	Gujarat	9.89	19.73
3	Haryana	12.33	24.66
4	Karnataka	10.74	21.47
5	Kerala	10.29	20.58
6	Maharashtra	9.73	19.46
7	Punjab	8.73	17.46
8	Tamil Nadu	10.43	20.86
9	West Bengal	10.64	21.28
	Overall	**10.49**	**21.08**
Middle and Low Income States			
10	Bihar	7.23	14.45
11	Chhattisgarh*	28.33	56.66
12	Jharkhand**	15.68	31.36
13	Madhya Pradesh	8.52	17.03
14	Odisha	10.86	21.71
15	Rajasthan	11.11	22.21
16	Uttar Pradesh	11.41	22.83
	Overall	**10.01**	**19.22**
	For All Sixteen States	**10.29**	**20.15**

* Data for Chhattisgarh are available since 2000-01.

** Data for Jharkhand are available since 2001-02.

Source: Handbook of Statistics on State Government Finances, Reserve Bank of India, 2010.

Growth rates of total public expenditure on health by individual states in India both at current and constant (2004-05) prices during the post-reforms period have been exhibited in Table 8.6. For all states, the annual average percentage growth rates at constant prices are above the ones at current prices. The growth rates computed both at current and constant prices for high income states are much above the corresponding growth rates computed for middle and low income states of India. Moreover, the growth rates for high income states are above the national averages of 10.29 and 20.15 per cents respectively. Thus in the post-reforms period, though all states have increased their allocations to health sector, it is faster among the high income states.

In the post-reforms period, all states of India irrespective of their level of economic development have increased their budgetary allocations to healthcare sector. This is indeed an encouraging feature of the state economies. These expenditures would be of little relevance if they lack allocative efficiency. Allocative efficiency can be judged from the benefits achieved out of the expenditure borne. This requires combining the spending on healthcare and health outcomes. This combination would indicate the value of the money put into the healthcare sector by the governments. Of course, this is a difficult task in India due to non-availability of appropriate and comparable data[6]. In spite of this, in the present context an approximation has been made to find the value of the spending on healthcare by the individual states (Table 8.7). While healthcare spending is made proxy by per capita public expenditure on health, health outcomes have been computed from IMR, LEB, MMR and CDR corresponding to each state. High income states, on an average, indicate high per capita health expenditure in comparison to that of the middle and low income states of India. At the same time, the high income states display higher scores on each of the four health outcomes than the middle and low income states of India. Viewed from this angle, high income states have achieved relatively better distributional impact and allocative efficiency of healthcare expenditure.

Per Capita Health Expenditure of States in India—Its Convergence

Stated elsewhere in this study, increase in public expenditure on healthcare per capita could be one of the direct and instant sources

Table 8.7: State-wise per Capita Health Expenditure and Health Outcomes

Sl. No.	States	Per Capita Health Expenditure (Rs.)	IMR 2010	LEB 2011	MMR 2007-09	CDR 2010
High Income States						
1.	Andhra Pradesh	388.13	46	64.4	134	7.6
2.	Gujarat	289.93	44	64.1	148	6.7
3.	Haryana	390.55	48	66.2	153	6.6
4.	Karnataka	349.59	38	65.3	178	7.1
5.	Kerala	446.88	13	74.0	81	7.0
6.	Maharashtra	288.46	28	67.2	104	6.5
7.	Punjab	407.04	34	69.4	172	7.0
8.	Tamil Nadu	408.97	24	66.2	97	7.6
9.	West Bengal	313.32	31	64.9	145	6.0
Middle and Low Income States						
10.	Bihar	156.14	48	61.6	261	6.8
11.	Chhattisgarh	356.11	51	58.0	335	8.1
12.	Jharkhand	328.59	42	62.6	269	8.0
13.	Madhya Pradesh	208.92	62	58.0	269	8.3
14.	Odisha	296.64	61	59.6	258	8.6
15.	Rajasthan	332.05	55	62.0	318	6.7
16.	Uttar Pradesh	277.17	61	60.0	359	8.1

IMR: Infant Mortality Rate
LEB: Life Expectancy at Birth
MMR: Maternal Mortality Rate
CDR: Crude Death Rate

Sources: Tables 8.1 and 8.5.

of mitigating health inequality in the cross-section. This is an empty hypothesis which needs no reality search. Per capita health expenditure of the states in India is not uniform. High income states exhibit higher per capita health expenditure in the post-reforms period than the middle and low income states which is evident from their averages computed in Table 8.8. But West Bengal is a lone exception. Its average per capita health expenditure is computed to have been less than the average per capita health expenditure of Rajasthan. It has been computed in Table 8.7 that high income states having higher per capita public health expenditure are with better health outcomes (IMR, LEB, MMR and CDR) than the middle and low income states having less per capita public health expenditure. Thus, the high income states have realised larger value for their money put into the health sector. The presence of divergence in health outcomes on the one hand

and in per capita health expenditure on the other between high income states and middle and low income states together point to the inefficiency of the healthcare system of the country. Convergence in per capita public health expenditure can be a formal test for the degree of inequality in health outcomes between the states of India.

Table 8.8: State-wise Average and Growth Rates of Per Capita Public Health Expenditure during 1991-92 – 2009-10

Sl. No.	States	Per Capita Health Expenditure (Rs.)		Average (Rs.)	Annual Average Growth Rate (%)
		1991-92	2009-10		
High Income States					
1.	Andhra Pradesh	56.78	388.13	147.61	10.68
2.	Gujarat	69.03	289.93	146.80	7.97
3.	Haryana	63.06	390.55	146.77	10.13
4.	Karnataka	66.85	349.59	156.93	9.19
5.	Kerala	79.67	446.88	211.25	9.58
6.	Maharashtra	69.49	288.46	155.40	7.91
7.	Punjab	104.24	407.04	209.12	7.57
8.	Tamil Nadu	78.52	408.97	167.18	9.17
9.	West Bengal	60.35	313.32	139.23	9.15
Middle and Low Income States					
10.	Bihar	65.39	156.14	83.15	4.84
11.	Chhattisgarh	64.98	356.11	129.01	9.45
12.	Jharkhand	65.39	328.59	130.98	8.97
13.	Madhya Pradesh	64.98	208.92	118.82	8.49
14.	Odisha	54.26	296.64	108.53	9.44
15.	Rajasthan	66.73	332.05	145.04	8.91
16.	Uttar Pradesh	51.78	277.17	111.24	9.32

Sources: Handbook of Statistics on State Government Finances, Reserve Bank of India, 2010.
Economic Survey 2010-11, Government of India.

In order to test the possibility of convergence/divergence in per capita public health expenditure between the states of India during a 19-year time period (1991-92 – 2009-10), the theoretical outlines due to Barro and Sala-i-Martin (1992) and Sal-i-Martin (1996) have been considered. Though in the present context, the model of inequality convergence has been used for per capita public expenditure on health in general, the model in fact seeks to enquire the possibility of catching-up in both the phenomena of per capita health expenditure and health outcome in particular in the cross-section of 16 non-special category major states of India as the latter is an upshot of the former. In Barro-Martin literature, three approaches to convergence are located. These include: (1) absolute β-convergence, (2) conditional β-convergence, and (c) σ-convergence. Each one befits to a particular situation. Absolute β-convergence works if all the spaces exhibit similar characteristics and finally, each follows a growth path in the concerned variable over time which is globally stable. The facts of experience confirm that spaces seldom exhibit comparable characteristics. With passage of time, the spaces would tend to exhibit differential growth configurations leading to a situation of different steady state balance for each space. This is referred to as conditional β-convergence. σ-convergence is defined as cross-sectional dispersion over time which is computed from the coefficients of variation. Conditional β-convergence is built on the rationality of the inevitability of spatial spill over and spatial-interdependence (Rey and Montouri, 1999). Viewed from the fundamental points of difference between the two approaches to convergence, its conditional version is the reality as no space is an 'island' on its own. Once the possibility of peripheral externalities and spill over both positive and negative (Mohanty, 2011) is ruled out as a matter of convenience, conditional β-convergence gets replaced by absolute β-convergence. Accordingly, in the present context absolute β-convergence model due to Sala-i-Martin (1996) has been used to locate convergence or otherwise in per capita public health expenditure of Indian states in the post-reforms period 1991-92 – 2009-10. The following is the model with white noise disturbance which has been applied to the state level time-series data on per capita public health expenditure in India.

$$\ln\left(\frac{y_{i,t+T}}{y_{it}}\right) = \alpha + \beta \ln(y_{it}) + \varepsilon_t \qquad \ldots(1)$$

where

y = per capita public health expenditure,

i = 1, 2, 3, ... 16 (States),

t = 1991-92, 1992-93, ... 2009-10 (Time), and

α and β are the parameters of the regression of which the latter is defined as the 'convergence' coefficient.

Absolute β-convergence holds across the states if the sign of β-coefficient is negative and statistically different from zero at appropriate level of probability, say 5 per cent. Due to difference in structural characteristics of these 16 states, they have been categorised as under 'high income states' and 'middle and low income states'. Coincidentally, these low-income states are seven out of eight Empowered Action Group (EAG)[7] states of India. The regression (1) has been applied to (1) all states taken together, (2) the club of high income states, and (3) the club of middle and low income states separately and the results are shown in Table 8.9. The convergence coefficient (β-coefficient) is negative everywhere but significant at 5 per cent level only in case of the club of middle and low income states. Accordingly, these states exhibit convergence in per capita public health expenditure among themselves not with the per capita health expenditure of high income states during the period under reference. This is indeed an encouraging symptom. They are tending to bridge up the gap in per capita public health expenditure within themselves. As shown in Table 8.1, poor states are equally poor in terms of health outcomes and these health outcomes are seen to have been directly related to per capita health expenditure (Table 8.7). After reforms these states have made significant efforts to strengthen their healthcare system in their attempt to be comparable with that of the high income states of India. If the middle and low income states continue to maintain the existing speed in their per capita public health expenditure, sooner or later, the Indian states are believed to encounter a situation of least (or tolerable) level of health inequality. However, the relevance of the inference is not free from limitation. Since all the states taken together exhibit non-convergence, with increase in per capita expenditure on health by the governments of the middle and low income states if the high income states increase the speed in their own per capita health expenditure, it would be in a perennial state of non-convergence for all states. Gaps will persist between the health outcomes relating to these two categories of states of India. In this case, the model would not be supportive of catching up both the phenomena of per capita public health expenditure and health outcomes convergence. Since middle and low income states constitute one component that again a weaker component, a mere convergence in their per capita health expenditure would not be enough to cause convergence in per capita public health expenditure for the whole.

Table 8.9: Estimates of Convergence Coefficient and other related Parameters

Model Estimates	*All States*	*High Income States*	*Middle and Low Income States*
α	3.368	6.855	4.388
	(1.979)*	(1.310)	(3.377)*
β	–0.430	–1.305	–0.648
	(–1.061)	(–1.028)	(–2.127)*
R^2	0.075	0.175	0.393
DW	2.640	2.035	3.017

Sources: Handbook of Statistics on State Government Finances, Reserve Bank of India, 2010.
Economic Survey 2010-11, Government of India.
* Significant at 5 per cent level.

Results and Policy Recommendations

Income inequality is a primary source of health inequality. The gradient measurement of health inequality can thus be displaced by alleviating income inequality. This is more a logic than a practice. Some of the developed countries of the world display worst economic inequality and at the same time, they have one of the best healthcare systems. Of course, richer countries are better equipped to address the problems of health inequalities faster. Mitigation of health inequality needs at the first instance improving the health outcomes and achieving an appreciable standard within not-so-long a period of time. Individuals on their own will not be successful in improving these health outcomes which are macro aggregates. State intervention is inevitable. The international forums and national governments have recommended the relevance of public expenditure on public health as a cause for improving health related parameters for all countries irrespective of their economic and social progress. Between the absolute level of public expenditure on health and its per capita version, the latter is more powerful than the former in achieving the goal. High income states of India have equally high per capita public health expenditure and have reaped better value from expenditure on health and healthcare. These states have achieved relatively better distributional impact and allocative efficiency of healthcare expenditure. The middle and low income states together have pulled down the national averages of health outcomes because of their relatively poor performance in these parameters. One of the mitigating forces for existing health inequalities between the states of India is to increase the per capita health expenditure more particularly by the governments of middle and low income states. After reforms, they are seen to have increased per capita health expenditure on health. In spite of this, there is no catching up with the per capita public health expenditure of the high income states of India. However, the model of inequality convergence has proved for the catching up process in per capita health expenditure being effective between the middle and low income states of India.

The current structure of the healthcare system of India is fragmented which may be one of the reasons for health inequality between the constituent states. These fragments consist of (1) public provision of public healthcare services, (2) large private sector that is financed out of the pocket of the healthcare consumers, and (3) scanty health insurance. The first one is again split into two: (i) the provisions made out of the central resources/grants, and (ii) the funding of the services by the federating states of India. While allocating resources for the purpose, the Central Government treats all states equally which aggravates the problem of health inequality. The structure of the healthcare system of the states is not uniform throughout. The states do not work in cohesion while spending for their respective healthcare sector out of their own resources. It is true that the health sector in India comes under the State List. This has given autonomy to the states to decide their own way of putting money for the health sector development. While exercising their autonomy, the states should recognise the most critical common area for intervention by keeping in view the national interest. This would increase the cost effectiveness of the intervention by the state governments. Limited health insurance is a major handicap in India on the programme of augmenting health equality between groups, states and regions. Less than 15 per cent of the population in India have some form of health insurance coverage. Lack of universal health insurance is held to be a source of health inequality. If equity is the major objective of the healthcare system of India, healthcare reforms are to be at the top of the domestic policy. These reform measures must continue with the provision of universal health insurance, cohesive approach to health sector development by the federating states of India, strengthening the programmes for health education and extension programme, and of all, putting maximum efforts to remedy the health and nutrition related problems of the most disadvantaged sections of the Indian society.

NOTES

1. The socio-economic rating scale consists of the socio-economic status score points of the socio-economic groups (SEGs) which range between 0 and 100. The final score point for each SEG is a composite index. This index for each group which is scalar quantity is computed from the factors like occupational attainment (employment status), level of education (literacy), income per capita, poverty (percentage of the members of the group living below poverty line), mortality rates (IMR, MMR and CDR), morbidity status (DALY), and life expectancy at birth. However, it is not an exhaustive list. It may vary over countries as in several countries; ethnicity of SEGs is also counted as a major factor.
2. It is an obvious fact that lower the socio-economic position of a group (individual), worse is their (his/her) health. And accordingly, the gradient in health runs from top to bottom on the socio-economic rating scale. Thus gradient in health determines health inequities (World Health Organisation, 2008).
3. Goal 4 (Reduce child mortality), Goal 5 (Improve maternal health) and Goal 6 (Combat HIV/AIDS, malaria and other diseases).
4. DBC is the socio-economic rating scale which has a kink at B, being steepening before B and flattening beyond B. Since the gradient (slope) of the segment DB exceeds that of the segment BC, socio-economic groups (SEGs) which have socio-economic status (SES)

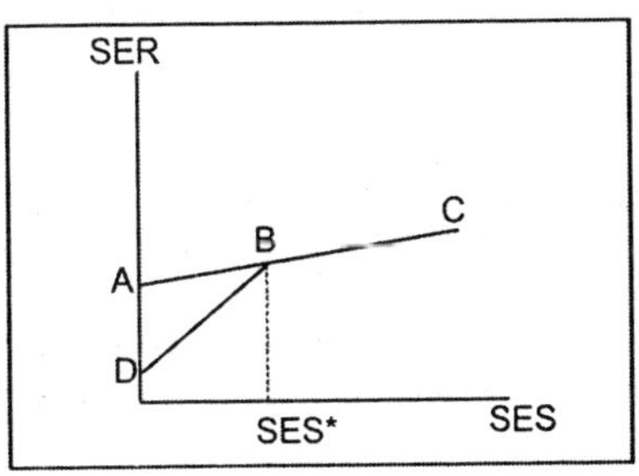

defined on the portion DB are lower positioned than those relating to the segment BC. Though absolute equality is the most ideal situation (in that case the line ABC should have been parallel to horizontal axis) can never be anticipated in a market economy. Market economies are always dynamic and thus with passage of time, they open up the vistas for new opportunities which are available to all categories of SEGs without any physical restraints. As the initial situation was a situation of inequality, the pool of new opportunities will not be equally shared between SEGs. More capable SEGs may capture relatively larger share than the others. Accordingly, under market economies there would always be gaps between SEGs. On consideration of equity, this gap should have been liberated from being much skewed having several kinks. It must have been of the shape ABC which is mildly rising throughout indicating the presence of minimum or tolerable level of inequality among the SEGs at all times. The social gradient of ABC thus measures the 'natural rate of subjective inequality' (Lambert *et al.*, 2003). Two issues are likely to arise. How much inequality between SEGs is tolerable/acceptable by the society and what determines the kink at B or how is it determined that the SEG having socio-economic status SES^* is at the border point that defines B? Socially acceptable level of inequality is that level of difference in socio-economic status that does not cause any subjective aversion to inequality among the SEGs or all SEGs are equally least averse to this level of inequality. The median value of the distribution of socio-economic rating (SER) scores of the SEGs (SES*) defines B. Mitigating inequality means raising DB to the level of AB in which case DB will squeeze in length per episode. This is obvious as with reduction in inequality among SEGs positioned on the segment DB, their socio-economic status score points will come closer, thus the limiting value of the length of DB over time would be that of AB. With upward shift of DB, health inequality among the SEGs positioned on this segment would reduce. In other words, reducing the gradient of DB towards the gradient of BC is identified with reducing socio-economic inequality among the SEGs to the level of the 'natural rate of subjective inequality'.

5. The following are the criteria used by WHO for healthcare ranking of countries:
   1. Responsiveness,
   2. Fairness of Financial Contribution,
   3. Overall level of Health,
   4. Distribution of Health in the Population, and
   5. Distribution of Financing.
6. For determining the value of spending on health sector by the state governments, year-wise data on health outcomes for each state

should have been available. While expenditure data on health are available for each year, data on health outcomes are available over intervals only. This causes incompatibility.

7. *Empowered Action Group (EAG)*: The states having high fertility and high (declining) mortality rates together are put under this category. The Government of India had constituted an Empowered Action Group (EAG) under the Ministry of Health and Family Welfare following 2001 Census to undertake measures for stabilising population in eight states—Bihar, Chhattisgarh, Jharkhand, Madhya Pradesh, Odisha, Rajasthan, Uttar Pradesh, and Uttarakhand (called EAG states), that were lagging in containing population. As per the latest Census (2011), EAG states have shown little improvement in population stabilisation. These states cover over 45 per cent of India's population.

REFERENCES

Acemoglu, Daron and James A. Robinson, (2002). 'The Political Economy of the Kuznets Curve', *Review of Development Economics*, 6(2): 183-203.

Barro, R. and Xavier Sala-i-Martin, (1992). 'Convergence', *Journal of Political Economy*, 100(2): 223 51.

Barraza-Llorens, Marina, Stefano Bertozzi, Eduardo Gonzalez-Pier and Juan Pablo Gutierrez, (2002). 'Addressing Inequities in Health and Health Care in Mexico', *Health Affairs*, 21(3): 47-56.

Batista-Foguet, J.M., J. Fortiana, C. Currie and J.R. Villalbi (2004). 'Socio-economic Indexes in Surveys for Comparison between Countries', *Social Indicators Research*, 67(3): 315-32.

Bhaduri, Amit. (2008). 'Growth and Employment in the Era of Globalisation: Some Lessons from the Indian Experience', *ILO Asia-Pacific Working Paper Series*, Sub-Regional Office for South Asia, New Delhi.

Deaton, Angus (2003). 'Health, Inequality, and Economic Development', *Journal of Economic Literature*, 41(1): 113-58.

Dev, Mahendra S. and C. Ravi (2007). 'Poverty and Inequality: All India and States, 1983-2005', *Economic and Political Weekly*, 42(6): 509-21.

Government of India (2002). *National Health Policy 2002* (India), New Delhi: Ministry of Health and Family Welfare.

House of Commons (2009). *Health Inequalities, Third Report of Session 2008-09*, Vol. 1, Health Committee. London: The Stationery Office Limited.

Lambert, Peter J., Daniel L. Millimet and Daniel Slottje (2003). 'Inequality Aversion and the Natural Rate of Subjective Inequality', *Journal of Public Economics*, 87: 1061-90.

Leigh, Andrew, Christopher Jencks and Timothy M. Smeeding (2009). 'Health and Economic Inequalities', in Wiemer Salverda, Brian Nolan and Timothy M. Smeeding (eds.), *The Oxford Handbook of Economic Inequality*, Oxford: Oxford University Press, pp. 384-405.

Mohanty, B.K. (ed.) (2011). *Economic Development in India: Issues and Challenges*. New Delhi: New Century Publications.

Mohanty, B.K. (2011). 'Convergence in Public Expenditure and Public Revenue across Indian States: Implications for Sustainable Economic Growth', *Asian Journal of Empirical Research*, 1(1): 14-24.

Mohanty, B.K. (2012). 'The Convergence Hypothesis: India under Neo-liberalism', *Man and Development*, 34(1): 1-14.

Mohanty, S.K. and F. Ram (2010). 'Life Expectancy at Birth among Social and Economic Groups in India', *IIPS Research Brief*, 13, November, Mumbai: International Institute for Population Studies.

OECD (2011). *Society at a Glance 2011— OECD Social Indicators*. Paris: OECD.

Rey, Sergio J. and Brett D. Montouri (1999). 'US Regional Income Convergence: A Spatial Econometric Perspective', *Regional Studies*, 3(2): 146-156.

Sal-i-Martin, Xavier (1996). 'The Classical Approach to Convergence Analysis', *Economic Journal*, 106 (437):1019-36.

Sarkar, Sandip and Balwant Singh Mehta (2010). 'Income Inequality in India: Pre- and Post-Reform Periods', *Economic and Political Weekly*, 45(3): 45-55.

Smith, James P. (2004). 'Unravelling the SES-Health Connection', *Population and Development Review*, 30 (Supplement 04):108-132.

United Nations (2003). *Indicators for Monitoring the Millennium Development Goals*. New York: United Nations Organisation.

UNDP (2010). *Human Development Report 2010*. New Delhi: Oxford University Press.

Wilkinson, Richard G. (1996). 'Unhealthy Societies: The Afflictions of Inequality'. London: Rutledge.

Wilkinson, Richard G. (1997). 'Socio-economic Determinants of Health: Health Inequalities: Relative or Absolute Material Standards?' *British Medical Journal*, 314(7080): 591-595.

World Bank (2008). 'Public Spending in Russia for Health Care: Issues and Options, Europe and Central Asia Region', *Human Development Report*, Russian Federation Country Management Unit.

World Bank (2012). *Health Expenditure, Total (%GDP)*.

World Health Organisation (1978). *Primary Health Care: Report of the International Conference on Primary Health Care* (Alma Ata, USSR, 6-12 September). Geneva: World Health Organisation.

World Health Organisation (2000). *World Health Report 2000*, Geneva: World Health Organisation.

World Health Organisation (2007). 'Achieving Health Equity: From Root Causes to Fair Outcomes, Commission on Social Determinants of Health', *Interim Statement*. Geneva: World Health Organisation.

World Health Organisation (2008). *Closing the Gap in a Generation, Commission on Social Determinants of Health* 2005-2008, Geneva: World Health Organisation.

9

Economically Backward People (EBP)

Criteria for Identification, Backwardness Measurement Issues and Policy Measures

D.K. Verma

Backwardness in India, as identified and measured by various national or state level commissions and committees, invariably referred to collectivities which is also upheld and further substantiated by judiciary too. Albeit, academicians and even subject experts in such commissions and committees have debated and also dissented on such identification and measures. Empirically, however, the beneficiaries (target) under so identified backward classes (collectivities) are in fact individuals and affirmative action by legislative, judiciary and executive including reservation and welfare measures are aspired and achieved for individuals only. Thus, the state creates a class of such individuals who get benefits through state interventions and affirmative action.

There is no denying the fact that SCs, STs and OBCs have made progress and their representation in various fields is visible but still they are in need of state support (reservation in promotion and private sector) because greater emphasis is still missing to accelerate their respective achieved status so as to generate enough escape velocity altering their ascribed status which is so far unchangeable. Because of this caste-gravitational-pull of backwardness, there has emerged another type of status in the post-independent India and particularly during the post-reform period, which cannot be defined and explained under traditional understanding of ascribed or achieved statuses as described by Ralph Linton. The author of the present paper has coined and described such newly emerged status as *affirmed status* and has also explained the process of such new status emergence as *social devolution* (Verma, 2004). The present paper reviews the approach and modalities to identify backwardness in our country on the basis of ascribed collectivities and discuss backwardness measurement issues based on achieved individualities so as to recommend policy measures for affirmative status of people in post-reform India who are not currently included in the existing lists of reserved categories but are in need of affirmative action, the Economically Backward People (EBP).

Backwardness: A Review

Expression of Backward Classes first appeared in 1870s in Madras Presidency where the British Government had grouped scheduled castes and untouchable castes under the label of Backward Classes and gradually their number increased from 39 in 1870 to 131 in 1920. Though the term 'backward class' has appeared more than once in the Constitution of India but it has not been defined adequately in order to adopt suitable criteria and identify those who come under backward class category.

Several commissions/committees were set up at national and state level to identify backward classes. Some of the important such commissions/committees were—Justice L.C. Miller Committee, Mysore (Karnataka) was constituted during 1918-20. In Karnataka four other commissions set up to identify backwardness include Naganna Gowda Commission (1961), L.G. Anna Havenoy Commission (1972-75), T. Venkataka Swami Commission 1986 and Chinnappa Reddy Commission (1989-90). In Kerala also a commission on backwardness was constituted in the colonial period during 1935 under the chairmanship of Justice C.D. Nokes. Thereafter three commissions were constituted in Kerala including V.K. Vishvanathan Commission (1961-63), J. Kumar Pillai Commission (1964-66), and M.P. Damodran Commission (1967-70). Backward Classes Commissions constituted in Tamil Nadu include A.M. Sattanathan Commission

(1969-70) and J.M. Ambasankar Commission (1982-86). In Andhra Pradesh also three backward class commissions were constituted for the purpose include Manohar Pershad Committee (1968-69), Ananta Raman Commission (1970), and Murlidhar Rao Commission (1982). Mungeri Lal Commission was set up in Bihar during 1971-76. In Gujarat the commissions set up to identify backward classes were: A.R. Bakshi Commission (1972-76), Justice C.V. Rane Commission (1981-83) and Justice R.C. Mankad Commission (1987). Justice Gajendragadkar Commission (1967-68); Justice J.N. Wazir Commission (1969); Justice Adarsh Anand Commission (1976-77); and Gurnam Singh Commission (1990) were set up in Haryana. Similarly, O.H.B. Starte Committee (Bombay Presidency, 1928-30) and B.D. Deshmukh Committee (1961-64) in Maharashtra; Brish Bhan Committee (1965-66) in Punjab; Chhedi Lal Sathi Commission in Uttar Pradesh and Mahajan Commission (1980-1983) in Madhya Pradesh were constituted to identify backward classes. In the year 1932, Madan Mohan Malviya, the signatory on behalf of Caste Hindus and B.R. Ambedkar on behalf of the depressed classes, signed the Poona Pact. That was the first occasion when British Government recognized the depressed classes as a separate element in Indian politics.

The debate remained focused on social and educational backwardness which had its roots in the *Pax Britanica*. The initial construction of the larger criteria of social and educational backwardness was in negative terms, wherein the Madras Presidency all sections, apart from Brahmins, was by definition, considered backward. Thus, no technical or scientific definition of backwards was evolved but non-Brahmins and later on non-upper castes, continued to be included under a larger umbrella 'socially and technically backward classes'. Community based census of 1931 was mainly exploited to identify the population of (such) backward classes. Thus, two categories emerged whereby caste and tribe were together constructed into a homogenous mass for the purpose of public policy. Irrespective of understanding of social reality, all families and communities belonging to upper caste and lower caste were respectively categorized as non-backward and backward.

Dr. B.R. Ambedkar was elected to Constituent Assembly of India from Bengal and later from Bombay and on August 29, 1947 became the Chairman of the Drafting Committee of the Constitution of India. On February 21, 1948, Ambedkar submitted the draft Constitution and in the revised draft Constitution of November 1949 the term 'backward class' was incorporated as suggested by him. In the Constituent Assembly, Ambedkar stated that India was a society based on the principle of graded inequality that meant elevation of some and degradation of others.

Dr. Ambedkar apprehended that the free India might revert to the old traditions and downtrodden sections of the society might get further marginalized in the absence of proper state intervention. While the question of identifying scheduled castes and scheduled tribes was settled before independence, largely due to efforts of B.R. Ambedkar, who composed them as a backward class in the Constitution, the question of 'other backward classes', as Jawaharlal Nehru quoted 'left for subsequent generations'.

Thus, in the past in independent India the criteria and identification of backward class other than scheduled castes and schedule tribes remained a more political and less academic debate. Under Article 340[1] of the Constitution of India, it is obligatory for the state to promote the welfare of the Backward Classes[2]. The first commission indicated that caste was an important measure of backwardness, however, 5 out of 11 members of the commission including the chairman himself, raised strong objections on considering caste as a criterion to identify backwardness. In his dissent-note annexed with the report of the first backward class commission, its chairman expressed that "the caste system is the greatest hindrance in the way of our progress towards an egalitarian society, the recognition of the specified class backward may serve to maintain and even perpetuate the existing distinction on the caste basis" (Government of India, Backward Class Commission Report, page 2). The then Central Government rejected the report of the first Backward Class Commission on the ground that the commission had not applied more objective criteria such as income, education and literacy to determine backward status. Thereafter, a number of state commissions were constituted to devise methods for identifying backwardness.

In 1978, the second Backward Classes Commission popularly known as Mandal Commission was constituted on December 20, 1978. The Commission headed by B.P. Mandal identified 3743 castes/communities representing over 52 per cent of Indian population as backward. During 1970s and 1980s, a number of castes including Yadavs, Kurmis, Koris and Vokkaligas emerged as important political forces and launched political agitations in the name of OBCs and when Janata Party came to power in 1977 many of them represented their respective communities or the castes in governance. That was the background under which the second Backward Classes Commission was set up. On August 7, 1990, the then Prime Minister announced the government's acceptance of the Mandal Commission Report in the parliament reminding the nation that the Constitution envisaged that social and educational backwardness be identified, their difficulties removed and their conditions be improved in terms of Article 340(1) read with Article 314(4) as well 16(4). The government decided to adopt in the first phase the castes common to both the Mandal list and lists prepared by various states to introduce 27 per cent reservation in services for Socially and Educationally Backward Classes, SEBCs (the Constitutional term for OBCs); but that policy was not extended to educational institutions.

Though the Mandal Commission had recommended reservation in educational institutions but the commission also state that "the initial part of the battle against social backwardness is to be fought in the minds of backward people in India....Government services have always been looked upon as (status) prestige and power by increasing the representation of OBCs in government services, we give them an immediate feeling of participation in the governance.

In 1992, the Apex Court gave its approval to the legitimacy of the government order to empower the Mandal report subject to the exclusion of the social advanced sections (creamy layer) amongst identified as backward classes. However, the Parliamentary Standing Committee on Personnel, Public Grievance, Law and Justice in its 8th report on the SC/ST/OBCs (Reservation in Posts and Services Bill, 2004) found that many of the castes, tribes and classes among the SC/ST/OBCs had been deprived of the benefits of reservations in services as these were restricted to certain upper sections among backward classes. It was expressed that "exclusion of some castes from the benefit of reservation has pushed them far behind which is violation of the principles of social harmony and social equality as embodied in the Indian Constitution."

The above discussion makes it clear that there was no thinking about backward classes other than SCs and STs in the pre-independence period at central level yet in provinces such as Bombay, Madras and Mysore Presidencies there were some reservations of jobs and seats for them in the field of education. The recognition of the first Backward Class Commission were not accepted and before accepting recommendation of second Commission report, some states had already given reservation to OBCs, for example, in 1970 on the basis of recommendations of the Manohar Pershad Commission, Andhra Pradesh Government reserved 25 per cent of seats in colleges. Inclusion of Sikhs and Buddhists opened a new debate because Sikhism, Buddhism and Jainism emerged as protest/movements against the institution of caste. The lists for SCs and OBCs were prepared on the basis of caste as the major criteria. Christianity and Islam were also opposed to the recognition of caste, but only backward Muslims were included among OBCs by Mandal Commission. Thereafter, emerged the issue of SC converts to the Christianity and Islam, as the two faiths were not included in the list for SCs.

The confusion was confounded with conversion itself and when that was compared on caste or tribe basis. In several studies in the country either Muslims in general or Muslim OBCs as part of the General OBCs are on the positive discrimination list. In Madhya Pradesh, Joshi and Verma (1998) conducted empirical studies to investigate the social, educational and economical conditions of Muslim communities whose applications were received by the Government of Madhya Pradesh for inclusion in the OBC List. The main criteria adopted for identification of backward communities among Muslims, was comparison of their socio-economic status with that of a local community already included in the list of OBC. For that study referent community elected was Patidar. Based on the findings, 32 Muslim communities were studied and recommended for inclusion in the list of OBCs.

Therefore, philosophically and in democratic social set up, the concept of backwardness needed to be understood in the context of issues like justice and equality irrespective of caste, race, religion and gender. Accordingly, the concept of backwardness was extended to non-Hindu communities by the Mandal Commission which declared over 80 Muslim groups as backward and, thus, in fact half of the Muslim population was identified as backward

(Galantar, 1994). Thus, it was a major policy shift to consider backwardness on religion basis. However, Mandal Commission refused to declare Muslims as a whole a backward community enjoying the same status as SCs and STs. Though backward communities among Muslims have been included in the OBC List but they were not getting actual benefits as was evident in the representation at various levels.

B.K. Roy Berman has mentioned that when he was chairman of the technical committee of the second Backward Class Commission, he found lack of transparency and many aberrations and congruities in the functioning of the commission (Mainstream, 2nd June, 2006). In a letter sent to the author of this paper he expressed that he firmly believed in formative action in favour of socially and educationally backward classes. He also mentioned that Mandal Commission did not make use of available information to correctly quantify the numerical strength of the population belonging to the socially and educationally backward classes.

Besides, there was a question of developing a strategy to prevent casteism being more deeply entrenched through formative action. He expressed that for a long time he had held that there should be transformation strategy in dealing with socially and educationally backward classes so that the focus could shift from caste and community, primarily to caste and income and secondarily to community only. In his aforementioned article, he mentioned that the state governments were asked to undertake *ad hoc* survey with a major focus shifted away from caste after the refusal of the Government of India to accept the recommendations of the first Backward Class Commission.

As In-charge of the Cultural Research Institute, Government of West Bengal, Roy Berman suggested that 50 per cent or more of persons depending on any non-agricultural occupation belonging to the scheduled castes or the scheduled tribes, and at the same time, the persons whose dependent having less than 50 per cent average literacy of the state could be considered as socially and educationally backward. On behalf of the Government of West Bengal that was presented to Government of India and was accepted with a rider that per capita income limited to Rs. 1000 per annum was also to be kept in view. That was considered to be a deft interlacing of caste and/or community and occupation to go beyond casteism.

I.P. Desai was associated as a member of the Expert Committee constituted by first socially and educationally backward class commission appointed by the Government of Gujarat in 1972, popularly known as Bakshi Commission. He expressed that some members of the Expert Committee including him were left with a certain dissatisfaction, particularly when Bakshi Commission made caste as a unit of identification for a collectivity being included in the socially and educationally backward classes and that their dissatisfaction enhanced when the Mandal Commission (1978-82) said that the survey had no pretension of being a piece of academic research and that had been used as rough and ready made tool for evolving a simple criteria for identification of socially and educationally backward classes. Desai also observed that leaving aside SCs and STs, the Constitution left us with an option to consider backwardness on the basis other than caste or on secular basis.

The Mandal Commission was assisted by three bodies, *viz.* a panel of experts led by M.N. Srinivas, a research planning team of sociologists, and a support committee of experts constituted by technical committee. The commission mentions in Part 11.1, Page 50, Vol. I that the experts panel agreed with the observations of the research planning team that the task before the commission was to lay down the criteria for identifying recognizable and persistent collectivities and not individuals. By that it was meant that those groups, which followed low and impure occupations, were socially backward and also educationally backward. They had low income also. In other words, all these backwardness were related to the concept of pollution and impurity. This is an important consideration to identify the criteria and indicators about social and economic backwardness among religious minorities, whether to consider collectivities or individuals.

Economically Backward Classes

The term 'Economically Backward Classes' is generally used to denote people, communities and castes/classes from any religion or region who do not currently qualify for reservation benefits which are meant for scheduled castes, scheduled tribes and for other backward classes (OBC) but they comprise a section of society which is economically backward or poor.

It was the Central Government under Prime Minister P.V. Narasimha Rao that proposed in 1991 a separate reservation quota of 10 per cent in government jobs for the poor among the General Category (GC) in Central Services.

However, the idea on the part of the government to give 10 per cent quota to the poor among GC was not a new one. It was in 1980-81 when the Government of India was processing Mandal Commission report to table its recommendations before the Parliament wherein it maintained the stand that the benefits of affirmative action should also reach the poor irrespective of caste and religion. A Member of the Parliament (Shri Rajiv Gandhi) speaking in the Parliament on September 6, 1990 (during the time Shri V.P. Singh as Prime Minister was about to implement recommendations of Mandal Commission) had explained his party's stand (the speech is at Annexure 12) on affirmative action which is as follows: "Is this government looking at one particular vested interest or is the government looking at the socially and educationally backward classes? This is the question I put to the Prime Minister. The point is within a particular class who you want to help. The fact is that within a class when you want to give some assistance it should go to the poorest. …In fact every objection that I am hearing is only confirming my fear that this government is aiming these benefits at a privileged group and not looking at the really poor...... I think the honourable Prime Minister has totally missed the point."

The thrust of Shri Rajiv Gandhi's speech was that a class (or a caste) could be taken up for affirmative measure on the basis of social backwardness criteria but beyond that it should be ensured that the poorest in the class got the benefit and it did not go to the well to do segments within the caste/class. He had further argued that such underprivileged groups should receive affirmative measures irrespective of caste or religion. The thinking of Congress Party as articulated in the 1990 speech of Shri Rajiv Gandhi in Parliament was reflected in the form of a Central Government Memo dated September, 25 1991 giving 10 per cent reservation in jobs and other opportunities to other economically backward sections of the people who are not covered by any of the existing schemes.

The Supreme Court subsequently struck down the order as unconstitutional while adjudicating in Indra Sawhney *vs.* Union of India in 1992. The Court's observation was, "A backward class of citizens cannot be exclusively identified by economic criterion. It is, of course, possible for government or any other authority to identify a class based on occupation-cum-education without reference to caste if it is so advised. There is no constitutional barrier to define more backward and less backward." As for the view of Bharatiya Janata Party on the issue, its General Secretary Shri Venkiah Naidu had clarified in 1992 that his party had all along been supportive of the idea and reminded the public that Jan Sangh, in its National Executive Meeting in 1985 had adopted a resolution endorsing reservation for economically backward classes in the General Category.

When National Democratic Alliance Government thereafter came to power in 1993 it appointed a Group of Ministers (GOM) to study the possibility of constitutional amendment Bill to provide job reservation to GC on economic ground. A Commission was subsequently set up in 2004 by the NDA led government (with Shri Atal Behari Vajpayee as Prime Minister) to work out modalities for reservation to the poor among the GC. However, that report was not submitted and this Commission could not make a reference of that.

Thereafter, when the United Progressive Alliance (UPA) Government came to power, it constituted a Commission[3] in 2006 to go into the issue of separate reservation for the Economically Backward Classes among the General Category. Thus, it may be seen that both UPA and NDA led Governments had taken steps to extend reservation to economically backward classes in GC. Among the states, only Rajasthan[4] had proposed to the Centre a 10 per cent quota for EBCs among its GC.

Identification of Economic Backwardness

In India, both during pre- and post-Independence period several attempts have been made to identify indicators for measuring backwardness among various sections of the society. In Andhra Pradesh, backward classes were categorized into four major groups, namely Aborigine tribes; Vimukti Jati; Nomadic and semi-Nomadic tribes; occupational and service class; scheduled castes who were converted to Christianity; and other communities. In Karnataka, a different approach to the problem of backwardness and determination of backwardness was followed by Havanor Commission. The Commission first of all prepared a list of educationally backward classes on the basis of indicators wherein "a caste or a community whose student per thousand of its population passing out SCLC examination was below state average."

Then on the basis of the list of educationally backward classes so drawn, further categories identified were: backward communities identified on the basis of criteria as "student average per thousand of population was below state level", backward caste identified with the indicator as "whose student average per thousand of population was below 50 per cent of the state average", and backward tribes identified with the indicator as "whose student average per thousand of population was below 50 per cent of the state average except Dombars and Voddars (nomadic and denotified tribes)." The commission under the chairmanship of L.G. Havanor did not take caste as the criteria to identify backwardness. However, the emphasis remained on caste, tribes and communities. Later on, Justice Chinappa Reddy Commission constituted by the state government in 1989-90, however, again considered caste as the "sufficient criteria" to identify backward classes.

In Bihar two categories of other backward classes were prepared, one containing 79 castes who were deemed more backward than the other list of 30 castes. However, the Patna High Court declared those two lists of backward castes as unconstitutional. Therefore, the Bihar government appointed a Backward Classes Commission under the Chairmanship of Mungeri Lal which remained in office during 1971-76. Based on the indicators like social status, educational backwardness, representation in Government service and adequacy of share in trade, commerce and industry, the Mungeri Lal Commission prepared two lists of other backward communities and most backward classes, the later contained 93 castes.

A Backward Class Commission was set up in August 1972 under the Chairmanship of A.B. Bakshi by the Government of Gujarat. The Commission considered the following ten factors in determining the social and educational backwardness in Gujarat: social backwardness in general; poverty and economic backwardness; illiteracy and educational backwardness;

occupational factors; representation in public sector services; social status in general; mode of living, customs and beliefs; caste only as one of the relevant factor; nomadic way of living and backwardness in other ways. The Bakshi Commission identified 82 castes as socially, economically and educationally backward.

The basic understanding and the conceptual framework for measuring multiple deprivation is reflected in the writing of Alpock 1997 — "we must know what poverty is before we can identify where and when it is occurring or attempt to measure and before we begin to do anything to alleviate it. The office of the Deputy Prime Minister of London commissioned the Socially Disadvantaged Research Centre at the Department of Social Policy and Social Research at the University of Oxford to update the indices of deprivation for the country.

The index of multiple deprivations was published in April 2004 in which domains and indicators for measuring multiple deprivations are discussed. And the account of poverty in U.K. in which Townsend (1979) sets out the case for defining poverty in terms of relative deprivation has "individuals, families and groups can be said to be in poverty if they lack the resources to obtain the type of diet, participate in the activities and have the living conditions and amenities which are customary or at least widely encouraged or approved in the societies to which they belonged. Following seven domains of deprivation were considered: Income deprivation; Employment deprivation; Health deprivation and disability; Education, skill and training deprivation; Barriers to housing and services; Living environmental deprivation; and Crime. Each domain contained a number of indicators totalling to 37 in all.

As per the National Commission for Backward Classes guidelines for Inclusion in the central list of OBCs there are three main criteria including social, economic and education[5&6]. These are the exiting criteria for identification of backwardness in the country.

Measures of Economic Backwardness

Monthly per capita expenditure (MPCE) is the monthly per capita expenditure on basic food and a few other items which the National Sample Survey Organization (NSSO) rounds track. It is a measure of the economic status of a household in terms of consumption of basics. While half of the OBCs and EBCs among General Castes (GCs) in rural areas have MPCE below the average MPCE, about 64 per cent OBCs had the same status. Both GC and OBC in rural India had better consumption status compared to ST and SC as 79.6 per cent and 77.4 per cent of them respectively have MPCE below the state average.

The difference between GC and OBCs was higher in urban areas where GCs appeared considerably better in their MPCE status. However, more than relative comparison, GCs was about 54 per cent of them, both in urban and Rural areas, had below state average MPCEs. Average MPCE of GC as a whole was admittedly higher than OBC and considerably higher than SC and ST. However, the fact remained that half of GC population shared the same status as most of other social groups in their consumption capacity.

Average MPCE of GCs at Rs. 685.31 was 22.5 per cent higher than the all groups average (Rs. 558.78) which was almost the same as average MPCE of OBCs (Rs. 556.72). SC and ST consumption averages were considerably lower at 15 per cent and 23.6 per cent respectively from the average for all groups. The MPCE average was highest for non-agricultural and non-self employed occupations at Rs. 924.44. The lowest occupation was Agricultural Labour with MPCE of Rs. 415. The difference of MPCE average between GC and OBC was higher in value added occupations such as "self-employed in non-agriculture" and "other" occupations and lowest in "labour" as occupation.

In the category of "self-employed in agriculture", GCs and OBCs had higher MPCE compared to ST/SC irrespective of size of land holding. Even at 4 acres level, MPCE of GC was of 29.4 per cent higher than STs holding same quantum of land. However, the difference between GC and OBC was only 10 per cent in the same land holding category. GCs having lower land holding but engaged in agriculture had a lower economic status than OBCs with equivalent land holding. But that did not hold true for SC/ST. Even with higher land holding their MPCE was lower than GC/OBC households having less land.

Below Poverty Line Population

Poverty line is officially fixed as the expenditure needed to meet cost of basic food and a few other items. The poverty line for rural and urban areas fixed by Planning Commission in 2004-05 were Rs. 368 expenditure per person per month on basic food and a few other items for rural and Rs. 559 for urban areas. NSSO gave the following as the proportion of households with MPCE below the poverty lines: Rural – SC (49.7%), ST (39.3%), OBC (28.8%) and GC (17.5%) and for Urban it was: SC (36.9%), ST (45.7%), OBC (37 %) and GC (19.3%). According to estimate about 17.5 per cent of GC in rural and 19.3 per cent in urban India together constituted about 5.8 crore poor among the GC. The total population of BPL is estimated at 31.70 crore (30.8 %). Category-wise population among Below Poverty Line is: ST 4.25 crore (48.4%); SC 7.74 crore (38.7%); OBC 13.86 crore (33.1%) and GC 5.85 crore (18.2%). As could be seen total number of poor that was BPL of GC at 5.85 crore was only 2 crore less than BPL among SCs (7.74 crore) and was higher than BPL-STs.

Thus, number of poor households among General Category was higher than that of STs. Poverty line was considered an absolute measure of poverty and uniformly applicable to all social groups. But its value changed state-wise to accommodate local cost differences. The official method of computation was to build BPL proportions state-wise based on state-wise poverty lines factoring local costs and then have a total of BPL ratios of all states each state ratio weighted in proportion to its population.

The official BPL ratio on that basis was about 26 per cent for the country. BPL ratios were worked out for the states based on state-wise MPCE distribution provided by NSSO (2004-05), applying to them poverty lines for the country uniformly so that it was possible to compare. The proportions were different when state-wise poverty lines were applied. While the status against average MPCE of all population was a relative comparison of economic status of a class, the Below Poverty Line was an objective matrix. BPL was not just poverty but almost abject poverty because the poverty standards/lines were equal to the cost of basic foods to meet calorie needs.

Occupational Pattern and Economic Backwardness

The analysis of 61st Round (2004-05) of NSSO gave percentage distribution of occupation among social groups in urban and rural India separately, and the following picture emerges: Self-employed in agriculture comprising engaged ST, OBC and GC almost to the same extent from each group 42.3 per cent, 42 per cent and 48.7 per cent respectively. Status of SC was lower at 21.2 per cent presumably because a larger percentage of them did not possess land unlike STs and other categories. Self-employment in Non-agriculture engages OBC, GC and SC almost to the same extent at 18.7 per cent, 17.7 per cent and 15.4 per cent respectively. SCs lacking land were more engaged in non-agriculture than agriculture in rural India. STs were engaged less at 6.7 per cent in non-agriculture. It could either be due to lack of skills or higher engagement in their lands and agriculture. A remarkable status of equity was the uniform percentage of engagement in regular salaried jobs in urban India by all four groups.

The percentage participation from GC at 42 in fact was equal to ST/SC of 42.5 and 42.9, if anything OBC engagement in jobs was a shade lower. Only 5.7 per cent of GC in urban India was casual labourers. The overall picture emerged was one of uniformity than differences in major occupational groups such as farming in rural and jobs in urban areas. However, share of GC and OBC was considerably lower compared to SC/ST as labour. There were bound to be more differences when we undertook stratified analysis of each occupation.

Unreserved category did not appear to enjoy any advantage in jobs or self-occupations except that fewer of them join "labour" as an occupation compared to SC/STs both in urban and rural areas. SCs and STs were more into "labour" as an occupation as they were under-represented in "self-employment" especially in non-agriculture fields—a pointer perhaps towards lack of skills, social deprivation and motivation. In rural areas, there was remarkable similarity between GC and OBC in terms of their participation in various occupations. In urban areas, GC and OBC were comparable in "self-employed" occupation while proportion from OBCs was somewhat less into salaried jobs compared to GCs. In rural areas 35.3 per cent of GC did not possess any land. The landless proportion of GC was not too different from OBCs (39.1%). It was reported that the reason behind the apparently high landless status among GCs and OBCs could be the cultivation structure in rural India.

The above review makes it clear that collectivities of all categories (SCs, STs, OBCs, minorities and BPL among unreserved) share common characteristics of backwardness except social backwardness. Further, transformation of occupational castes (collectivities) into work categories (as enumerated by Census) supports identification of economic backwardness on individualities, which is in other words, economically backward people (EBP).

Identification of Backwardness at Individual Level

According to the Article 46, the welfare measures that are directed to state for weaker sections include:

(i) promote with special care their economic interests,
(ii) promote with special care their educational interests,
(iii) protect them from social injustice, and
(iv) protect them from all forms of exploitation.

It would be appropriate to understand economic interest of EBP. For poverty has been a much debated phenomenon. East and West have remained divided on conceptualizing poverty. Is poverty simply about the level of income obtained by households or individuals? Is it about lack of access to social services? Or is it more correctly understood as the inability to participate in society, economically, socially, culturally or politically? In Western world, the understanding about poverty could be traced back to the codification of poor laws in medieval England. But the empirical studies appeared, at the turn of the 20th century. Rowntree (1901) was the first to develop a poverty standard for individual families, based on estimates of nutritional and other requirements.

In the 1960s, the main focus was on the level of income, reflected in macro-economic indicators like Gross National Product per head. In the 1970s, poverty became prominent, notably as a result of Robert MacNamara's celebrated speech to the World Bank Board of Governors in Nairobi in 1973, and the subsequent publication of *Redistribution with Growth*. Townsend (1979), in particular, helped redefine poverty: not just as a failure to meet minimum nutrition or subsistence levels, but rather as a failure to keep up with the standards prevalent in a given society. The second shift was to broaden the concept of income poverty, to a wider set of 'basic needs', including those provided socially. New layers of complexity were added in the 1980s with the incorporation of non-monetary aspects, particularly as a result of Robert Chambers' work on powerlessness and isolation which helped to inspire greater attention to participation.

Further broadening of the concept of poverty to a wider construct, livelihood appeared in the report '*Our Common Future*' (Brundtland Commission on Sustainability and the Environment, WCS, 1980) which popularized the term sustainable livelihood. Thereafter, theoretical work by Amartya Sen (1973), emphasized that income was only valuable in so far as it increased the 'capabilities' of individuals and thereby permitted 'functioning' in society. Finally, the 1980s was characterized by a rapid increase in the study of gender. In 1990s the idea of well-being came to act as a metaphor for absence of poverty, with concomitant emphasis on how poor people themselves view their situation. At the same time, inspired by Sen, UNDP developed the idea of human development: 'the denial of opportunities and choices to lead a long, healthy, creative life and to enjoy a decent standard of living, freedom, dignity, self-esteem and the respect of others.'

The social sciences offer a wide range of theoretical literature on the causes of poverty. This debate has been broadly distinguished between the individualistic and the structural perspectives (Taylor-Gooby, 1991: 40–45; Roche, 1992: 57). The focus on the individual approach is on the behavioural and cultural factors. Poverty is seen as a result of internal factors, such as undesirable behaviour of the poor, lack of intelligence or living an indecent way of life. Such a lifestyle generates a culture of poverty characterized by various interacting social, economic and psychological features. These include lack of education, poor financial situation, suspicion, deviant values and lack of participation in society or in any other social functioning outside the immediate family (Lewis, 1965, 1969).

An essential feature of this approach is the intergenerational transmission of poverty. A strong nuclear family that creates strong ties and dependence between family members ensures the transmission of poverty, as the younger generations inherit values and customs from their parents (Lewis, 1969). In addition, families on welfare become trapped in poverty because receiving welfare benefits often changes the values and behaviour of both parents and children (Mead, 1992). While the individualistic approach emphasizes individual reasons as an explanation for poverty, the structural approach focuses on the external factors (Merton, 1968; Wilson, 1987, 1996). The structural approach emphasizes that the poor are in an unfavourable position in structural hierarchies. It regards poverty as a result of external forces, such as lack of education or low income.

The poor are victims of social structures. For example, in his study of inner city ghettos, Wilson (1987) argues that poor public transport and loss of manufacturing jobs in inner cities are reasons for poverty and the urban underclass, and that these factors reduce the chances of escaping poverty. In Indian perspective, despite rapid economic growth in our country and in spite of surviving against global recession because of strong economy, achieving the goal of poverty reduction remains a major challenge.

While accelerated growth in India has been widely attributed to the reforms of the early 1990s, their impact on poverty is still much debated among scholars with regard to three main issues: the divergence between the NAS and NSS consumption expenditure, the adjustment procedure to make the 55th round comparable to the previous rounds and the choice of the poverty line (Siggel, 2010). Some social scientists (Lal, Mohan and Natarajan, 2001; Bhalla 2002, 2003; Sundaram and Tendulkar, 2003; Datt, Kozel and Ravallion, 2003; Kulshreshtha and Kar, 2003; Deaton and Cozel, 2005) believe that poverty has been reduced in post-reform period (evident from NSS rounds) as accelerated growth is likely to lead to rapid poverty reduction.

While Sen and Himanshu (2004) hold that poverty did not decline as sharply as the official numbers claimed, and that the worsening situation of inequality is to be held responsible for that. Historically also, it has been observed that economic growth leads to improved living conditions for most, but not all individuals. The notion of poverty is usually taken to mean lack of material well-being, but it does equally apply to non-material aspects of well-being, especially education and health. It has been found useful to measure poverty by counting the number of individuals that are lacking in well-being. Human Poverty Index (HPI), is an indicator of deprivation in the three categories of average income, education and health.

The Planning Commission reports the HDI for each Indian state as well as a ranking according to the HDI. Among the 15 large states, Bihar maintained the lowest position for 1981, 1991 and 2001. At the other end, Kerala occupied the highest rank over the whole period. A basic and promising fact is that the composite HDI has increased for all-India as well as for all states. Although all the states have improved their performance over time, but at different rates, their rankings have not changed much.

Bihar, Madhya Pradesh, Uttar Pradesh, Rajasthan, Odisha and Assam were, and are, still the poorest and the lowest ranking states. Kerala, Punjab, Tamil Nadu, Maharashtra, Gujarat and Haryana, on the other hand, have remained the richest and the highest-ranked states. Further, human development finds a counterpart in the current debate about social exclusion. The focus is on multiple deprivation (low income, poor housing, poor access to education and health), but also on the process by which multiple deprivation occurs. The key arenas for exclusion include democratic and legal systems, markets, welfare state provisions, and family and community: rights, resources and relationships are all important.

The Approach Paper to the Eleventh Five-Year Plan (2007-12) chose 'faster and more inclusive growth' as its central theme. It recognized the need to make growth 'more inclusive' in terms of benefits of growth accruing to those sections of population, which have been bypassed by the high rates growth achieved in recent years. But both exclusive and inclusive models will take us to the domain of caste and ascribed status characteristics. However, in the theoretical frame of present context, poverty needs to be understood first and foremost as a problem at the individual rather than caste or community level.

Also, 'being in poverty' is a temporary status as people move in and out of poverty. In designing poverty programmes, it is wise to respect the vision of poverty articulated by poor people themselves. For many decades, the concept of poverty has been mostly identified with economic deprivation. People are considered as poor when they lack sufficient purchasing power (Akindola, 2010). In the individualistic view, poverty is the product of factors operating at the individual level, such as personal traits and behaviour of the poor themselves as against the social explanation that poverty is a result of structural factors (economic, political and/or cultural) operating at the supra individual and social level (van Oorschot and Halman, 2000; Gallie and Paugam, 2002).

Thus, the Directive Principles of State Policy lay foundations for a 'Welfare State' which needs to work for weaker sections of society. Empirical evidences and academia also support that, there is a need to identify specific target people for whom specific welfare measures could be designed and ensured.

Identification of Economic Backward People and Welfare Measures

There are certain people who are in need of state support on priority. Such EBP are being suggested to design and provide specific welfare measures, like:

- Old Age People:
- Identification: All people of age 60 and above in general and priority target beneficiaries including
- Old Age Single Widows; Old Age People without any source of Income; Old Age People with chronic diseases; and Old Age Widow heading a Household with no regular source of income.

It would be a greater challenge for state to help older single widows. Because they are old, they cannot move much distance, no-one within their houses can help them in time of emergency and they do not have any source of income except pension that too if the husband was in pensionable job. Therefore, their priorities include health, food, and shelter.

Social Reservation

It is time now to have social reservation policies in the country. A Policy of Social Reservation for Old Age People is needed in the country where all citizens of the country in order to pay respects to the old people reserve at least 10 per cent share of their services and trade for above mentioned target people. Suitable tax rebates could be given to those practising social reservation policies, for which modalities could be worked out.

Old Age Free Health Insurance: Whereby in all health centres and clinics (in both public and privately owned) certain hour/beds need to be reserved for free treatment of old age people.

At least 10 per cent reservation could be provided voluntarily by medical practitioners (including private medical practitioners) as their social obligation towards old age people. Millions of tonnes of food grains are rotting and there are no places to store that. The Central Government in an affidavit to the Supreme Court admitted that 12,418 tonnes of food grains—2,689 tonnes of wheat, 9,647 tonnes of rice and 82 tonnes of paddy, stored in FCI warehouses were damaged by August 1, 2010. It is pathetic that rats, insects and fungi consumed that food but that was not available to the needy and hungry people. All such food in excess must be distributed free to above mentioned target beneficiaries through PDS.

There are lakhs of agencies including NGOs and Civil Societies, social organizations, clubs like Rotary, Lions, Rotract and Inner Wheels, Charity Organizations, Employers' Associations, Trade Unions, People's Organizations, Registered Societies which can come forward to help Backward Communities (BCs) in this regard. Free comprehensive health facilities (cashless in all respects) in all private and government hospitals under a scheme may be designed as Free Comprehensive Insurance for Old Age People.

Eradication of Forced Livelihood

Identification: All those people who do not have freedom to earn their livelihood in general and priority Target EBP beneficiaries include:

- Child Labour—as defined under the relevant Act;
- Bonded Labour—as defined under the relevant Act;
- Landless Migrant Workers;
- Forced Female Sex Workers (FFSW); and
- Unorganized Female Domestic Workers.

Child and Bonded labourers are in larger numbers in the state like Madhya Pradesh. A state-wise study conducted by Dr. Babasaheb Ambedkar National Institute of Social Sciences (BANISS), Mhow revealed the fact that thousands of bonded labourers were working in pathetic conditions. Another state-wise study on handicraft artisans also revealed the fact that children who were supposed to be in schools were engaged as child labour.

A study on migrant labourers by the Institute also revealed pathetic working conditions of migrant labourers. In spite of having stringent legislative measures forced child and bonded labour is common in Madhya Pradesh. Such forced labourers belonging to SC and ST get protection under the SC and ST (Prevention of Atrocities) Act. But those belonging to OBCs and EBCs get protection under Minimum Wages Act only. For the purpose of rehabilitation and checking forced labour, all Child and Bonded Labourers belonging to EBP, could be identified as a special group like Most Vulnerable Group. Special packages could be designed and modalities could be worked out for their proper rehabilitation.

Domestic violence, illiteracy, unemployment, poverty; unsafe migration and child marriage were found as the major reasons for the increasing rate of illegal human trafficking in a study conducted by Shakti Vahini under United Nation Development Programme (UNDP) sponsorship. It was reported that there were 4 million prostitutes nationwide and out of 593 districts in India, 378 or 62.5 per cent were affected by human trafficking. About, 44 per cent of the women were into flesh trade due to poverty. Of the total women who were in sex work in the country, 60 per cent were from the lower and backward classes.

Sustainable Livelihood for EBP

In general for EBP, sustainable livelihood measures meant for SCs, STs and OBCs may not be appropriate as these emphasize upon a framework that help in ameliorating traditional socio-economic disabilities and discrimination. Sustainable livelihoods and welfare measures for EBP may include: Guaranteed availability and improved access to high-quality education, information, technologies and vocational training; improvement in dietary habits, checking malnutrition and insured health services; more equitable distribution, secured access, and better management of natural resources and common property resources, particularly their living environment and ecological linkages; increased and subsidized public-private partnership towards better access to basic and facilitating infrastructure to EBP; timely availability and easy accessibility to micro credit needs; a state policy and institutional environment that supports multiple livelihood strategies and promotes equitable access to competitive markets for all; and reorientation of bureaucratic machinery and functionaries to work as change agents rather than working as passive and target conscious state instrumentality. Special economic package could be considered for EBP living within 5 km of LOC area, Tsunami affected areas, snow-clad areas, dessert, famine and flood affected regions, victims of communal violence, terrorism, separatist activities and natural disasters, disturbed areas, and in the islands of poverty/deprivation due to extreme climatic conditions. Centre of Excellence need to be set-up in the state to conduct research and regular monitoring and evaluation of welfare schemes meant for betterment of EBP.

Conclusion

The current approach of Indian polity towards inequality favours sub-categorization of reserved categories based on collectivises, which is detrimental for an egalitarian order because politics favours nominal and ordinal levels of measurements for capturing power. Objectively as well as methodologically target for removing inequality can never be a family or caste or community (nominal or ordinal level measures) because parameters of identification and measurement of inequality can be worked out only at interval or ratio levels of measurements available with individuals.

Therefore, for an egalitarian order within the democratic framework and in the post-reform era we need to address inequality not as a result of ascribed status within the unchangeable caste-ridden hierarchical society but as opportunities through capacity building of individuals particularly identified as Economically Backward People (EBP) so as to strengthen their respective achieved status in different working sectors.

NOTES

1. Article 340(1) states: "The President may by order appoint a commission consisting of such persons as he thinks fit to investigate the conditions of socially, economically and educationally backward classes within the territory of India and the difficulties under which they labour and to make recommendations as to the steps that should be taken by the Union or any state to remove such difficulties and as

to improve their conditions and as to grants that should be made and the order appointing such commission shall define the procedure to be followed by the commission." Article 340(2) states: "A commission so appointed shall investigate the matters referred to them and present to the President a report setting out the facts as found by them and making such recommendations as they think proper."

2. The first attempt to identify those backward classes other than SCs and STs at national level was made in 1953 when the first backward class commission was set up by a Presidential Order on January 29, 1953 under the chairmanship of Kaka Kalekar which submitted its report on March 30, 1955. The first commission included 2399 castes or communities as backward and among them listed 837 as the 'most backward'. The Commission recommended CASTE as the criteria to determine the backwardness and all women as a class was considered backward. The main aim of such identification was to provide maximum opportunity to backward classes, with a major means of reservation policy. The policy of reservations policy was largely criticized as often preceded independently of ethical basis, practical efficacy and sustainability particular response to contingent political compulsions.
3. A Commission was constituted by the Government of India, Ministry of Social Justice and Empowerment (Backward Classes Division) *vide* its Notification No. 20012/10/2003-BCC dated 6th July, 2004 and resolved to continue that Commission *vide* resolution dated 3rd March, 2005. The Government of India, Ministry of Social Justice and Empowerment (Backward Classes Division) resolved to reconstitute a commission for Economically Backward Classes not covered under the existing Reservation Policy *vide* Gazette Notification No. 20012/10/2003-BCC dated 10th July, 2006.
4. The Government of Rajasthan, Department of Personnel (A-Gr2) had issued a notification dated 18.9.2009 with effect to 14 per cent reservation of seats in Educational Institutions in the State and Appointments and Posts in Services under the State for Economically Backward Classes. However, the Rajasthan High Court stayed the quota provided by the State Government to Gujjars and other economically backward communities as that extended the 50 per cent limit set on reservations (total reservation in Rajasthan went up to 68%). The main barrier to implementation of reservation for the economically backward classes appeared to be Constitutional, as according to the Supreme Court, classes seeking reservation under the existing constitutional provision of 15(4) and 16(4) had to be 'backwards' first either on ground of caste discrimination or on occupation-cum-education.

5. Criteria for identification of backwardness:

A. Social:

1. Castes and communities generally considered as socially backward.
2. (a) Castes and communities, which mainly depend on agricultural and/or other manual labour for their livelihood and are lacking any significant resource base.
   (b) Castes and communities, which, for their livelihood, mainly depend on agricultural and/or other manual labour for wage and are lacking any significant base.
   (c) Castes and communities, the women of which, as a general practice, are for their family's livelihood, engaged in agricultural and/or other manual labour for wage.
   (d) Castes and communities, the children of which, as a general practice, are, for family's livelihood or for supplementing family's low income, mainly engaged in agricultural and/or manual labour.
   (e) Castes and communities, which in terms of caste system, are identified with traditional crafts or traditional or hereditary occupations considered to be lowly or undignified.
   (f) Castes and communities, which in terms of the caste system, are identified with traditional or hereditary occupations considered to be 'unclean' or stigmatized.
   (g) Nomadic and semi-nomadic castes and communities.
   (h) Denotified or Vimukta Jati castes and communities.
3. Castes and communities, having no representation or poor representation in the State Legislative Assembly and/or district-level Panchayati Raj Institutions during the ten years preceding the date of the application.

B. Educational:

1. Castes and communities, whose literacy rate is at least 8 per cent less than the State or district average.
2. Castes and communities of which the proportion of matriculates is at least 20 per cent less than the State or district average.
3. Castes and communities, of which the proportion of graduates is at least 20 per cent less than the State or district average.

C. Economic:

1. Castes and communities, a significant proportion of whose members reside only in *Kachcha* houses.
2. Castes and communities, the share of whose members in number of cases and in extent of agricultural lands surrendered under the Agricultural Land Ceiling Act of the State, is nil or significantly low.

6. Castes and communities, the share of whose members in State Government posts and services of Groups A & B/Classes I & II, is not equal to the population-equivalent proportion of the caste/community.

REFERENCES

Adiseshiah, Malcolm S. (1990). 'Sustainable Development: What It is and Its Coverage', in *Sustainable Development: Its Content, Scope and Prices*, Lancer International in association with India International Centre, New Delhi.

Akerlof, George (1976). 'The Economics of Caste and of Rat Race and Other Woeful Tales', *Quarterly Journal of Economics*, XC 4, November.

Akindola, Rufus B. (2010). 'Towards a Definition of Poverty: Poor People's Perspectives and Implications for Poverty Reduction', *Journal of Developing Societies*, Vol. 25(2): 121–150.

Angel, J., Jimenez, M., & Angel, R. (2007). 'The economic consequences of widowhood for older minority women', *The Gerontologist*, 47(2), 224-234.

Bhalla, Surjit S. (2003). 'Recounting the poor: Poverty in India, 1983–1999', *Economic and Political Weekly*, 37(4), 338-49.

Bullock, H.E. (1999). 'Attributions for Poverty: A Comparison of Middle-Class and Welfare Recipient. Attitudes', *Jr of Applied Social Psychology* 29: 2059–82.

Bullock, H.E. (2004). 'From the Front Lines of Welfare Reform: An Analysis of Social Worker and Welfare. Recipient Attitudes', *Journal of Social Psychology*, 114: 571-88.

Corson, Walter H. (1995). 'Priorities of a Sustainable Future: The Role of Education, the Media and Tax Reform', *Journal of Social Issues*, Vol 51, No.4, pp. 37-62.

Datt, Gaurav, Valerie Kozel and Martin Ravallion (2003). 'A model-based assessment of India's progress in reducing poverty in the 1990s', *Economic and Political Weekly*, 37, 355-61.

Deaton, A. and Jean Drèze (2002). 'Poverty and inequality in India: A Re-examination', *Economic and Political Weekly*, 7 September, 3729-48.

Deaton, A. and Valerie Kozel (2005). 'Data and dogma: The great Indian poverty debate', *The World Bank Research Observer* 20, 177–99.

Dworkin, R. (1981). 'What is Equality? Part I: Equality of Welfare and Part II: Equality of Resources'. *Philosophy of Public Affairs*. 10, 185-246 & 283-345.

Ferro, M., Rosenblatt, D. and Stern, N. (2004). 'Policies for pro-poor growth in India', in Basu, K. (ed.) *India's Emerging Economy*. Oxford University Press, 153-81.

Fukuoka, M. (1978). *'One Straw Revolution: The Natural Way of Farming. Emmaus, Pennsylvania'*, Rodalel Press.

Galanter, Marc (1984). 'Competing Equalities: Law and the Backward Classes India'. Delhi: Oxford University Press, pp. 154-155.

Garrett, Hardin (1968). 'The Tragedy of the Commons', *Science*, 13 December, 162, pp. 1243-48.

Ghosh, Madhusudan (2009). 'Dynamics of Agricultural Development and Rural Poverty in Indian States'. *Margin—The Journal of Applied Economic Research*, 3:3: 265–295.

Hussain, Monirul; Lipi Ghosh (2002). 'Religious minorities in South Asia: selected essays on post-colonial situations', New Delhi: Manak Publications.

Khan, K. Rahman (1995). 'Report of High Power Committee on Socio-Economic and Educational Survey – 1994 of Religious Minorities in Karnataka', Karnataka State Minorities Commission.

Khoshoo, T.N. (1986). 'Environmental Priorities in India and Sustainable Development', *Presidential Address*, Indian Science Congress Association, 73rd Session.

Lal, Deepak, Rakesh, Mohan and Natarajan, I. (2001). 'Economic Reforms and Poverty Alleviation: A Tale of Two Surveys', *Economic and Political Weekly*, 36(12), 1017–28.

Leekok, Lee (1989). *Social Philosophy and Ecological scarcity*. London: Routledge.

Lewis, O. (1969) 'The Culture of Poverty', in D.P. Moynihan (ed.) *On Understanding Poverty*, New York: Basic Books, pp. 187–200.

McGarry, K., & Schoeni, R. (2005a). 'Medicare gaps and widow poverty', *Social Security Bulletin*, 66(1), 58-74.

McGarry, K., & Schoeni, R. (2005b). 'Widow(er) poverty and out-of-pocket medical expenditures near the end of life'. *Journals of Gerontology: Psychological Sciences and Social Sciences*, 60B (3), S160-S168.

Mead, L.M. (1992). *The New Politics of Poverty: The Non-Working Poor in America*. New York: Basic Books.

Misturelli, Federica and Claire Heffernan (2010). 'The Concept of Poverty: a Synchronic Perspective', *Progress in Development Studies* 10: 35.

Moon, Vasant (1987). 'Dr. Babasaheb Ambedkar Writings and Speeches: Philosophy of Hinduism', *The Hindu Social Order – Its Essential Features*. Vol. 3, pp. 1-94.

Narake, Hari, M.L. Kasare, N.G. Kamble and Ashok Godghate (2003). 'Dr. Ambedkar and His Egalitarian Revolution'. In *Dr. Babasaheb Ambedkar Writings and Speeches*, Vol. 17 (part 1, 2, 3).

Olson, Robert L. (1995). 'Sustainability as a Social Vision', *Journal of Social Issues*, Vol. 15, No.4, 15-36.

Palmer, J.A., (1998). 'Environmental Education in the 21st Century: Theory, Practice', *Progress, and Promise*, Routledge.

Parameswara, S. (1990). *Development of Backwardness, Coexistence or Confrontation?: A Study of Leather Workers of Karnataka*, New Delhi: Reliance Publishing House.

Population Resource Center (2005). *Older women and poverty: A demographic profile*. Retrieved from www.prcdc.org/summaries/AgingSeries05/womenandpoverty.html.

Sandell, S., & Iams, H. (1997). 'Reducing women's poverty by shifting social security benefits from retired couples to widows'. *Journal of Policy Analysis and Management*, 16(2), 279-297.

Sen, A. (1973). *On Economic Inequality*, Delhi: Oxford University Press.

Sen, A. (1996). 'Radical Needs & Modern Reforms', In Jean Dreze & Amartya Sen (eds.) *Indian Development: Selected Regional Perspective*, Delhi: Oxford University Press.

Sen, Abhijit and Himanshu (2004). 'Poverty and inequality in India – I', *Economic and Political Weekly* 18 and 25 September, 4247–63 and 4361-75.

Siggel, Eckhard (2010). 'Poverty alleviation and economic reforms in India'. *Progress in Development Studies*,10, 3, pp. 247–59.

Siggel, E. (2007). 'Economic reforms and their impact on the manufacturing sector: Lessons from the Indian experience', *Asia-Pacific Development Journal*, 14, 73–104.

Siggel, E. (2010). 'The Indian informal sector under the influence of globalization and reforms', *International Labour Review*, 149, 93–105.

Sundaram, K. and Tendulkar, S.D. (2003). 'Poverty has declined in the 1990s: A Resolution of comparability problems in NSS consumer expenditure data', *Economic and Political Weekly*, 25 January, 327–37.

Sundaram, K. and Tendulkar, S.D. (2003). 'Poverty in India in the 1990s: Revised Results for all-India and 15 major states for 1993–94', *Economic and Political Weekly*, 15 November, 4865–72.

Thorat, S.K. (1996). 'Ambedkar on Economics of Hindu Social Order: Understanding Its Orthodoxy and Legacy' in Walter Fernandes (ed.), *The Emerging Dalit Identity*, Indian Social Institute, Delhi.

Thorat, S.K. (1999). 'Caste and Labour Market Discrimination', *Indian Journal of Labour Economics*, Conference Issue, November (with R.S. Deshpande).

United Nations (2005). 'Poverty and Economic Growth: Challenges to Human Rights'. *Economic and Social Council*.

Van Oorschot, W. (2000). 'Who Should Get What, and Why? On Deservingness Criteria and the Conditionality of Solidarity among the Public', *Policy & Politics*, 28: 33–48.

Van Oorschot, W. and Halman, L. (2000). 'Blame or Fate, Individual or Social? An International Comparison of Popular Explanations of Poverty', *European Societies*, 2: 1–28.

Verma D.K. (1993). 'Intergenerational Equity: environmental right of the child', *AJSDJ*, Vol. 3, 163-168.

Verma, D.K. (1999). 'Sustainable Development', *Madhya Pradesh Journal of Social Sciences*, Vol. 4, (2): 37-59.

Verma, D.K. (1993). 'Role of Environmental Education in Social Development and Justice (in Hindi)', *Dr. Ambedkar Samajik Vigyan Shodh Patrika*.

Verma, D.K. (1994). 'Ecoethical Approach for Sustainable Development and Justice', *AJSDJ*, Vol. 2: 37-59.

Verma, D.K. (1995). 'Ecological Sustainability in Social Development', in R.G. Singh & R.D. Gadkar (eds.) *Social Development & Justice*, New Delhi: Radiant Publication, 225-229.

Verma, D.K. (1997). 'Dr. Ambedkar's Views on Planning, Development and Conservation of Environmental Resources', *AJSDJ*, Vol. 5, 1-8.

Verma, D.K. (1999). 'Concept and Dimensions of Social Environment Needed for Sustainable Development', in Y.G. Joshi and D.K. Verma (eds.) *Social Environment & Sustainable Development*, Jaipur: Rawat Publications.

Verma, D.K. and A. Sohrot (2003). 'The Concept of Social Justice in Post-modern Society: Some Reflections on Sustainable Development', in B.R. Purohit and S. Joshi (eds) *Social Justice in India*, Jaipur: Rawat Publications, 174-197.

Verma, D.K. (2004). 'Social Devolution—A Sociological Perspective Affirmed Status of Dalits in India'. *The Asianists' Asia*, Vol. August 5, ISSN 1298-0358.

Verma, D.K. (2008). 'Tribal Livelihood Options: Socio-ecological Changes, State Intervention and Sustainable Development', in S.N. Chaudhary (ed.) *Tribal Development since Indepeudence*, New Delhi: Concept Publishing Company, ISBN: 81-8069-622-7, pp. 171-205.

Verma, D.K. (2010). 'Economics and Development of Castes and Tribes', in Arun Kumar (ed.) *Dalits and Economic Reforms*, Jaipur: Rawat Publications, ISBN: 8131603079, pp. 16-50.

Verma, D.K. (2011). 'Politics of Social backwardness and Empowerment of Other & Economically Backward Classes', *Journal of Social and Political Studies*, pp – 64-83, Vol. II (2), (ISSN: 2229-3647), December.

World Bank (1990). *World Development Report, Poverty*, The World Bank.

World Bank (2000). *World Development Indicators* Washington, D.C.

10

Growth, Poverty and Land Distribution in Odisha

R.K. Panda

It is well recognized that the growth-led strategy of development coupled with a number of public intervention programmes followed in the post-liberalization period have ushered in faster decline in the incidence of poverty at the all-India and cross-state levels. However, the magnitude of the problem continues to be quite staggering in certain parts of the country, particularly in relatively backward states/regions and among the weaker sections. The state, Odisha characteristically a backward agricultural state with more than 65 per cent of its population depending on agriculture for livelihood, suffers from high incidence of poverty despite experiencing high growth rate and significant reduction in poverty during the last decade. The study of Ghosal (2010) reveals that between 2000 to 2005 and 2005 to 2010 the per capita NSDP in the state has grown at the annual compound rates of 3.58 per cent and 6.75 per cent respectively. The NSSO poverty estimates shows that between 1993-94 and 2009-10 the incidence of poverty in the state has declined from 59.10 per cent to 37.0 per cent with rural poverty from 63.00 per cent to 39.20 per cent—the annual decline in poverty works out to 1.47 percentage points for the state in aggregate and 1.52 percentage points for rural poverty. The state with 15.32 million poor is placed in the third position among the states in the country in terms of number of people below the poverty line after Bihar and Uttar Pradesh. Analyzing the relation between economic growth and poverty reduction in case of Odisha, during the period 1993-94 and 2004-05, Panda (2008) has observed that despite higher economic growth witnessed in the state, the rate of poverty reduction has not been faster. His study reveals that the rise in the per capita income in the state has been found associated with rise in inequality in the income distribution leading to elasticity of poverty with respect to per capita income remaining low at 0.084. As often stated, in the context of poverty reduction, composition of and growth in economic sectors (agriculture industry and services) make significant contribution in case of developing countries. Studies conclude that growth in agriculture is highly beneficial for poverty reduction. However, a look at the sectoral contribution to growth of Odisha's GSDP we find that the Tertiary/Service Sector contributes more than 53.0 per cent followed by Secondary Sector 30.0 per cent and Primary Sector 17.0 per cent. There is on-going debate among the researchers that in view of the state witnessing a service sector-led growth, pace of poverty reduction in the state has remained below the desired level, the growth has not been inclusive.

Brief Review of Literature

Studies on poverty analysis in case of poor and developing countries including India are many and varied. While majority of such studies are concerned with estimating the poor and measuring poverty following different methodologies, quite a number of studies have made in-depth analysis as to why poverty persists despite high growth achieved in developing countries in recent years. Studies analyzing persistence of poverty in case of developing countries characterized by a large majority of population dependent on agriculture for livelihood reveal that inequality in the distribution of assets (especially land) has a bearing on the success or failure of poverty reduction in these countries (Kube, 2009). The findings of Janvry and Sadoulet, 1993 and Carter, 2000 show that in developing countries with agrarian structure which is traditionally unequal creates exclusionary pattern of growth deepening inequality and blunting the potentially positive impact of growth on rural poverty. Kakwani study (1993) in respect to India reveals increased income inequality in India over time resulting in a lower growth elasticity of poverty reduction.

Given the brief review of the studies in which growth has not resulted in substantial reduction of poverty and the recent development in the Odishan economy, the present study is an attempt to discuss the trends in the growth rates in per capita NSDP and reduction in poverty in the state, Odisha, the changes in the pattern of land distribution over time, the extent of landlessness and the state government efforts in redistributing land among the poor and landless with possible areas of action to be taken up in reforming agrarian structure to achieve faster reduction of poverty in the state.

Trends in Growth Rate in Per Capita NSDP and Reduction in Poverty

Table 10.1 presents data on growth rates of per capita NSDP and reduction in poverty during 1993-94 to 2009-10. As shown in the table, the per capita NSDP which was Rs. 11546 in 1993-94 has gone to Rs. 17650 in 2004-05 and further to Rs. 22846 in 2009-10. The annual compound growth rate of per capita NSDP which was 3.32 per cent during 1993-94 to 2004-05 has increased to 6.06 per cent during 2004-05 to 2009-10, thus showing nearly doubling in the latter period over the previous one. During this period, the poverty incidence in terms of Head Count Ratio has declined in the state. The proportion of people living below the poverty line has fallen from 59.1 in 1993-94 to 57.2 in 2004-05 and further to 37.0 in 2009-10. The rural poverty ratio which was 63 per cent in 1993-94 has declined to 60.8 per cent in 2004-05 and further to 39.2 per cent in 2009-10. The average annual reduction in the poverty in the state in terms of headcount ratio has gone from 0.17 percentage points in first period to 4.04 percentage points in the second period. The decline in rural poverty has been from 0.20 percentage points in the first period to 4.32 percentage points in the latter period. This implies that, the growth in NSDP during the period has not benefited the poor and vulnerable sections much and the pace of poverty reduction has remained slower in the state.

Land Ownership among Farm-Sizes

Given that the pace of decline in poverty has been slow in Odisha, let us discuss the existing land ownership distribution among different farm categories, social groups and across regions in the

Table 10.1: Trends in Growth Rate of Per Capita NSDP and Changes in Poverty Incidence in Odisha

Sl. No.	Items	1993-94	2004-05	2009-10
1.	Per capita NSDP at 2004-05 prices (Rs.)	11546	17650	22846
2.	Total Poverty (HCR)	63.00	60.80	39.20
3.	Rural Poverty (HCR)	59.10	57.20	37.00
4.	Annual Compound Growth Rate in Per Capita NSDP (Between 1993-94 to 2004-05 and 2004-05 to 2009-10)	—	3.32	6.06
5.	Annual Percentage Point Change in Total Poverty (Between 1993-94 to 2004-05 and 2004-05 to 2009-10 and 1993-94 – 2009-10)	—	0.17	4.04 1.47
6.	Annual Percentage Point Change in Rural Poverty (Between 1993-94 to 2004-05 and 2004-05 to 2009-10 and 1993-94-2009-10)	—	0.20	4.32 1.52

state. Table 10.2 presents data on distribution of owned land among different farm categories. Considering the marginal farm households having less than one hectare of land, about 60.5 per cent at the bottom own only 26.6 per cent of the total cultivated area, while 4.5 per cent of having land more than 4 hectares own 18.0 per cent of total cultivated area. The small and semi-medium farms in the size-groups of 1-2 and 2-4 hectares constituting 25.5 and 10.8 per cent holdings own 30.4 and 25 per cent of total area. Between 1995-96 to 2005-06, the number as well as area under ownership holding for marginal farms has increased, and their share in the total area under ownership has improved. For the farms more than 4 hectares (medium and large size-groups), their number and area under ownership have declined between 1995-96 to 2005-06. While in case of farms between 1-2 hectares while their number has fallen their area has gone up between 1995-96 to 2005-06, for farms 2-4 hectares both number and area under ownership have declined during the period. All these reveal that though in terms of both number and area under ownership holding of upper farm-sizes (semi-medium, medium and large farms) have declined and that of marginal farms have increased, yet not much significant changes in the agrarian structure in terms of land ownership are noticed and the pattern of land ownership remains skewed in rural Odisha (Fig. 10.1).

Table 10.2: Land Ownership Distribution among different Size-groups in the State (%)

Size Class (Hect)	*1995-96*		*2000-01*		*2005-06*		*Average Area (in Hect)*		
	Number	*Area*	*Number*	*Area*	*Number*	*Area*	*1995-96*	*2000-01*	*2005-06*
Marginal (<1 Hect)	55.84	21.16	57.06	21.99	60.48	26.58	0.48	0.49	0.50
Small (1-2 Hect)	26.37	28.20	26.03	28.49	25.50	30.43	1.37	1.38	1.37
Semi-Medium (2-4 Hect)	13.29	27.69	12.57	26.76	10.82	24.97	2.67	2.69	2.65
Medium (4-10 Hect)	04.09	17.75	03.96	17.69	02.90	13.97	5.55	5.65	5.52
Large (> 10 Hect)	0.41	05.21	00.38	05.07	00.29	04.05	16.16	16.68	15.96
All	100.00	100.00	100.00	100.00	100.00	100.00	1.28	1.26	1.15

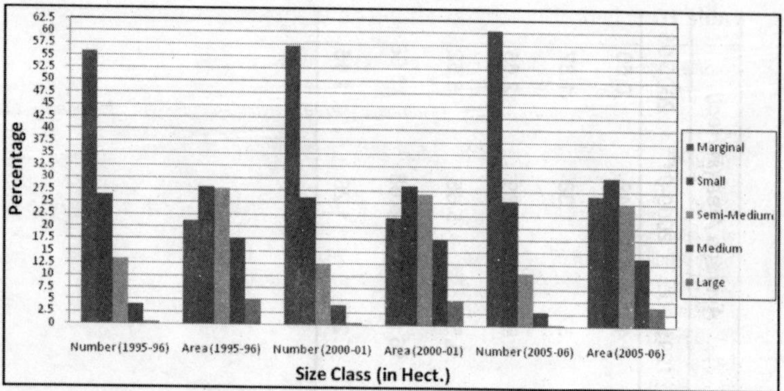

Fig. 10.1: Wholly Owned and Self Operated Holdings

Land Ownership among Social Groups

The Scheduled Castes and Scheduled Tribes constituting quite a sizeable percentage of the total population of the state (17.1% in case of former and 22.4 in case of latter, Census, 2011) are considered to be the most marginalized and vulnerable sections in rural society. In this context it would, therefore, be appropriate to examine their status of land ownership in relation to the general category population. Table 10.3 shows distribution of land ownership among major social groups in the state. As it is seen, majority of SC farm households (73%) are in the marginal size group followed by 20 per cent in the size group of 1-2 hectare and 6 per cent in the size group of 2-4 hectares. Only 1.6 per cent S.C. households are in the size group of 4 hectares and above. In case of STs, about 56 per cent households are in the marginal size group followed by 28.4 per cent in 1-2 size group and 12.3 per cent in the 2-4 size group of holdings. Only 3.3 per cent households are in the 4 hectares and above size group. As regards other category of households (General Caste including OBCs), about 60 per cent belong to the marginal category followed by 25.2 in the 1-2 hectares, 11.1 per cent in the 2-4 hectares and only 3.6 per cent in the 4 hectares and above category. Thus, it is revealed that marginal farms are more concentrated among SC households followed by the general castes and the STs. The common understanding that STs are poorer in respect to land ownership is not found true from data available.

Table 10.3: Land Ownership among different Social Groups in 2005-06 (%)

Size Class (Hect)	*SC*		*ST*		*Others*		*All*	
	Number	*Area*	*Number*	*Area*	*Number*	*Area*	*Number*	*Area*
Marginal (<1 Hect)	72.95	40.77	56.02	25.02	60.01	25.49	60.48	26.58
Small (1-2 Hect)	19.92	32.51	28.38	32.03	25.24	29.56	25.50	30.43
Semi-Medium (2-4 Hect)	6.07	19.24	12.28	26.60	11.15	25.32	10.82	24.97
Medium (4-10 Hect)	1.00	6.50	3.09	13.79	3.26	15.51	2.90	13.97
Large (> 10 Hect)	0.06	0.98	0.24	2.56	0.34	4.13	0.29	4.05
All	100.00	100.00	100.00	100.00	100.00	100.00	100.00	100.00

Land Ownership across Regions

National Sample Surveys as well as studies of some scholars have identified backward regions with high concentration of poor and landless households. The state economy of Odisha presents wide variation in agro-economic conditions across regions. Broadly we can divide the state economy into two broad regions – the Coastal Plain and the Inland Region, the former being a relatively developed region with plain land, fertile soil, better irrigation facility, higher agricultural productivity, developed infrastructure and better communication and transport as compared with the latter having uneven and mountainous terrain with widespread forest, rain-fed agriculture with low productivity, unhealthy climate, poor infrastructure with inadequate communication and transport facilities. The former region having higher per capita income has lower incidence of poverty as compared to the Inland Region having lower per capita income has higher incidence of poverty. In view of the prevailing regional divergences in various agro-economic indicators including poverty incidence it is pertinent to examine land ownership status across regions. Table 10.4 shows the pattern of land ownership among major farm sizes between the two regions in the state. It would be seen that in the Coastal Region, the marginal farms (within one hectare of holding size) constituting around 70 per cent of the total holdings are the largest farming community, followed by 21 per cent holdings between 1-2 hectares, 8 per cent holdings between 2-4 hectares, and 1.7 per cent holdings in the 4 hectares and above size-group. In the case of Inland region, around 55 per cent farms belong to the marginal farm category followed by 28.1 per cent in the 1-2 size group, 12.6 per cent in the 2-4 size-group and the rest 4 per cent in the 4 hectares and above size-group. Thus, as per the revelation, land ownership distribution is more skewed in the Inland Region as compared to the Coastal Plain.

Land Ownership Status in Scheduled Areas

The Scheduled Tribes constituting nearly 22 per cent of the state's total population are considered to be the most marginalized and vulnerable section having the highest poverty incidence and lowest HDI (Orissa Human Development Report, 2003). Latest poverty estimates (NSS, 2009-10) for rural Odisha by social groups reveals that the STs are the poorest communities in the state. In view of this it would be appropriate that the land holding status of this section is examined separately.

Studies on land ownership pattern in scheduled areas of tribal districts reveal that nearly three-fourth of the land in these districts are owned by the state and the tribals have no or very little rights on these lands either individually or collectively. About 20 per cent households are landless and another 65 per cent own only 13 per cent land. Among the households owning land a sizeable percentage (41%) belong to the marginal farm category having average holding size 0.44 acres (Kumar *et al.*, 2007). Besides, as reported, land alienation is more often seen in scheduled areas of the state due to irregular transfer and sale of land to non-tribals, acquisition of land for development projects and changes in government policies (Viegas, 1991, Singh, 2005, Government of Odisha, various reports). In view of this it becomes imperative to look at the land status of the STs in the Scheduled Areas of the state. It would be seen from Table 10.5 that in the ten scheduled areas of the state the share of government land in the total land area comes to 76 per cent leaving private land 25 per cent. There is also wide variation in the private land in the scheduled areas across district—varying from the lowest 12.95 per cent in Mayurbhanj District to the largest 35.9 per cent in Kalahandi district. The percentage of landless is also quite high in different tribal districts.

Table 10.4: Region and Size class-wise Land Ownership Distribution in the State (2005-06)

Regions	Number						Area(Ha)					
	Marginal	*Small*	*Semi-medium*	*Medium*	*Large*	*All Classes*	*Marginal*	*Small*	*Semi-medium*	*Medium*	*Large*	*All Classes*
Coastal	69.76	20.78	7.75	1.58	0.13	100.00	35.17	30.82	22.05	9.18	2.78	100.00
Inland	55.17	28.12	12.65	3.67	0.38	100.00	23.28	30.10	26.22	15.88	4.52	100.00
Odisha	60.65	25.36	10.81	2.89	0.29	100.00	26.82	30.31	24.98	13.89	4.01	100.00

Table 10.5: Tribal Land Status in Scheduled Areas

District	Percentage of Government Land to Total Land Area	Percentage of Private Land to Total Land Area	Percentage of Landless (less than one standard acre)
Gajapati	84.61	15.39	89.45
Kalahandi	64.10	35.90	66.30
Keonjhar	79.80	19.01	84.93
Kondhmal	85.53	14.47	88.55
Koraput	69.13	30.87	59.04
Malkangiri	82.12	17.88	63.44
Mayurbhanj	89.38	12.95	88.82
Nabarangpur	68.13	31.87	73.22
Rayagada	81.83	18.17	74.08
Sundargarh	78.13	21.87	70.43

Source: Revenue Department, Government of Odisha, Bhubaneswar, 2006-07.

All these reveal that not only landlessness is very high in different tribal districts but also private land required for cultivation is quite meagre to provide livelihood support to the tribals.

Status of Landlessness and Near Landless in the State

Inequality in land distribution as such may or may not be a problem but high incidence of landlessness and near landlessness (marginalization of land holdings) pose a threat to the livelihood security of a large number of rural poor households in the state and consequently social harmony and security. As it is observed the proportion of rural landless households has remained very sizeable in the state in spite of government efforts under several schemes to distribute cultivable and homestead land to the landless poor. Data available from the 59th NSSO (2003-04) show that in Odisha, the proportion of households without owning any type of land comes to 9.6 while those having ownership of only homestead land are 38.5 as compared to the all-India figures of 10.0, 41.6 per cent respectively (Table 10.6). This shows that while the incidence of landlessness in the state is more or less at par with the all-India average, as regards the near-landlessness the state having lower percentage of households in this group is in a better position over the all-India average. A calculation by the State Government reveals that in absolute sense the number the landless population works out to 4.45 lakh in the state in 2006 with varying concentration across districts—the coastal districts having higher incidence of landless population as compared to the inland and tribal districts (Government of Odisha, 2006). Besides, the proportion of near of landlessness (sub-marginal land ownership) is quite large in the state. During 2003-04, the farm households within 0.4 hectare and those between 0.4 -1.0 hectare land holding constitute 32.33 and 22.96 per cent of the total farm households in the state which is higher than the all-India average of 29.82 and 18.96 per cent respectively (Table 10.7). In view of the fact that these categories of households have very lower level of literacy this poses challenges of providing livelihood support to these households through different off-farm activities.

Table 10.6: Proportion of Landless Households in Odisha *vis-à-vis* all-India (2003-04)

(%)

State/All-India	*% of Households Not owning any Land*	*% of Households owning only Homestead Land*
Odisha	9.6	38.5
All-India	10.0	41.6

Table 10.7: Distribution of Land Ownership within Marginal Farms in Odisha and India in 2003-04

(%)

State/All-India	*Proportion of Households*		*Proportion of Area Owned*	
	Less than 0.4ha.	*0.4-1ha.*	*Less than 0.4*	*0.4-1ha.*
Odisha	32.33	22.96	10.82	30.82
All-India	29.82	18.97	5.11	16.89

State Government Initiatives in Securing Land to the Landless

Realizing the crucial role of land reform in alleviating poverty and achieving higher growth, the Government of Odisha after independence has enacted several progressive laws. So far as land to the landless is concerned three significant measures have been taken by the state of Odisha. They are: (a) distribution of ceiling surplus land, (b) distribution of government land and (c) distribution of Bhoodan land. The study of Sahoo and Dharmalingam (1994) in this context, reveals that in the initial years of land reform (during 1960s) the redistribution of land among the landless remained as mere policy pronouncement without any matching practical action. In 1974 the government enacted Land Ceiling Act for acquiring surplus land and distributing among the landless. The Bhoodan Act, 1953 was also replaced by another The Bhoodan Act, 1970 to make land transfer from donations received under Bhoodan more meaningful. Further, in 2006 the government launched the project 'Vasundhara' aiming at providing house sites to all homestead-less families within a period of three years. In 2007, the government started a campaign 'Mo Jami Mo Diha' (My Land and My Homestead Land) so as to enforce possession of land to the beneficiaries allotted lease of Government lands. In view of all these efforts made by the state government it is revealed that between 1974 and 2007 the total ceiling surplus land and government waste land allotted among landless have come to 8.96 lakh acres, covering 6.21 lakh beneficiaries of whom 153029 belong to Scheduled Castes, 284564 Scheduled Tribes and 458282 other categories. However, as it is seen there lies differences in the allotment of land and its actual possession. Some empirical studies conducted on re-distribution of ceiling surplus land in different districts, however, opine that there lies big gap between legislation and implementation (UNDP, 2008). Land distribution under Bhoodan has not achieved much success. Not only a large area of Bhoodan land remains undistributed due to illegal encroachment, but also land donated has been taken back due to want of official records. Inter-district disparity in the land distributed under Bhoodan continues greatly (*Ibid.*, 2008).

Conclusion and Future Policy Direction

The findings of the study reveal that poverty reduction in Odisha has remained slow in spite of an appreciable rise in per capita NSDP in recent years. Along with this, the land ownership distribution in the state remains very much unequal across farm-sizes, social groups and regions. Though, over time, there has been some increase in access to land of the small and marginal holders, yet land ownership concentration continues with the upper farm sizes. Landlessness is also quite high in the state and the government's efforts to redistribute ceiling surplus and other lands have remained far from impressive. In scheduled areas, landlessness among tribals continues to be a serious concern as a significantly large percentage of land in these areas is owned by the government in which the tribals have no ownership rights and the illegal transfer and sale of private land continues in tribal areas. In view of the high incidence of poverty coexisting with landlessness and growing marginalization of land holding in the state, regulatory measures prohibiting or restricting land transfer from marginal and sub-marginal holders to upper farm sizes and non-farmers are very much needed. Since a substantial proportion of cultivated area remains under large ownership holdings, there exists the potential for land redistribution. In scheduled areas, land transfer from tribals to non-tribals needs to be strictly prohibited. To achieve this land should be jointly owned by male and female heads of the tribal households. The Ceiling Law of the state needs to be amended to take into account Operational Area instead of Ownership Area for fixing land ceiling. This will discourage reverse tenancy and release more land for distribution among the landless. It is often alleged that the quality of government land allotted to the beneficiaries is mostly inferior and hence unsuitable for crop cultivation. More so, the plot size being small, the scope of getting institutional credit and other support services to develop the plot for any economic activity becomes very remote. In this context, these beneficiaries should be encouraged to form SHGs for getting improved institutional support for undertaking different economic activities on the allotted land. In view of the fact that the agriculture cannot provide livelihood to increasing number of people, as the per capita land size is declining in the state due to increase in population pressure on land, as a long term measure, the rural youth should be imparted proper education and training for skill formation to take up various off-farm activities within and outside villages. The sub-sectors like animal husbandry, fishery and forestry having a lot of potential and high positive linkage with agriculture need to be developed for generating higher growth and employment in the rural economy of the state.

REFERENCES

Agarwal, Bina (1994a). *A field of One's Own: Gender and Land Rights in South Asia*, Cambridge: Cambridge University Press.

Cotula, Lorenzo *et al.* (2006). 'Better Land Access for the Rural Poor-Lessons from Experiences and Challenges Ahead', IIED, FAO, Paper presented in the *International Conference on Agrarian Reform and Rural Development (ICARRD)*, Porto Alegre, Brazil, March.

Deininger, K. and L. Squire (1998). 'New Ways of Looking at Old Issues: Inequality and Growth', *Journal of Development Economics*, 57(2).

Government of India (2013). *Draft National Land Reforms Policy*, Department of Land Resources, Ministry of Rural Development, July 24.

Government of India, *Report on Consumer Expenditure, 1993-94, 2004-05 and 2009-10*, National Sample Survey Organization.

Government of India (2006). *Report of the Expert Group on Prevention of Alienation of Tribal Land and its Restoration*, Ministry of Rural Development.

Government of Odisha, *Economic Survey 2012-13*, Planning and Coordination Department.

Government of Odisha, *Agricultural Census, 1995-96, 2000-01, 2005-06*, Board of Revenue, Odisha, Cuttack.

Hanstad, Tim *et al.*, (2008). 'Improving Land Access for India's Rural Poor', *Economic and Political Weekly*, March 8.

Jayne, T.S. *et al.*, (2003). 'Smallholder Income and Land Distribution in Africa: Implications for Poverty Reduction Strategies', *Food Policy*, 28.

Jha, Praveen (2009). 'Conceptualizing land and rural Poverty Linkages with Some Reflections on Madhya Pradesh and Chhattisgarh, Agrarian Reforms', in D. Narasimha Reddy (ed) *Land Markets and Rural Poor*, Centre for Rural Studies, LBSNAA, Mussoorie.

Kubo Kensuke (2009). 'Poverty and Asset Distribution Inequality in Rural India', in S. Hirashima & Hisaya Oda (eds) *Approach Towards Inclusive Growth: India's Challenges*, Institute of Developing Studies, Tokyo.

Mearns, Robin (1999). 'Access to Land in Rural India: Policy Issues and Options', *World Bank Policy Research Working Paper No: 2123*, May.

Misra, Baidyanath (1990). *Agriculture Development – Problems and Prospects*, New Delhi: Ashish Publishing House.

Panda and Tripathy (2009). 'Land Distribution and Tenancy in Orissa', in D. Narasimha Reddy (ed) *Agrarian Reforms, Land Markets and Rural Poor*, Centre for Rural Studies, Lal Bahadur Shastri National Academy of Administration (LBSNAA), Mussoorie.

Patnaik, Sanjoy (2008). *Status Report: Land Rights and Ownership in Orissa*, UNDP.

Patnaik, Utsa (2009). 'The Problem of Tenancy Reforms and Land Reforms in Relation to Productivity and Rural Poverty', in D. Narasimha Reddy (ed) *Agrarian Reforms, Land Markets and Rural Poor,* Centre for Rural Studies, LBSNAA, Mussoorie.

Rawal Vikas (2008). 'Ownership Holdings of Land in Rural India: Putting the Record Straight', *Economic and Political Weekly,* March 8.

Sahoo, B. and G. Dharmalingam (1994). 'Problems and Prospects of Land Distribution in Orissa', in A. Mitra and B. Sahoo (eds) *Agricultural Planning and Technology in Rural Development,* M.D. Publications Pvt. Ltd.

Sahu, Basanta K. (2009). 'Access to Land, Land Markets and Poverty: The Orissa Experience, Agrarian Reforms', in D. Narasimha Reddy (ed) *Land Markets and Rural Poor,* Centre for Rural Studies, LBSNAA, Mussoorie.

The Hindu, December 9, 2007.

11
How Inclusive is Odisha's Economic Growth?

Amarendra Das and *Bibhunandini Das*

Introduction

The surge in growth rates of Odisha in the recent years generates much optimism among the planners of the state and the country. For a poor state like Odisha high economic growth is essential to alleviate poverty and raise the living condition of the people in general. But the question still remains whether the benefits of the growth reaches at all sections of the society or not? To put the question in direct, is the growth of Odisha inclusive? The 11th Five Year Plan of Government of India defines inclusive growth as 'growth process which yields broad-based benefits and ensures equality of opportunity for all' (Government of India, 2008). It implies that the output or income should grow and it should simultaneously generate equal opportunities for all sections of the society to take the benefit of the rapid growth. The inclusive growth represents the Gandhian view of *Sarvodaya* which means the rise of all sections of the society with the process of economic growth. This motivates us to examine whether the current growth process of Odisha is inclusive or exclusive? The rest of the paper is organized as follows. Section-2 analyzes the growth trend of Gross State Domestic Product (GSDP) of the state and its composition. In section-3 we examine whether the growth is spatially inclusive by comparing the growth of 30 districts. Section 4 provides the inter-district disparity in Monthly Per Capita Consumption Expenditure (MPCE). Section 5 examines whether the output growth has reduced poverty among various social groups and regions. Section 6 summarizes the findings and concludes the paper.

Growth Trend and Composition

Table 11.1 presents the annual average growth rate of GSDP and per capita NSDP (Net State Domestic Product) of Odisha from 1951-52 to 2009-10. The growth rate of GSDP in the 1950s was around 3 per cent. The growth rate accelerated in the next decade to a little above 4 per cent. The growth momentum again slowed down in the 1970s and GSDP grew at an average rate of around 2 per cent with a very high volatility of the growth rates. This is reflected from a very high standard deviation value for the growth rate of GSDP during this period. The GSDP growth again got momentum during 1980s to 5.75 per cent, which was highest as compared to the earlier decades. After the 1991 liberalisation of Indian economy the growth rate of Odisha fell down by almost half the rate of previous decade and GSDP of the state grew at an average rate of 2.68 per cent with relatively less fluctuation of the output with the SD value 7.95. The highest growth rate of GSDP is recorded in the year 2003-04 at 15.15 per cent. On an average the GSDP of the state grew at around 8 per cent per annum with relatively least degree of fluctuations during 2000-01 and 2009-10.

The growth trend of per capita NSDP also followed the trend of GSDP. The per capita NSDP of the state grew for the first time a little above 4 per cent during 1980s. After experiencing a slowdown in 1990s it has gone up to the highest level for ever during the last decade (2000-01 to 2009-10). If we consider the break point as 2003-04 then the average growth of output from 1951-52 to 2002-03 was 3.41 per cent, which is even below what Rajkrishna called as the Hindu rate of growth. The per capita NSDP grew at an average rate of 1.74 per cent per annum. The GSDP of the state grew at an average rate of 10.63 per cent between 2003-04 and 2009-10, which is even higher than the average growth rate of GDP of all-India. Similarly, the per capita NSDP grew at an average rate of 3.92 per cent during 2003-04 and 2009-10. What is the implication of this growth rate? If we look at the GSDP of 1950 and the time taken for doubling this value, it took 23 years (in 1973). Again it took another 24 years to double the GSDP in 1997. However, the GSDP of 1997 could be doubled within a span of 11 years that is in 2008. This has been possible due to rapid economic growth in the recent years. It is also noteworthy that the growth in the recent decade has witnessed less fluctuation as compared to all previous decades. However, we need to remember that although the growth of the cake size (GSDP) is important, so also the distribution of the cake among all population of the country. The SD of growth during 2000-01 and 2009-10 is only 5.79, which is lowest as compared to all other decades. Similarly, the per capita NSDP recorded highest annual growth rate of 6.39 per cent.

Table 11.1: Annual Average Growth Rate of GSDP and Per Capita NSDP of Odisha

Decades	*Growth rate of GSDP at 1999-2000 prices*	*Growth rate of per capita NSDP at 1999-2000 prices*
1951-52 to 1959-60	2.99 (6.26)	1.75 (7.20)
1960-61 to 1969-70	4.26 (7.23)	2.30 (6.02)
1970-71 to 1979-80	1.93 (10.12)	0.14 (11.12)
1980-81 to 1989-90	5.75 (8.99)	4.26 (9.80)
1990-91 to 1999-2000	2.68 (7.95)	0.83 (8.58)
2000-01 to 2009-10	7.84 (5.79)	6.39 (6.02)
1951-52 to 2002-03	3.41 (7.85)	1.74 (8.33)
2003-04 to 2009-10	10.63 (3.71)	9.27 (3.92)

Note: Values in the parentheses are corresponding standard deviations.
Source: Own computation based on data from Government of Orissa, Economic Survey 2009-10.

Does this high economic growth reflect the structural transformation of Odisha economy? Which sector of the state has driven the growth? Kuznets (1971) hypothesised that usually the structural change of an economy takes places from a predominant agricultural economy to industrially driven one and then to service sector driven economy. However, Odisha shows a different path of structural transformation. The structural transformation of Odisha economy took place in the year 1996-97 when the share of service sector surpassed the contribution of primary sector with the former contributing 42.1 per cent of GSDP (see Figure 11.1). However, in next two years the share of service sector went down as compared to the agriculture and again from 1999-2000 the share of service sector has exceeded that of agriculture and has been growing steadily.

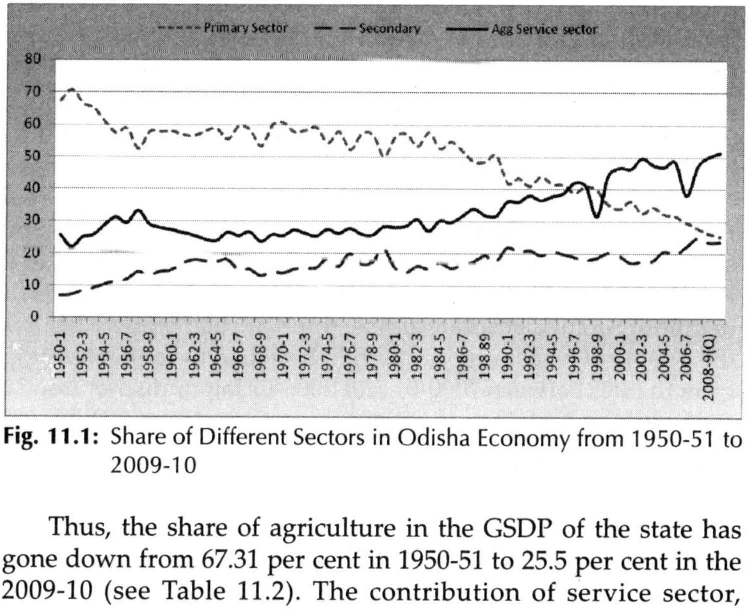

Fig. 11.1: Share of Different Sectors in Odisha Economy from 1950-51 to 2009-10

Thus, the share of agriculture in the GSDP of the state has gone down from 67.31 per cent in 1950-51 to 25.5 per cent in the 2009-10 (see Table 11.2). The contribution of service sector, reversely, has gone up from 25.75 per cent in 1950-51 to 51.28 per cent in 2009-10. The share of secondary sector has also gone up from 6.94 per cent to around 25 per cent in 2007-08. Therefore, we can conclude that the recent surge in the growth of Odisha economy is primarily driven by the service sector followed by agriculture. However, from early 2000s the secondary sector has shown a moderate rise in the growth rate and resultantly the share of secondary sector has become almost equal to that of agricultural sector and is about to surpass the share of latter.

Table 11.2: Share of Different Sectors in Odisha's GSDP

Year	Primary Sector	Secondary Sector	Service Sector
1950-51	67.31	6.94	25.75
1960-61	57.92	14.86	27.21
1970-71	60.60	13.87	25.53
1980-81	56.34	15.59	28.07
1990-91	42.04	21.83	36.12
2007-08	28.06	24.86	47.08
2008-09	26.39	23.48	50.13
2009-10	25.50	23.52	51.28

Source: Government of Odisha, Economic Survey 2009-10.

Inter-District Disparity in Income and Growth

Table 11.3 presents Per Capita Net District Domestic Product (PNDDP) of 30 districts and the annual average growth recorded between 2000-01 and 2006-07 and the rank of each district based on these two indicators. Based on the PNDDP for the year 2006-07, Angul district was the richest district of the state and Nabarangpur district was the poorest district of the state with the value of Rs. 33,377 and Rs. 9,722 respectively. Thus, on an average the people of Angul district are almost three and half times richer than the people of Nabarangpur district. Based on the annual average growth rates between 2000-01 and 2006-07 Jajpur district stood at first rank and Malkangiri district stood at last position. The maximum growth has been achieved by the mineral rich districts like Jajpur (9.85%), Kendujhar (9.45%), Sundargarh (9.14%) and Angul (8.27%). Only one coastal district which is not endowed with minerals comes at 4th rank. If we compare the PNDDP of each district with the average per capita NSDP of the state, 19 districts fall below the state average and only 11 districts have PNDDP higher than the state average. Thus, Rayagada, Bolangir, Debagarh, Dhenkanal, Ganjam, Gajapati, Baleshwar, Nuapada, Baudh, Bargarh, Puri, Kalahandi, Sonepur, Mayurbhanj, Bhadrak, Nayagarh, Malkangiri, Kendrapara, Nabarangpur can be considered as the poorer districts and Angul, Jharsuguda, Sundargarh, Khordha, Kendujhar, Sambalpur, Jagatsinghpur, Cuttack, Kandhamal, Jajpur, Koraput can be considered as rich districts of the state. The annual average growth rates of the 19 poor districts have also been lower than the average growth of the state during 2000-01 and 2006-07 except Bhadrak which has recorded 6.39 per cent annual average growth. Similarly, when we observe the rank of the 19 poor districts in the ranking based on annual average growth rates except Ganjam and Bhadrak, all other 17 districts come under the bottom 19 districts.

Table 11.3: Relationship between PNDDP and Growth Rate

District	*2006-07*	*PNDDP Rank*	*Average Growth*	*Growth Rank*
Angul	33377	1	8.27	5
Baleshwar	12576	18	4.79	18
Bargarh	12449	21	3.25	27
Bhadrak	10681	26	6.39	8
Bolangir	13885	13	5.62	11
Baudh	12503	20	4.68	19
Cuttack	18047	8	6.28	9
Debagarh	13700	14	2.60	28
Dhenkanal	13689	15	4.97	15
Gajapati	12793	17	3.70	25
Ganjam	13076	16	5.71	10
Jagatsinghpur	18478	7	8.46	4
Jajpur	16298	10	9.86	1
Jharsuguda	32521	2	7.19	7
Kalahandi	11754	23	3.35	26
Kandhamal	16801	9	5.22	13
Kendrapara	9998	29	4.67	20
Kendujhar	19765	5	9.45	2
Khordha	23556	4	7.37	6
Koraput	15969	11	4.90	17
Malkangiri	10406	28	0.78	30
Mayurbhanj	10986	25	4.10	23
Nabarangpur	9722	30	2.22	29
Nayagarh	10419	27	5.58	12
Nuapada	12550	19	3.93	24
Puri	12236	22	4.66	21
Rayagada	13950	12	4.98	14
Sambalpur	19681	6	4.38	22
Sonepur	11664	24	4.93	16
Sundargarh	25614	3	9.14	3
Odisha	**15760**	—	**6.01**	—

Source: Estimated based on the data from Government of Odisha, *Economic Survey 2010-11.*

PNDDP-Per capita Net District Domestic Product.

PNDDP Ranks are based on the of 2006-07 and Rank based on annual average growth rate.

If the poor districts are to catch up with the rich districts, then their income has to grow faster than the richer districts. However, we do not observe such a trend. Rather, the rich districts are continuing to grow faster and poorer districts are growing much slower. The relationship between the PNDDP rank and growth rank of the 30 districts of the state are plotted in Figure 11.2. Thus, we can infer that the richer districts of the state are continuing to grow faster than the poor districts. Therefore, there is no sign of convergence between districts.

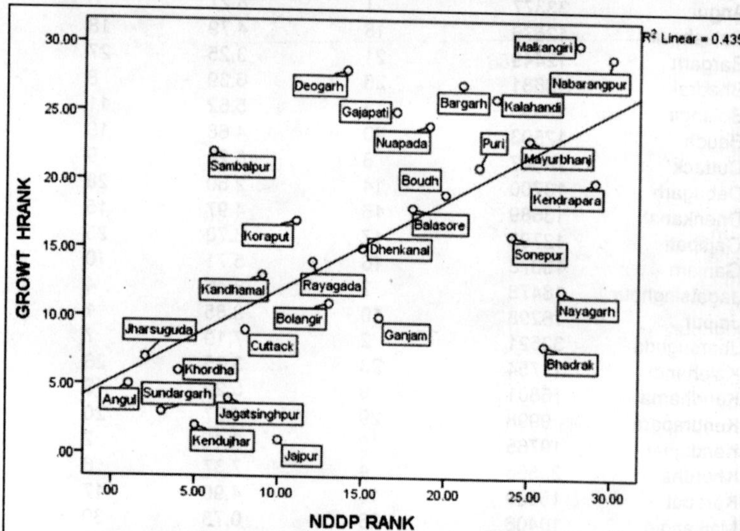

Note: Horizontal axis presents the rank of districts based on Net District Domestic Product in the year 2006-07 at 1999-200 price and Vertical axis presents the rank of districts based on the annual average growth rates between 2000-01 and 2006-07.

Fig. 11.2: Relationship Between NDDP and Growth of NDDP

For a better comparison of the PNDDP of different districts *vis-à-vis* the average value of PNSDP (Per Capita Net State Domestic Product) of the state, the values have been converted into an index where the state average PNSDP is considered 100 and the PNDDP of each district is compared against this (*see* Table 11.4). This index has been constructed for two years 1999-2000 and 2006-07 to facilitate inter-temporal comparison of the position of each district. In 1999-2000, 10 districts had PNDDP higher than the average PNSDP and one district that is Jagatsinghpur had the equal value as that of the PNSDP. Other 19 districts had PNDDP less than the average PNSDP of the state. As mentioned earlier, in the year 2006-07, 19 districts had PNDDP less than the average PNSDP and 11 districts had PNDDP higher than the average PNSDP.

Table 11.4: Comparison of Per Capita NDDP at 1999-2000 prices in 1999-2000 and 2006-07

District	*1999-2000*	*2006-07*
Angul	186	212
Baleshwar	87	80
Bargarh	99	79
Bhadrak	66	68
Bolangir	93	88
Baudh	87	79
Cuttack	112	115
Debagarh	114	87
Dhenkanal	94	87
Gajapati	94	81
Ganjam	85	83
Jagatsinghpur	100	117
Jajpur	81	103
Jharsuguda	192	206
Kalahandi	90	75
Kandhamal	112	107
Kendrapara	69	63
Kendujhar	101	125
Khordha	136	149
Koraput	109	101
Malkangiri	95	66
Mayurbhanj	79	70
Nabarangpur	80	62
Nayagarh	68	66
Nuapada	94	80
Puri	84	78
Rayagada	95	89
Sambalpur	141	125
Sonepur	81	74
Sundargarh	138	163
Odisha	100	100

Note: Average Net State Domestic Product is considered as 100 and the Net District Domestic Product is compared against the Odisha average.

Source: Odisha Economic Survey, 2010-11.

The comparison of indices values conveys that nine districts have raised their position compared to the state average income in the year 2006-07 *vis-à-vis* that in 1999-2000, whereas other 21 districts have grown less proportionately than the average PNSDP. Thus we can infer that the PNSDP of Odisha has not benefited all the districts equally.

Inter-district Disparity in Monthly Consumption Expenditure

The backwardness of Odisha is also revealed from the low Monthly Per Capita Consumption Expenditure (MPCE) as compared to the all India average. As per the estimates of 66th National Sample Survey, as reported in Odisha Economic Survey for the year 2011-12, the all India average MPCE during July 2009 to June 2010 in rural areas was Rs. 953.05 and that of Odisha was Rs. 715.59. This implies that on an average a rural Odia monthly consumes only 75 per cent of what an average rural Indian consumes. Among 15 major states of India, rural Keralites spend maximum amount of money (Rs. 1763.14) for their monthly consumption. Therefore, MPCE of a rural Odia is only 60.58 per cent of the MPCE of a rural Keralite. The MPCE of an average urban Odia is Rs. 1468.84 and that of an average urban Indian is Rs. 1856.01. It implies that an urban Odia consumes only 79 per cent of what an average urban Indian consumes. Urban Keralites also spend maximum amount of money (Rs. 2267.16) in a month for their consumption as compared to the people of other major states. Thus, an average urban Odia spends only 64.79 per cent of what an urban Malayali spends in a month. Therefore, we can conclude that the rural Odias are more deprived than the urban Odias as compared to the average rural and urban Indian.

Within Odisha, the disparity between the MPCE of urban and rural areas is also very high. On an average urban Odias spend more than double what an average rural Odia spends in a month. The disparity is more in case of non-food expenditure. Urban Odias spend Rs. 607.96 and rural Odias spend Rs. 404.22 for food in a month. Similarly, urban Odias spend Rs. 860.88 and rural Odias spend Rs. 311.37 on non-food items in a month. Thus, a rural Odia spends 66 per cent of what an urban Odia spends on food items and only 36 per cent on non-food items.

The disparity within the state can also be assessed by analyzing the average MPCE of each district and the percentage of people in different quintiles of MPCE. Table 11.5 presents the average MPCE for 30 districts and the percentage of people in different quintiles of MPCE. Among the 30 districts of Odisha, MPCE is highest for Khordha district and lowest for Malkangiri with values Rs. 1694.78 and Rs. 368.94 respectively. Thus on an average the people of Khordha district spend 4.6 times higher than the people of Malkangiri district in a month. 17 districts report MPCE less than that of state average. The distribution of the MPCE also varies a great deal within the district. In an ideal distribution equal percentage of people should come in different quintiles.

Nevertheless, we find a very uneven distribution of MPCE in all 30 districts. The distribution is highly skewed in the poorer districts. In 10 poorest districts (in terms of MPCE) of the state, namely Balangir, Mayurbhanj, Sonepur, Baudh, Rayagada, Kalahandi, Nabarangapur, Nuapada, Koraput and Malkangiri more than 70 per cent people come in the first quintile of MPCE which ranges between Rs. 10 to 247.32. In Malkangiri district, the poorest district of the state and where the aggregate SC and ST population constitutes 78.78 per cent of the total population, more than 98 per cent people have MPCE in the lowest quintile. In another seven districts, Sundargarh, Nayagarh, Gajapati, Baleswar, Debagarh, Kendujhar and Kandhamal, namely between 50 to 70 per cent people come in the lowest quintile of MPCE. Only in five districts, namely Khordha, Cuttack, Jharsuguda, Sundargarh, Nayagarh, the percentage of people in the top quintile exceeds 10 per cent.

After analysing Tables 11.3 and 11.5 we can easily infer that although PNDDP is a better indicator to assess the regional spread of benefits of growth, it does not reveal the distribution of the income among the people within the same district. The PNDDP might be much higher but a large section of the population might be living below the poverty line. For example, the extraction of minerals by a few companies in a district may increase the PNDDP without benefiting the local people. Therefore, it is pertinent to examine the relationship between PNDDP and the average MPCE of each district. Based on the range of PNDDP and MPCE we divide all 30 districts into high medium and low category districts in Table 11.6. Table 11.6 also compares the rank of each district based on PNDDP in 1999-2000 and 2006-07 to observe the mobility of each district over this time period. Although Angul and Jharsuguda

Table 11.5: District-wise average Monthly Per Capita Expenditure and Quintile Distribution

District	*Average MPCE*	*10.00-247.32*	*247.40-325.40*	*325.45-410.33*	*410.37-590.50*	*590.71-16081.78*
		Q1	*Q2*	*Q3*	*Q4*	*Q5*
1. Khordha	1694.78	42.40%	22.60%	7.20%	15.50%	12.20%
2. Cuttack	1153.39	42.10%	14.80%	17.10%	14.80%	11.30%
3. Sambalpur	1151.09	43.60%	21.60%	16.10%	9.40%	9.20%
4. Jharsuguda	1062.69	37.10%	22.40%	16.30%	13.30%	10.90%
5. Jagatsinghpur	1047.27	22.90%	36.70%	14.60%	16.40%	9.40%
6. Sundargarh	1021.26	54.80%	16.50%	8.40%	6.90%	13.40%
7. Bargarh	985.78	42.40%	20.70%	22.90%	6.80%	7.20%
8. Dhenkanal	968.66	31.40%	33.40%	19.60%	8.30%	7.20%
9. Jajpur	968.49	41.10%	14.80%	26.80%	11.70%	5.70%
10. Angul	955.40	38.90%	28.60%	16.20%	10.40%	5.80%
11. Ganjam	940.30	36.50%	28.80%	20.40%	8.80%	5.50%
12. Nayagarh	934.57	59.50%	19.20%	9.00%	1.90%	10.50%
13. Kendrapara	917.78	36.60%	24.00%	24.30%	11.10%	4.00%
14. Puri	831.49	46.50%	30.90%	11.50%	7.90%	3.30%
15. Gajapati	822.44	60.60%	12.20%	18.30%	5.20%	3.70%
16. Baleshwar	818.92	60.10%	13.40%	14.00%	5.30%	7.10%
17. Bhadrak	788.82	48.40%	33.10%	13.30%	2.40%	3.00%
18. Debagarh	769.02	58.90%	24.00%	9.20%	4.80%	3.10%
19. Kendujhar	744.30	66.50%	11.00%	10.10%	9.80%	2.50%
20. Kandhamal	699.09	59.40%	17.20%	17.20%	3.50%	2.70%
21. Balangir	658.71	73.30%	16.80%	4.90%	2.00%	3.00%
22. Mayurbhanj	647.65	73.00%	12.90%	7.20%	5.80%	1.20%
23. Sonepur	642.92	71.70%	18.60%	5.60%	3.10%	1.00%
24. Baudh	634.44	71.30%	23.00%	2.60%	1.60%	1.50%
25. Rayagada	607.83	72.40%	14.30%	6.60%	5.60%	1.10%
26. Kalahandi	597.95	77.60%	12.20%	8.40%	1.30%	0.40%
27. Nabarangapur	577.30	84.60%	7.80%	3.70%	2.00%	1.90%
28. Nuapada	543.26	80.30%	15.20%	3.00%	1.30%	0.30%
29. Koraput	455.91	85.50%	3.10%	5.20%	4.10%	2.20%
30. Malkangiri	368.94	98.10%	1.10%	0.20%	0.50%	0.10%
All-Odisha	875.45	54.90%	19.10%	12.90%	7.50%	5.60%

Source: Computed from NSSO 66th round

districts consistently rank at the top with highest PNDDP their position in MPCE comes in the medium order. Only Khordha district, which includes the capital city of the state comes as the high ranked district in MPCE but is ranked in the medium order

Table 11.6: Relationship between PNDDP and MPCE of 30 districts

Rank	*PNDDP in 1999-2000 at 1999-2000 prices*	*PNDDP in 2006-07 at 1999-2000 prices*	*MPCE in 2009-10*
High	(15914.68—20382) Angul, Jharsuguda	(25493-33377) Angul, Jharsuguda	(Rs. 1252.84 to 1694.78) Khordha
Medium	(11447.34—15914.67) Sambalpur, Sundargarh, Khordha, Debagarh, Cuttack, Kandhamal, Koraput	(17608-25492) Sundargarh, Khordha, Kendujhar, Sambalpur, Jagatsinghpur, Cuttack	(Rs. 810.9 to 1252.83) Cuttack, Sambalpur, Jharsuguda, Jagatsinghpur, Sundargarh, Bargarh Dhenkanal, Jajpur, Angul, Ganjam, Nayagarh, Kendrapara, Puri, Gajapati, Baleshwar
Low	(6980 -11447.33) Kendujhar, Jagatsinghpur, Bargarh, Rayagada, Malkangiri, Gajapati, Dhenkanal, Nuapada, Bolangir, Kalahandi, Baudh, Baleshwar, Ganjam, Puri, Sonepur, Jajpur, Nabarangpur, Mayurbhanj, Kendrapara, Nayagarh, Bhadrak	(9722-17607) Kandhamal, Jajpur, Koraput, Rayagada, Bolangir, Debagarh, Dhenkanal, Ganjam, Gajapati, Baleshwar, Nuapada, Baudh, Bargarh, Puri, Kalahandi, Sonepur, Mayurbhanj, Bhadrak, Nayagarh, Malkangiri, Kendrapara, Nabarangpur	(Rs. 368.94 to 810.89) Bhadrak, Debagarh, Kendujhar, Kandhamal, Boalangir, Mayurbhanj, Sonapur, Baudh Rayagada, Kalahandi, Nabarangapur, Nuapada, Koraput, Malkangiri

Note: 1. Ranks based on PNDDP are estimated by taking the range of income; Angul with highest income Rs. 33,377 and Nabarangpur with lowest income Rs.9,722. The range (23655) was divided by 3 and the value (7885) was added on the lowest PNDDP to get the range for low income districts (9722-17607); the medium PNDDP districts were derived by adding 7885 upon 17607, i.e. between 17608 to 25492 and similarly, the range for high NDDP districts were derived, i.e. between 25493-33377.

2. PNDDP in 2006-07 at 1999-2000 prices.

Source: Ranks based on the estimations using the NSSO 66th round data and PNDDP from Government of Odisha, *Economic Survey 2010-11* and own computation based on Economic Survey data-2009-10.

in PNDDP indicator. Districts like Koraput, Kandhamal and Debagargh although ranked in the medium order of PNDDP in 1999-2000 slipped down to low rank in 2006-07.

Has the growth helped the districts helped to reduce the gap between all districts? For answering this question we have estimated the Gini-coefficient, for two indicators: PNDDP and MPCE at two points of time subject to data availability (see Table 11.7). Gini-coefficient for PNDDP has gone up from 0.226 in the year 1999-2000 to 0.302 in the year 2006-07. Similarly, the Gini-coefficient for MPCE has also gone up from 0.207 to 0.256 in the year 2009-10. The comparison of Gini-coefficient for both PNDDP and MPCE indicates a growing inequality among different districts. Along with the findings of Table 11.4, we can conclude that the growth has not benefitted all the districts equally.

Table 11.7: Gini-coefficients for District-wise PNDDP and MPCE

Gini-coefficient for PNDDP		*Gini-coefficient for District-wise MPCE*	
1999-2000	*2006-07*	*2004-05 NSSO 61st round*	*2009-10 NSSO 66th round*
0.226	0.302	0.207	0.256
Source: Computed from the data of Economic Survey 2010-11, Government of Odisha.		*Source:* Computed from the NSSO 61st and 66th data	

For explaining the reasons why some districts are performing better than the other we looked for the demographic and education profile of each districts. In Table 11.8 we present the MPCE of each district, percentage of SC and ST population and literacy rates. In Table 11.9 we provide the rank of every district based on these indicators and the Human Development Indicator. From this we observe that low literacy rate works as a sufficient condition for the economic backwardness. Although high literacy rates do not necessarily coincide with high MPCE, low literacy rates are highly associated with low MPCE. Similarly, by and large, the districts with a large percentage of SC and ST population have low literacy rates and MPCE. The association is also established in Figure 11.2.

Table 11.8: Share of SC/ST Populations, MPCE and Literacy Rates

District	MPCE	% of SC Population	% of ST Population	% of SC+ST Population	Literacy rates %
1. Angul	955.40	18.8	14.1	32.9	77.5
2. Baleshwar	818.92	20.6	11.9	32.5	79.8
3. Bargarh	985.78	20.2	19.0	39.2	74.6
4. Baudh	634.44	23.8	12.5	36.3	71.6
5. Bhadrak	788.82	22.2	2.0	24.2	82.8
6. Bolangir	658.71	17.9	21.1	39.0	64.7
7. Cuttack	1153.39	19.0	3.6	22.6	85.5
8. Debagarh	769.02	16.7	35.3	52.0	72.6
9. Dhenkanal	968.66	19.6	13.6	33.2	78.8
10. Gajapati	822.44	6.8	54.3	61.1	53.5
11. Ganjam	940.30	19.5	3.4	22.9	71.1
12. Jagatsinghpur	1047.27	21.8	0.7	22.5	86.6
13. Jajpur	968.49	23.7	8.3	32.0	80.1
14. Jharsuguda	1062.69	18.1	30.5	48.6	78.9
15. Kalahandi	597.95	18.2	28.5	46.7	59.2
16. Kandhamal	699.09	15.8	53.6	69.4	64.1
17. Kendrapada	917.78	21.5	0.7	22.2	85.2
18. Kendujhar	744.30	11.6	45.4	57.0	68.2
19. Khordha	1694.78	13.2	5.1	18.3	86.9
20. Koraput	455.91	14.2	50.6	64.8	49.2
21. Malkangiri	368.94	22.6	57.8	80.4	48.5
22. Mayrubhanj	647.65	7.3	58.7	66.0	63.2
23. Nabarangapur	577.30	14.5	55.8	70.3	46.4
24. Nayagarh	934.57	14.2	6.1	20.3	80.4
25. Nuapada	543.26	13.5	33.8	47.3	57.3
26. Puri	831.49	19.1	3.4	22.5	84.7
27. Rayagada	607.83	14.4	56.0	70.4	49.8
28. Sambalpur	1151.09	18.4	34.1	52.5	76.2
29. Sonepur	642.92	25.6	9.4	35.0	74.4
30. Sundargarh	1021.26	9.2	50.7	59.9	73.3
Odisha	**875.45**	**17.1**	**22.8**	**39.9**	**72.9**

Source: MPCE estimates computed from NSSO 66th round data. Literacy rates: 2011 Census; SC, ST populations 2011 Census.

Similarly, industrialisation also helps in raising the average MPCE of the concerned district.

Table 11.9: Rank of 30 Districts Based on Different Indicators

District	SC-ST rank	MPCE rank	PNDDP Rank	literacy rank	HDI rank	Industrialisation Rank
Khordha	1	1	4	1	1	3
Cuttack	6	2	8	5	3	1
Sambalpur	21	3	6	13	13	21
Jharsuguda	19	4	2	12	2	19
Jagatsingpur	4	5	7	2	19	15
Sundargarh	24	6	3	16	4	2
Bargarh	16	7	21	14	17	23
Dhenkanal	12	8	15	9	12	11
Jajpur	9	9	10	8	22	26
Angul	11	10	1	11	6	9
Ganjam	7	11	16	19	20	6
Nayagarh	2	12	27	10	15	20
Kendrapada	3	13	29	3	10	16
Puri	4	14	22	4	7	10
Gajapati	23	15	17	26	28	27
Baleshwar	10	16	18	7	18	5
Bhadrak	8	17	26	6	8	8
Debagarh	20	18	14	17	5	25
Kendujhar	22	19	5	20	24	4
Kandhamal	27	20	9	22	29	18
Bolangir	15	21	13	21	21	13
Mayurbhanj	26	22	25	23	9	7
Sonepur	13	23	24	15	16	28
Baudh	14	24	20	18	23	24
Raygada	29	25	12	27	25	12
Kalahandi	17	26	23	24	11	14
Nabarangapur	28	27	30	30	26	22
Nuapada	18	28	19	25	14	29
Koraput	25	29	11	28	27	17
Malkangiri	30	30	28	29	30	30

Source: HDI ranks based on Human Development Report of Orissa, 2004; MPCE ranks Based on MPCE data from NSSO 66th round; SC-ST ranks based on census 2011 data; rank 1 shows lowest per cent SC-ST population and rank 30 highest SC-ST population; Literacy rates rank based on Census 2011 data Industrialisation ranks are estimated from the number of large and Micro, Small and Medium Scale Enterprises based on the data provided by Government of Odisha http://as.ori.nic.in/diorissa/msme_dicwis_catwis.asp?distcd=20 data retrieved on January 28, 2012.

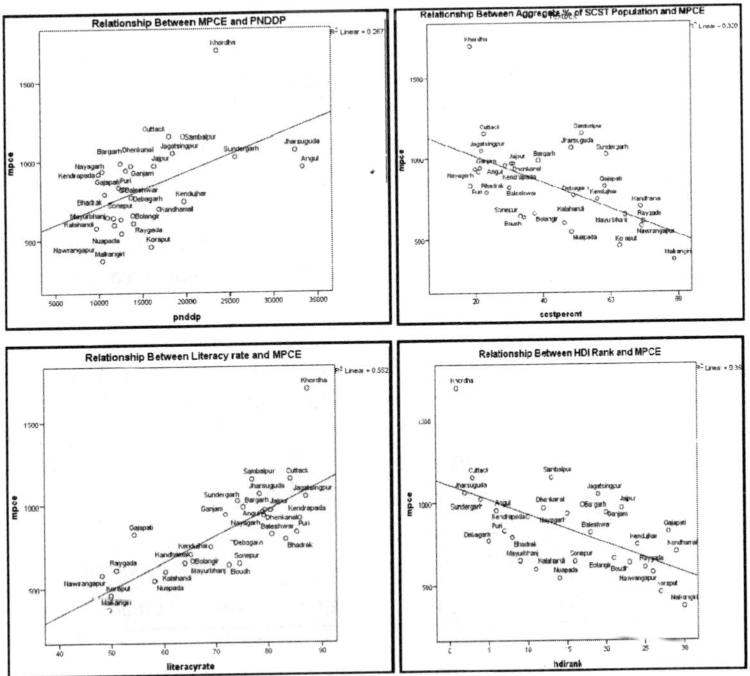

Fig. 11.3: Relationship Between MPCE with PNDDP, SC/ST Population, Literacy Rates and HDI Rank

Poverty Reduction across Regions and Social Groups

Raising the income of the households and reducing poverty is the principal objectives of any development policy. Therefore, it is pertinent to examine whether the growth in Odisha has been successful in reducing the poverty or not. It is noteworthy that the poverty estimates in India are shrouded with serious controversy for difference in methodology in estimation. Nevertheless, we take some standard sources of poverty estimates for comparison. Table 11.10 provides the poverty head count ratio for Odisha and India based on the methodology of Tendulkar Committee. The poverty ratio is much higher in Odisha as compared to all India average. However, the total poverty ratio in Odisha has fallen from 59.1 per cent in 1993-94 to 57.2 per cent in 2004-05 and 47.3 per cent in 2009-10. The rate of poverty decline is much higher in the recent years as compared to 1990s. Annual rate of poverty decline was 0.17 percentage points during 1993-94 and 2004-05 and 1.98 percentage points during 2004-05 and 2009-10. Poverty reduction was lower in Odisha as compared to that of all India average during the first phase and just opposite in the second phase. Within Odisha the incidence of poverty is much larger in rural areas as compared to the urban areas. In the year 2009-10 more than 50.5 per cent rural people were poor as compared to the 28.5 per cent in urban areas. More surprisingly, poverty ratios in urban area increased (0.28% points per annum) during the first phase and showed a declining trend in the second phase. Overall, fall in poverty has been greater in rural areas as compared to urban area. The fall in rural poverty of Odisha is also higher than that of rural India.

Table 11.10: Poverty Head Count Ratio (%) for Odisha and India by Tendulkar Committee Methodology

Time Period	*Poverty Head Count Ratio for Odisha*			*Poverty Head Count Ratio for all India*		
	Rural	*Urban*	*Total*	*Rural*	*Urban*	*Total*
1993-94	63.0	34.5	59.1	50.1	30.8	45.3
2004-05	60.8	37.6	57.2	41.8	25.7	37.2
2009-10	50.5	28.5	47.3	36.4	21.5	32.0
Total Poverty Reduction						
1993-94 to 2004-05	2.2	–3.1	1.9	8.3	5.1	8.1
2004-05 to 2009-10	10.3	9.1	9.9	5.4	4.2	5.2
Annual Rate of Poverty Reduction						
1993-94 to 2004-05	0.20	–0.28	0.17	0.75	0.46	0.74
2004-05 to 2009-10	2.06	1.82	1.98	1.08	0.84	1.04

Source: Computed from the data from Government of Odisha, *Economic Survey 2011-12.*

Table 11.11 presents the poverty head count ratio for Odisha and all-India as per the methodology of Lakdawala Committee. As per this estimate poverty HCR is much lower as compared to the estimates of Tendulkar Committee. More surprisingly, this estimate shows that poverty ratio is higher in urban Odisha as compared to rural Odisha starting from the year 2004-05. However, there are some common trends in both findings; urban poverty

Table 11.11: Poverty Head Count Ratio Estimates of Planning Commission using Poverty Line of the Lakdawala Committee

Time Period	*Poverty Head Count Ratio for Odisha*			*Poverty Head Count Ratio for all India*		
	Rural	*Urban*	*Total*	*Rural*	*Urban*	*Total*
1993-94	49.72	41.64	48.56	37.27	32.36	35.97
1999-00	48.01	42.83	47.15	27.09	23.62	26.1
2004-05	39.8	40.3	39.9	21.8	21.7	21.8
2009-10*	29.06	33.44	29.69	16.26	15.94	16.18
Total Poverty Reduction						
1993-94 to 1999-2000	1.71	–1.19	1.41	10.18	8.74	9.87
1999-2000 to 2004-05	8.21	2.53	7.25	5.29	1.92	4.3
2004-05 to 2009-10	10.74	6.86	10.21	5.54	5.76	5.62
Annual Rate of Poverty Reduction						
1993-94 to 1999-2000	0.29	–0.20	0.24	1.70	1.46	1.65
1999-2000 to 2004-05	1.64	0.51	1.45	1.06	0.38	0.86
2004-05 to 2009-10	2.15	1.37	2.04	1.11	1.15	1.12

* Tentative estimates

Source: Computed from the data from Odisha Economic Survey 2011-12.

rose by 0.20 percentage points per annum during 1993-94 to 1999-2000 but it has fallen afterwards. The decline in overall poverty of Odisha was lower during 1993-94 and 1999-2000 as compared to the decline in the all-India average. However, starting from 1999-2000 till 2009-10, fall in the poverty rate of Odisha has been higher than that of all-India average. This trend is also observed both at rural and urban level.

After analyzing the poverty reduction in urban and rural Odisha *vis-à-vis* all India average here we provide the poverty reduction among different social groups in different parts of Odisha. Table 11.12 presents the poverty estimates among social groups in different regions of Odisha based on the pooled data of NSS 61st and 66th round for rural Odisha. As per the estimates based on the NSSO 66th round data the incidence of poverty is maximum among the ST population followed by SC, OBC and other caste groups of Odisha with the HCR 54.01 per cent, 34.46 per cent, 18.79 per cent and 14.93 per cent respectively. Similarly, if we compare the poverty in coastal, southern and northern regions of Odisha, southern Odisha shows the maximum prevalence of poverty (47.03%), followed by northern region (25.07%) and coastal region (16.57%). As compared to the NSSO 61st round, poverty during 66th round has gone down for all groups at aggregate level. Poverty has fallen at maximum rate among STs followed by OBC, SC and other groups. During 2004-05 and 2009-10 the decline in poverty is highest in northern part of Odisha (18.62% points) followed by southern and coastal region. The fall in poverty is slowest in the coastal region. In this region poverty among ST and other category has gone up during this period.

Summary and Conclusion

After the 1991 liberalisation of Indian economy the growth rate of Odisha fell down by almost half the rate of previous decade and GSDP of the state grew at an average rate of 2.68 per cent with relatively less fluctuation of the output with the SD value 7.95. The highest growth rate of GSDP is recorded in the year 2003-04 at 15.15 per cent. On an average the GSDP of the state grew at around 8 per cent per annum with relatively least degree of fluctuations during 2000-01 and 2009-10. The GSDP of the state grew at an average rate of 10.63 per cent between 2003-04 and

Table 11.12: Social Group-wise and Region-wise Poverty (Head Count Ratio) Estimates based on Pooled Data, NSS Round: Rural Odisha

Method	*Social Group*	*Coastal*	*Southern*	*Northern*	*All*
MRP 66th round	ST	57.15	72.52	34.25	54.01
	SC	22.69	49.8	28.28	34.46
	OBC	10.48	30.77	15.56	18.79
	Others	14.63	17.61	12.67	14.93
	Total	16.57	47.03	25.07	29.65
MRP 61st round	ST	50.63	76.42	59.39	64.32
	SC	26.99	59.52	42.85	38.55
	OBC	13.52	45.26	33.58	24.48
	Others	11.71	41.38	22.52	15.57
	Total	18.38	62.5	43.69	35.54
Fall in Poverty between 2004-05 and 2009-10	ST	-6.52	3.9	25.14	10.31
	SC	4.3	9.72	14.57	4.09
	OBC	3.04	14.49	18.02	5.69
	Others	-2.92	23.77	9.85	0.64
	Total	1.81	15.47	18.62	5.89

Source:: Computed from the data of Directorate of Economics and Statistics as cited in Government of Odisha, *Economic Survey 2011-12*.

2009-10 which is even higher than the average growth rate of GDP of all-India. Similarly, the per capita NSDP grew at an average rate of 3.92 per cent during 2003-04 and 2009-10. Along with this fast economic growth the structural transformation of Odisha economy took place in the year 1996-97 when the share of service sector surpassed the contribution of primary sector with the former contributing 42.1 per cent of GSDP. Thus, the share of agriculture in the GSDP of the state has gone down from 67.31 per cent in 1950-51 to 25.5 per cent in the 2009-10. The contribution of service sector, reversely, has gone up from 25.75 per cent in 1950-51 to 51.28 per cent in 2009-10. The share of secondary sector has also gone up from 6.94 per cent to around 25 per cent in 2007-08. Therefore, we can conclude that the recent surge in the growth of Odisha economy is primarily driven by the service sector followed by agriculture.

If we compare the PNDDP of each district with the average per capita NSDP of the state, 19 districts fall below the state average and only 11 districts have PNDDP higher than the state average. The annual average growth rates of the 19 poor districts have also been lower than the average growth of the state during 2000-01 and 2006-07 except Bhadrak which has recorded 6.39 per cent annual average growth. If the poor districts are to catch up with the rich districts, then their income has to grow faster than the richer districts. However, we do not observe such a trend. Rather, the rich districts are continuing to grow faster and poorer districts are growing much slower.

As per the estimates of 66th National Sample Survey, as reported in Odisha Economic Survey for the year 2011-12, the all India average MPCE during July 2009 to June 2010 in rural areas was Rs. 953.05 and that of Odisha was Rs. 715.59. This implies that on an average a rural Odia monthly consumes only 75 per cent of what an average rural Indian consumes. Within Odisha, the disparity between the MPCE of urban and rural areas is also very high. On an average urban Odias spend more than double what an average rural Odia spends in a month. The disparity is more in case of non-food expenditure. We find a very uneven distribution of MPCE in all 30 districts. The distribution is highly skewed in the poorer districts. In 10 poorest districts (in terms of MPCE) of the state, namely Bolangir, Mayurbhanj, Sonepur, Baudh,

Rayagada, Kalahandi, Nabarangapur, Nuapada, Koraput and Malkangiri more than 70 per cent people come in the lowest quintile of MPCE which ranges between Rs. 10 to 247.32. Gini-coefficient, which measures the degree of inequality, for PNDDP has gone up from 0.226 in the year 1999-2000 to 0.302 in the year 2006-07. Similarly, the Gini-coefficient for MPCE has also gone up from 0.207 to 0.256 in the year 2009-10. The comparison of Gini for both PNDDP and MPCE indicates a growing inequality among different districts. We can conclude that the growth has not benefited all the districts equally.

The poverty ratio is much higher in Odisha as compared to all India average. However, the total poverty ratio in Odisha has fallen from 59.1 per cent in 1993-94 to 57.2 per cent in 2004-05 and 47.3 per cent in 2009-10. The rate of poverty decline is much higher in the recent years as compared to 1990s. As per the estimates based on the NSSO 66th round data the incidence of poverty is maximum among the ST population followed by SC, OBC and other caste groups of Odisha with the HCR 54.01 per cent, 34.46 per cent, 18.79 per cent and 14.93 per cent respectively. Similarly, if we compare the poverty in coastal, southern and northern regions of Odisha, southern Odisha shows the maximum prevalence of poverty (47.03%), followed by northern region (25.07%) and coastal region (16.57%). As compared to the NSSO 61st round, poverty during 66th round has gone down for all groups at aggregate level. Poverty has fallen at maximum rate among STs followed by OBC, SC and other groups. During 2004-05 and 2009-10 the decline in poverty is highest in northern part of Odisha (18.62%) followed by southern and coastal region. The fall in poverty is slowest in the coastal region. In this region poverty among ST and other category has gone up during this period.

It may, thus, be concluded that the rapid growth of Odisha economy from early 2000s brings much optimism. Nevertheless, the benefits of growth have not reached all sections of the society and regions equally. This may increase the discontentment of deprived people and aggravate the social unrest in the backward regions. Therefore, judicious steps need to be taken for transferring the benefits of growth to all the sections of society.

REFERENCES

Government of India (2008). *Eleventh Five Year Plan 2007-08-2011-12*. New Delhi: Planning Commission, Government of India.

Government of Odisha (2011). *Economic Survey 2010-11* (also for other years). Bhubaneswar: Planning and Coordination Department.

Kuznets, Simon (1971). *Economic Growth of Nations: Total Output and Production Structure*. Cambridge, Massachusetts: Harvard University Press.

12

Measuring the Effect of Foreign Aid on Economic Growth and Income Inequality in India

Kalpana Sahoo

Introduction

Since after Second World War foreign aid has been used as an important financial tool by the developed countries and the aid agencies to stimulate economic growth and reduce income inequality in poor countries. It acts as a major source of foreign exchange earnings for developing countries. Foreign aid is the international transfer of public funds in the forms of loans and grants directly from one government or an international financial institution to another government at the time of need. It takes two forms such as loans at concessional term (contains grant element of at least 25%) and grants which is non-refundable (OECD, 2009). The main purpose of the foreign aid programmes is to accelerate the process of economic development up to a point where a satisfactory rate of growth can be achieved on a self-sustaining basis. The major contribution of foreign aid programme towards underdeveloped economies can be evaluated by its role in filing three major gaps—(1) saving-investment gap, (2) export-import gap, and (3) technological gap. The strategic role of capital in accelerating the development process has traditionally been acknowledged in economics. In fact, Harrod-Domar model of growth has treated capital as the crucial factor in economic development. Capital is considered as the life-blood of all economic activities. Shortage of capital is a common feature of the developing economies. The solution is to have more and more capital. There are two ways to have capital, i.e., domestic capital and foreign capital. Developing Countries are characterized as capital poor or low saving and low investing economies along with technological backwardness. Due to insufficient capital formation, most of the developing nations depend on foreign capital to accelerate their development process. Foreign capital in terms of foreign aid helps in overcoming these drawbacks as it brings sufficient physical and financial capital, investment funds, technical know-how, skilled personnel, organizational experience, market information, advanced production techniques, innovations in products and foreign exchange resources (Morrissey, 2001).

In the era of globalization and economic integration, economies are so dependent on each other that impacts of one economy quickly affect the other economy. That's why many developed economies provide huge financial support to other developing nations to overcome from the unfavourable situation and to accelerate the process of development. Foreign aid is believed to address poverty and income inequality by supplementing domestic scarce resources such as savings, thus increasing the amount of investment and capital stock. Higher amount of investment will lead to faster and sustained economic growth. While economic growth should benefit the economy as a whole that does not mean that income inequality will lessen with rise in economic growth. In recent time, there have been considerable debates going on over the motives of foreign aid and its impact on income inequality. Foreign aid is accused of aggravating income inequality which it is proposed to reduce first (Shafiullah, 2011). Adding to this unproductive utilization of such huge amount of external assistance inflows may create threat for large amount of external debt burden in the long run. Over time this debt burden increases and acts as a major obstacle in attending the targeted rate of growth in future.

Up to the commencement of the Second World War, foreign aid was used as a profitable mode of investment by the donor community. Since after Second World War, developed economies have been providing hundreds of billions of dollars in terms of foreign aid to the developing world for welfare motive. Still the problems are not cured fully and even in some cases the existing problems are more aggravated than the past. Here the question arises who is responsible for the failure of the foreign aid programme? Whether the donor community or the recipient government or the aid providing system or the implementation strategy or something else? With the passage of time the issue has become a worldwide phenomenon. Both foreign aid donors and recipient governments have recognized the need to establish a possible link between foreign aid and its welfare motives. Studies on such relationship have often ended with conflicting conclusions.

In this context, the present study tries to empirically the impact of foreign aid on both economic growth and income inequality in India during 1960-61 to 2010-11. The study also tries to determine whether economic growth and income inequality of India is associated with other macroeconomic variables like GDP (Gross Domestic Product), trade, population, inflation, GCF (Gross Capital Formation), PCGNI (Per Capita Gross National Income) or not. The remaining part of this paper is organized into five sections including introduction. Section 2 describes the reviews both theoretical and empirical literatures. Section 3 presents the nature, sources and methodology of the study. Section 4 deals with the analysis of the empirical results and its discussion. Section 5 presents the summary, conclusion and limitation of the paper.

Foreign Aid, Growth and Economic Inequality

Foreign aid and its impact on economic growth and income inequality have remained as one of the major debatable issue since last few decades. A lot of debates and researches have been dedicated to finding the solution of this issue. Many supportive and controversial arguments have been found but the effectiveness of foreign aid is still questionable. The relationship between foreign aid, growth and income inequality has been difficult to interpret. Different researchers have given various views regarding the impact of foreign aid on economic growth and income inequality.

The Kuznets inverted U-curve indicates that income inequality will rise as the economy grows in the earlier stages of development and fall again when GDP per capita exceeds a certain amount (Kuznets, 1955). Studies carried out by Papanek (1972), Dowling and Hiemenz (1982), Gupta and Islam (1983), Hansen and Tarp (2000), Burnside and Dollar (1997), Gomanee, *et al.* (2005) and Dalgaard *et al.* (2004) find evidences for positive impact of aid on growth. Singh (1985) has found some evidence which states that foreign aid has positive and strong effects on growth when state intervention is not included. Snyder (1993) has found a positive relation between aid and growth by taking country size into account. Burnside and Dollar (1997) have argued that aid works well in the presence of good-policy environment particularly in the recipient country. A study carried out by Kosack (2003) has found that aid can directly increase welfare but only in the presence of democracies. Karras (2006) has concluded that the effect of foreign aid on economic growth is positive, permanent and statistically significant. Minoiu and Reddy (2009) have analyzed the growth impact of Official Development Assistance (ODA) to developing countries over 1960-2000 by using OLS and 2SLS techniques. It is different as it takes a longer study period and also divided the aid into two segments, i.e. developmental aid and non-developmental aid. It has found that only the developmental aid promotes long run growth. Sakyi (2011) has found that the impact of both trade openness and aid inflows on economic growth is positive and statistically significant in both short run and long run.

Some other researchers have found contradict results. Pedersen (2001) has argued that it is not possible to conclude that the foreign aid has a positive impact on growth. Using game theory technique, the study has found that the impact of aid on growth is not positive. Svensson (2000) has argued that large aid flow help to raise the welfare gain but in certain cases it result high expectation which may increase rent seeking and reduce the expected public goods quality. Knack (2000) in a cross-country analysis, has explained that higher aid amount degrade the quality of governance indexes, i.e. bureaucracy, corruption and the rule of law, which ultimately hinders the growth process of the nation. It is debated that high income inequality may be responsible for reduction of economic growth (Barro, 2000). Some empirical studies show that there is an inverse relationship exists between income inequality and economic growth (Herzer and Vollmer, 1998; Panizza, 2002). Easterly, *et al.* (2003) and Rajan and Subramanian (2008) have found that it is quite difficult to conclude that aid has significant positive impact on growth. Their studies state that foreign aid is found to be significantly and negatively correlated with growth. There are a number of underlying causes, such as the fungibility of aid, poor economic policies, aid dependency, bad economic management, corruption and poor coordination and cooperation among aid agencies which are responsible for this adverse result. Foreign aid has become ineffective in Bangladesh due to its utilization in unproductive expenditures (Quazi, 2005). Donors' conditionality may be partly responsible for the ineffectiveness of foreign aid (Dalgaard, 2008). Mallik (2008) has examined the effectiveness of foreign aid programme for economic growth in six poorest and highly aid dependent African countries by using the Johansen's co-integration tests. The empirical result showed that aid as a percentage of GDP and the long run effect of aid on growth was found to be negative for most of these countries. Ekanayake and Chatrna (2010) have analyzed the effect of foreign aid on the economic growth of 85 developing countries covering Asia, Africa, Latin America and the Caribbean countries for the period 1980-2007. They have found that foreign aid has mixed effects on economic growth in developing countries which depends on many factors like economic policies, geographic condition, human development and institutional efficiency etc.

From the findings of the above literature reviews, it is clear that the interrelationships between foreign aid, economic growth and income inequality vary from country to country and that is dependent on many factors like economic policy, institutional quality, good governance, mode of utilization of the foreign aid, growth of the population, demographic features, etc.

Methodology of the Study

In the light of many empirical as well as theoretical studies taken up earlier, the present study makes an attempt to examine the impact of foreign aid on both economic growth and income inequality in India during the period 1960-61 to 2010-11. The study uses the variables like Gross Domestic Product (GDP as the indicator of economic growth), Per Capita Gross National Income (PCGNI as the indicator of economic development), Official Development Assistance (ODA as the proxy of foreign aid), Wholesale Price Index (WPI as the proxy of inflation rate), population, Gross National Expenditure (GNEx), Gross Capital Formation (GCF, as a proxy of domestic investment), Trade and Gini Index (as the indicator of income inequality) for its empirical analysis. The whole study is based on the secondary annual time series data which is collected from the World Development Indicators published by the World Bank and the online database of Standardized World Income Inequality Database (SWIID), Version 3.1 (2011). The missing data on income inequality is collected from the World Income Inequality Database (WIID). This study uses the statistical package E-views 5.0 for its empirical analysis. The study uses GDP and Gini Index as the proxy of economic growth and income inequality respectively. The data have been taken at current prices for all the variables. Owing to high variation in their absolute values, all the variables are expressed in terms of their log value to minimize their differences. The study makes use of the following simple econometric methods to carry out the empirical analysis.

Firstly, calculation is made for the descriptive statistics of all the variables. In order to examine the impact of foreign aid on both economic growth and income inequality in India, Ordinary Least Squares (OLS) technique is used. Before going to use OLS technique one should test the stationary properties of the variable in case of time series data. As our data is time series in nature, the study tests the stationary aspects of the variables using unit root tests, namely Augmented—Dicky Fuller (ADF), Phillips-Perron (PP) (1988) and Kwiatkowski-Phillips-Schmidt-Shin (KPSS) test to avoid the spurious regression results. Among three Unit root tests only the KPSS test without trend shows the stationary properties of all the variables (see Table 12.1).

In the light of this, the following equation is used as the basic model to find out the impact of foreign aid on economic growth of India. Here GDP is considered as the proxy of economic growth.

$$\text{Growth in terms of GDP} = f\{\text{GCF, ODA, Trade, WPI, GNEx, Popu, PCGNI, GI}\}$$

Here, GDP is taken as the dependent variable and other variables are considered as independent variables. The following model is specified to find out the impact of foreign aid on economic growth. We estimate the effects of independent variables on

Table 12.1: Unit Root Tests Result

Variables	*ADF*		*PP*		*KPSS*	
	Without Trend	*With Trend*	*Without Trend*	*With Trend*	*Without Trend*	*With Trend*
PCGNI	0.63	–0.93	0.63	–1.04	0.93*	0.16*
GDP	1.5	–0.29	1.5	–0.17	0.95*	0.19*
GCF	0.52	–1.57	0.91	–1.54	0.95*	0.17**
GI	–2.13	–2.29	–2.01	–2.19	0.16***	0.1
ODA	–1.2	–4.2*	–2.1	–4.1**	0.81*	0.08
Trade	1.1	–0.79	1.19	–0.84	0.96*	0.18*
WPI	–0.84	–2.18	–0.95	–1.69	0.95*	0.18*
GNEx	1.48	–0.42	1.59	–0.45	0.95*	0.19*
Popu	2.8	–2.3	–3.67*	2.94	0.95*	0.23*

Notes: *, ** and *** indicate significance at 1%, 5% and 10% level respectively.

Source: Author's calculation (by using the software E-views 5.0).

economic growth by ordinary least squares (OLS) techniques which can be written as:

$$(g_t) = \alpha_0 + \alpha_1 \text{GCF}_t + \alpha_2 \text{ODA}_t + \alpha_3 \text{Trade}_t + \alpha_4 \text{WPI}_t + \alpha_5 \text{GNEx}_t + \alpha_6 \text{Popu}_t + \alpha_7 \text{PCGNI}_t + \alpha_8 \text{GI}_t + u_t \quad \ldots(1)$$

Here,

g_t = Economic growth in terms of GDP current US $ during the time period t

GCF_t = Gross Capital Formation in terms of current US $ during the time period t

ODA_t = Net Official Development Assistance in terms of current US $ during the time period t

Trade_t = Total monetary valuation of trade in terms of current US $ during the time period t

WPI_t = Weighted Price Index during the time period t

GNEx_t = Gross National Expenditure in terms of current US $ during the time period t

Popu_t = Total population during the time period t

PCGNI_t = Per Capita GNI in terms of current US $ during the time period t

GI_t = Gini Index as in terms of ratio during the time period t

u_t = Disturbance term

In the second equation, GI (Gini Index) is considered as the dependent variables. The following equation is used as the basic model to find out the impact of foreign aid on income inequality in India. Here GI is considered as the proxy of income inequality.

Inequality in terms of GI = *f* {GCF, ODA, Trade, WPI, GNEx, Popu, GDP, PCGNI}

Here GI is taken as the dependent variable and other variables are considered as independent variables. The following model is specified to find out the impact of foreign aid on income inequality. We estimate the effects of independent variables on income inequality by ordinary least squares (OLS) techniques which can be written as:

$$(GI)_t = \alpha_0 + \alpha_1 GCF_t + \alpha_2 ODA_t + \alpha_3 Trade_t + \alpha_4 WPI_t + \alpha_5 GNEx_t + \alpha_6 Popu_t + \alpha_7 GDP_t + \alpha_8 PCGNI_t + u_t \quad ...(2)$$

Here,

$(GI)_t$ = Income Inequality in terms of Gini Index during the time period t

GCF_t = Gross Capital Formation in terms of current US $ during the time period t

ODA_t = Net Official Development Assistance in terms of current US $ during the time period t

$Trade_t$ = Total monetary valuation of trade in terms of current US $ during the time period t

WPI_t = Weighted Price Index during the time period t

$GNEx_t$ = Gross National Expenditure in terms of current US $ during the time period t

$Popu_t$ = Total population during the time period t

GDP_t = Gross Domestic Product in terms of current US $ during the time period t

$PCGNI_t$ = Per Capita GNI in terms of current US $ during the time period t

u_t = Disturbance term

Empirical Analysis

This section deals with the analysis of the empirical results and its discussion. The empirical result is calculated by using the simple regression analysis. Before going to use OLS test, the present study has examined the stationary property of the time series data. After that the descriptive statistics of the variables have been calculated. Next the simple OLS technique is used to measure the impact of foreign aid on both economic growth and income inequality.

Test of Stationary

The study has used annual time series data of 51 years which contains some trend. Before using any econometric technique in any time series data, the first step is to identify whether the series is stationary or not. If the variables of a time series data do not satisfy the stationary property, then the regression result become spurious one which have no practical implication. Unit root test is used to test the stationary property of the variables. Stationary of the variables are very much desired as non-stationary series will produce spurious regression estimates. Unit root test is a pre-requisite of testing long run relationship between two or more time series data (Granger, 1981). Augmented Dickey-Fuller (ADF), Phillips-Perron (PP) and Kwiatkowski-Phillips-Schmidt-Shin (KPSS) tests are widely used in empirical research. Here, to test the stationary of the variables the study has conducted all the three tests. The criterion of selection for unit test is that the absolute value of the test statistics should be higher than the critical value of the variables. The result of unit root test is shown in Table 12.1. The test result suggests that all the variables are stationary in KPSS without trend.

Descriptive Statistics

Table 12.2 shows the results of descriptive statistics. The mean values of the GCF, GDP, ODA, Population and GNEx are similar to some extent. The mean values of GI, PCGNI, Trade and WPI are also same to some extent. The variability present among the variables is measured by the standard deviation. From the descriptive statistics result, it is clear that the variability among GDP and GNEx are similar to some extent and variability among PCGNI, Population and ODA are also same to some extent. The maximum and the minimum values show the range in between which the values of the variables are lying. Here all the values of the variables are lying in between 1.4 to 27.61. Skewness helps us to determine the nature and extent of the concentration of the

Table 12.2: Descriptive Statistics

	GCF	*GDP*	*GI*	*GNEx*	*ODA*	*PCGNI*	*Popu*	*Trade*	*WPI*
Mean	24.6202	26.12324	3.508891	26.13153	21.93479	5.644845	20.45752	3.26273	3.22984
Median	24.4675	26.0345	3.505046	26.0477	21.9315	5.549098	20.48055	3.25992	3.27065
Max	26.5523	27.59374	3.605498	27.61226	22.84907	6.659478	20.92589	3.31826	4.89696
Min	22.9793	24.86812	3.412945	24.88355	20.49395	4.810591	19.91996	3.21420	1.42214
Std. Dev.	0.96476	0.755624	0.052975	0.758286	0.541328	0.474408	0.310932	0.02893	0.09374
Skew	0.27670	0.223759	0.311721	0.236618	-0.53379	0.309517	-0.15288	0.19475	-0.13926
Kurto	2.22002	2.032252	2.151053	2.028937	3.132733	2.495379	1.73184	2.01299	1.70184
Jar-Bera	1.9436	2.415717	2.357459	2.479696	2.459373	1.355419	3.616154	2.39252	3.74591
Prob	0.3784	0.298837	0.307669	0.289428	0.292384	0.507779	0.163969	0.30232	0.15366

Source: Author's calculation (by using the software E-views 5.0).

observations towards the highest or the lowest values of the variables. The skewness values of GDP, PCGNI, GCF, Trade, GNEx and GI are positive which indicates that the frequency curve of all the distributions are not symmetric bell shaped curve rather they are stretched more to the right side or have a longer tail towards the right side. Rest three variables ODA, population and WPI are negatively skewed. Kurtosis is concentrated with the flatness or peakedness of the frequency curve. The kurtosis values of all the variables except ODA are greater than 3, which show that all the variables (except ODA) have leptokurtic curve (more peaked than normal curve).

Regression Results

Next, we examined equation-1 with applying the Ordinary Least Square (OLS) method. Here we calculate the simple regression to find out the impact of foreign aid on economic growth where GDP is considered as the proxy of economic growth. The following Table 12.3 shows the result of the simple regression test. Here GDP is considered as the dependent variable. But the result is not quite good because of low value of the Durbin-Watson d-statistics (Enders, 1995) which shows the existence of auto-correlation problem and to avoid this situation we will take the AR (1) model to minimize the problem. The following major criterions are considered to know whether a model is good fit or not. The result of this simple OLS technique and the OLS test with the AR (1) model is presented in Table 12.3.

Table 12.3: Selection Criterion of a Good Model (for Euqation-1)

Major Criterion	*Simple OLS test*	*OLS with AR(1)*	*Ideal Value*
R-squared Value	0.99	0.99	1
Adjusted R-squared Value	0.99	0.99	1
Durbin Watson Stat	1.13	1.87	2
Akaike Info Criterion (AIC)	–6.68	–6.94	Should be lower
Schwarz Info Criterion (SIC)	–6.34	–6.56	Should be lower

Source: Author's calculation (by using the software E-views 5.0).

From Table 12.3 it is clear that the result which is drawn from the simple OLS technique can't be considered as good one. Though

Table 12.4: Simple OLS Results—Impact of Foreign Aid on Economic Growth in India

Dependent Variable: GDP		
Variable	*Coefficient*	*t-Statistic*
C	124.19	4.98*
GCF	−0.0078	−0.46
GI	−0.014	−0.48
GNEx	2.67	7.22*
ODA	0.088	2.33*
PCGNI	0.36	5.64*
Population	0.78	5.33*
Trade	−56.92	−5.08*
WPI	−0.027	−1.07

Note: R-squared: 0.99, Adjusted R-squared: 0.99, Durbin Watson stat:1.87, Akaike Info Criterion (AIC): -6.94, Schwarz Info Criterion (SIC): -6.56

Source: Author's calculation (by using the software E-views 5.0).

the values of both R^2 and adjusted R^2 are nearer to 1 which show the goodness of the fit but at the same time the Durbin-Watson (DW) statistic is very low, i.e. 1.13 which indicates the presence of auto-correlations and violates normal assumptions of OLS test. This value should be nearer to 2 (Gujarati, 2004). Both Akaike Info Criterion (AIC) and Schwarz Info Criterion (SIC) are also taken to find a good model. Here both the values of AIC and SIC is lower in case of AR (1) model than the simple OLS test result. The result of the OLS test with AR (1) model is considered as good one for the analysis. The result of the OLS technique with AR (1) is presented in Table 12.4.

The above Table 12.4 shows that the result which is drawn from the OLS test with AR (1) model can be used for analysis, as it satisfies all the criteria of a good model. The value of both R^2 and adjusted R^2 are nearer to 1 which shows the goodness of fit of the model. The value of DW-statistics (1.87) is nearer to 2 which indicates lower chances of the presence of auto-correlations in the error term (Gujarati, 2004). The R^2 or coefficient of determination is used to show how much variation in the dependent variable is captured by the independent variables taken in the model. R^2 and adjusted R^2 values are nearer to 1 which shows that the economic growth of India can be explained by the independent variables included in the model. Both Akaike Info Criterion (AIC) and

Schwarz Info Criterion (SIC) are used for the selections of better model which have relatively lower values, i.e. –6.94 and –6.56 respectively in the AR (1) model. Therefore, the regression results of Table 12.4 are used for the analysis of equation 1, as the estimated regression results satisfy all the criteria for a good model. The estimated regression test result value helps to find out the impact of foreign aid on economic growth:

$$(g_t) = \alpha_0 + \alpha_1 GCF_t + \alpha_2 ODA_t + \alpha_3 Trade_t + \alpha_4 WPI_t + \alpha_5 GNEx_t + \alpha_6 Popu_t + \alpha_7 PCGNI_t + \alpha_8 GI_t + u_t \quad \ldots (1)$$

$$(g_t) = 124.19 - 0.0078\,GCF_t + 0.088\,ODA_t - 56.92\,Trade_t - 0.027\,WPI_t + 2.67\,GNEx_t + 0.78\,Popu_t + 0.36\,PCGNI_t - 0.014\,GI_t + u_t \quad \ldots (1)$$

t-statistics (4.98*) (–0.46) (2.33*) (–5.08*) (–1.07) (7.22*) (5.33*) (5.64*) (–0.46*)

From the above regression results it is found that, the coefficients of GNEx, ODA, Population, Trade and PCGNI have significant impact on economic growth of India during the study period. The coefficients of all the five variables are statistically significant at 1 per cent level. Only the coefficients of GCF, GI and WPI are statistically insignificant, so no inference can be drawn about the impact of these three variables on GDP. It cannot be said that these variables have any positive or negative impact on economic growth of India during this study period. The impact of these variables on growth is ambiguous. On the other hand, the estimated coefficient of GNEx, PCGNI, Population and ODA are positive and statistically significant which indicate that all the four variables have positive impact on economic growth. Among them, GNEx has highest significant positive impact on economic growth of India, which may be the reason that a major share of public fund is invested in both industrial and service sector whose contributions are more to GDP of India. PCGNI has also shown significant positive impact on economic growth as growth is a major part of development process (Sen, 1997). Official capital inflows (ODA) has also shown significant positive impact on economic growth of India as aid supplements to the scarce domestic resources and acts as a source of foreign exchange earnings (Morrissey, 2001). Only trade has shown significant negative impact on economic growth of India during the study period which may be due to the balance of trade deficit in current account.

Next, we examined equation-2 with applying the Ordinary Least Square (OLS) method. Here we calculate the simple regression to find out the impact of foreign aid on income inequality where GI (Gini index) is considered as the indicator of income inequality. The following Table 125 shows the result of the simple regression test. Here GI is considered as the dependent variables. But the result is not appropriate due to the low value of the Durbin-Watson statistics (Enders, 1995). To avoid this situation, the AR (1) model has been taken. The following major criterions are considered to know whether a model is good fit or not. The result of this simple OLS technique with comparison to AR (1) model is presented in Table 12.5.

Table 12.5: Selection Criterion of a Good Model (for Equation-2)

Three Major Criterion	*Simple OLS Test*	*OLS with AR (1)*	*Ideal Value*
R-squared Value	.87	0.94	1
Adjusted R-squared Value	.78	0.96	1
Durbin Watson stat	1.08	2.01	2
Akaike Info Criterion (AIC)	−3.35	−3.68	Should be lower
Schwarz Info Criterion (SIC)	−3.01	−3.3	Should be lower

Source: Author's calculation (by using the software E-views 5.0).

From the above Table 12.5 it is clear that the result which is drawn from the OLS test with AR (1) model is more appropriate than the simple OLS test. In the simple OLS test, both the values of R^2 and adjusted R^2 are far away from 1 and the Durbin-Watson (DW) statistic is also very low 1.08 which indicate the presence of auto-correlations problem. Here both the values of AIC and SIC is more than the AR (1) model. By comparing all the criteria, it is found that the result of the OLS test with AR (1) model is used for the analysis of equation-2. The result of the OLS technique with AR (1) is presented in Table 12.6.

Table 12.6 shows that the result which is drawn from the OLS test with AR (1) model can be used for analysis as it satisfies all the criteria of a good model. The value of both R^2 and adjusted R^2 are nearer to 1 which shows the goodness of fit of the model. The value of DW-statistics (2.01) is nearer to 2 which indicate lower

Table 12.6: Simple OLS results – Impact of Foreign Aid on Income Inequality in India

Dependent Variable: GI (Gini index)		
Variable	*Coefficient*	*t-Statistic*
C	199.44	1.12
GCF	0.027	0.33
GDP	0.62	2.12*
GNEx	–3.71	–4.19*
ODA	–0.023	–1.75
PCGNI	–0.19	–3.78*
Population	0.32	3.37*
Trade	–87.41	–1.09
WPI	0.28	2.16*

Note: R-squared: 0.94, Adjusted R-squared: 0.96, Durbin Watson Stat: 2.01, Akaike Info Criterion (AIC): –3.68, Schwarz Info Criterion (SIC): –3.3

Source: Author's calculation (by using the software E-views 5.0).

chances of the presence of auto-correlations in the error term (Gujarati, 2004). R^2 and adjusted R^2 values are nearer to 1 which shows that the income inequality of India is completely explained by the independent variables included in the model. Both Akaike Info Criterion (AIC) and Schwarz Info Criterion (SIC) are used for the selections of better model which have lower values –3.68 and –3.3 respectively in comparison to the simple OLS test. Therefore, the regression results of Table 12.6 are used for the analysis of equation 2, as the estimated regression results satisfy all the criteria for a good model. The estimated regression test result value helps to find out the impact of foreign aid on income inequality:

$$(g_t) = \alpha_0 + \alpha_1 GCF_t + \alpha_2 ODA_t + \alpha_3 Trade_t + \alpha_4 WPI_t + \alpha_5 GNEx_t + \alpha_6 Popu_t + \alpha_7 PCGNI_t + \alpha_8 GDP_t + u_t \quad \ldots(2)$$

$$(g_t) = 199.44 + 0.027\,GCF_t - 0.023\,ODA_t - 87.41\,Trade_t + 0.28\,WPI_t - 3.71\,GNEx_t + 0.32\,Popu_t - 0.19\,PCGNI_t + 0.62\,GDP_t + u_t \quad \ldots(2)$$

t-statistics (1.12) (0.33) (–1.75) (–1.09) (2.16*) (–4.19*) (3.37*) (–3.78*) (2.12*)

From the above regression results it is found that, the coefficients of GNEx, GDP, WPI, Population and PCGNI has significant impact on income inequality of India during the study period. The coefficient of all the above variables is statistically significant at 1 per cent level. Only the coefficients of ODA, Trade and GCF are statistically insignificant, so no inference can be drawn about the impact of these three variables on the dependent variable. On the other hand, the estimated coefficients of GDP, Population and WPI are statistically significant at 1 per cent level and have positive impact on income inequality of India. The positive relationship of these three variables with the income inequality shows that the changes in the direction will go in the same way. It means when any one of the three variables increases income inequality also rises and *vice-versa*. This result shows that these three variables seem to increase income inequality in India which may be the reason that growth is not translated into meaningful development. The benefits of economic growth are not equally distributed among the individuals of the country. Adding to this unequal distribution of growth benefits heavy population growth and unwanted inflation rate also aggravated the situation. In the other hand, GNEx and PCGNI have shown negative and significant impact on income inequality of India during the study period. This inverse relationship of these two variables with income inequality shows that both government expenditure and per capita income help in the reduction of the income inequality in India during the study period. Though ODA and Trade have shown statistically insignificant impact on income inequality but both are negatively related with the income inequality in India. If proper plans and programmes will be executed for the effective use of the foreign aid and trade benefits, then both will help in the reduction of income inequality problem in future.

Conclusion

This paper contributes to the recent empirical literature of aid effectiveness and its contribution towards economic growth. The paper empirically analyses the impact of foreign aid on both economic growth and income inequality using the OLS technique for India over the period 1960-61 to 2010-11. The empirical results show that foreign aid has significant positive impact on economic growth of India. This study conforms to the findings given by Hansen and Tarp (2000) and Karras (2006) that foreign aid has significant positive impact on economic growth of the aid recipient country. On the other side, it has found that aid has no significant impact on the reduction of income inequality in India. But the inverse relationship between foreign aid and income inequality variables indicates a ray of hope for the future. It seems that aid contributes positively to the process of economic growth but its impact on the reduction of income inequality is not statistically significant in case of India. Inefficient utilisation of the foreign aid is one of the major causes of the failure of aid programme in India. Adding to this unequal distribution of growth benefits, corruption, bad economic policies, lack of human capital and mass poverty are some of the factors which hinder the path of aid programmes in achieving its welfare goals. The growth can be translated into meaningful development only when there will be. The study concludes that equitable distribution of growth benefits along with effective utilisation of foreign aid programmes in different developmental projects (i.e. infrastructural development, agricultural development, irrigation, transport, education etc.) should be the main agenda of the national policy.

Reduction of income equality and higher economic growth are the two primary objectives of foreign aid programme *via* stimulating the process of economic development. So both objectives should be given equal importance in case of India. One should not be compromised or neglected with the other objective. The findings of this study suggest that a developing country like India should try to fully utilize its own resources and abilities and then try to utilize the foreign capital as a supplement to its scarce domestic resources. If it really feels the need of foreign aid, then it should learn some management techniques to make aid effective. Foreign aid should utilize in those welfare activities, i.e. employment generation, infrastructural development, human capital development where the rate of return shall be more than the investment in the long run. Donor countries should provide some technical assistance to recipient countries related to the proper allocation of aid. So foreign aid needs cooperation from both donors as well as recipient country to be effective. Negligence or miss-utilization of one can give adverse result. However, the study is not without its limitations. The analysis and conclusion presented in this study are subject to certain limitation. Certain variables like good economic policy, sector-wise distribution of foreign aid have to be dropped due to the non-availability of reliable data. The present study can hopefully provoke further empirical research in find out the appropriate way by which the benefits of growth can by distributed equally among the each and every individuals of the economy.

Acknowledgements: The author of the article is thankful to Dr. Narayan Sethi, research supervisor for his valuable suggestions in the preparation of this paper and also to UGC, New Delhi for providing the necessary financial assistance (JRF) during the research.

REFERENCES

Barro, R.J. (2000). 'Inequality and Growth in a Panel of Countries', *Journal of Economic Growth*, 5(1): 5-32.

Burnside, C. and Dollar, D. (1997). 'Aid, Policies and Growth', *American Economic Review*, 90(4): 847-68.

Dalgaard, C.J. Hansen, and F. Tarp (2004). 'On the Empirics of Foreign Aid and Growth', *Economic Journal*, 114: 191–216.

Dalgaard, C.J. (2008). 'Donor Policy Rules and Aid Effectiveness', *Journal of Economic Dynamics and Control*, 32: 1895-1920.

Dicky, D.A. and W.A. Fuller (1981). 'Like-hood Ratio Statistics for Autoregressive Time Series with a Unit Root'. *Econometrica*, July, 49: 1057-72.

Dowling, M. and U. Hiemenz (1982). 'Aid, Savings and Growth in the Asian Region', *Economic Office Report Series 3*, Asian Development Bank, Manila.

Ekanayake, E.K. and D. Chatrna (2010). 'The Effect of Foreign Aid on Economic Growth in Developing Countries', *Journal of International Business and Cultural Studies.*

Enders, Walter (1995). *Applied Econometric Time Series*, John Wiley & Sons, New York.

Easterly, W., Levine, R., and Roodman, D. (2003). 'New Data, New Doubts: A Comment on Burnside and Dollar's Aid, Policies and Growth', *NBER, Working Paper No 9846*.

Gomanee, K., S. Girma and O. Morrisey (2005). 'Aid and Growth in Sub-Saharan Africa: Accounting for Transmission Mechanisms', *Journal of International Development*, 17 (8): 1055-75.

Granger, C.W.J. (1981). 'Some Properties of Time Series Data and Their Uses in Econometric Model Specification', *Journal of Econometrics*, 16.

Gujarati, Damodar N. (2004). *Basic Econometrics.* The McGraw Hill Companies, 4th Edition.

Gupta, K.L., and Islam, M. A. (1983). *Foreign Capital, Savings and Growth: An International Cross-Section Study.* Dordrecht: Reidel Publishing Company.

Hansen, H., and F. Tarp (2000). 'Aid Effectiveness Disputed', *Journal of International Development*, 12: 375–98.

Herzer, D. and S. Vollmer (2011). 'Inequality and Growth Evidence from Panel Cointegration'. (This article is published with the open access at *Springerlink.com*)

Karras, G. (2006). 'Foreign Aid and Long-run Economic Growth: Empirical Evidence for a Panel of Developing Countries', *Journal of International Development*, 18 (7): 15–28.

Knack, Stephen, (2000). 'Aid Dependence and the Quality of Governance: A Cross-Country Empirical Analysis', *World Bank Policy Research Paper.*

Kosack, S. (2003). 'Effective Aid: How Democracy Allows Development Aid to Improve the Quality of Life', *World Development*, 31(1): 1-22.

Kuznets, S. (1955). 'Economic Growth and Income Inequality', *American Economic Review*, 45: 1-28.

Mallik, G. (2008). 'Foreign Aid and Economic Growth: A Co-integration Analysis of the Six Poorest African Countries', *Economic Analysis & Policy*, 38(2): 251-260.

Minoiu, Camelia and Sanjay G. Reddy (2009). 'Development Aid and Economic Growth: A Positive Long-Relation Approach', *IMF Working Paper*, WP/09/118.

Morrissey, O. (2001). 'Does Aid Increase Growth?', *Progress in Development Studies*, 1:(1).

Organization for Economic Cooperation and Development (2009). *Online Database.*

Quazi, R.M. (2005). 'Effects of Foreign Aid on GDP Growth and Fiscal Behaviour: An Econometric Case Study of Bangladesh', The *Journal of Developing Areas*, 38(2): 95-117.

Panizza, U. (2002). 'Income Inequality and Economic Growth: Evidence from American Data', *Journal of Economic Growth*, 7(1): 25-41.

Papanek, G.F. (1972). 'The Effect of Aid and Other Resource Transfers on Savings and Growth in Less Developed Countries', *Economic Journal*, 82(327): 935–50.

Pedersen, K.R. (2001). 'The Samaritan's Dilemma and the Effectiveness of Development Aid', *International Tax and Public Finance*, 8: 693-703.

Rajan, R. and A. Subramanian (2008). 'Aid and Growth: What Does the Cross Country Evidence Really Show?' *The Review of Economics and Statistics*, 90(4): 643-65.

Sakyi, Daniel (2011). 'Trade Openness, Foreign Aid and Economic Growth in Post-Liberalisation Ghana: An Application of ARDL Bound Test', *Journal of Economics and International Finance*, 3(3): 146-56.

Sen, A. (1983). 'Development: Which Way Now'? *Economic Journal*, 93(372): 745-62.

Shafiullah, Muhammad (2011).'Foreign Aid and Its Impact on Income Inequality'. *International Review of Business Research Papers*, 7 (2): 91-105.

Singh, D. Ram (1985). 'State Intervention, Foreign Economic Aid, Savings and Growth in LDCs: Some Recent Evidence', *KYKLOS*, 38(2): 216-32.

Snyder, W. Donald (1993). 'Donor Bias Toward Small Countries: An Overlooked Factor in the Analysis of Foreign Aid and Economic Growth', *Applied Economics*, 25: 481-88.

Svensson, J. (2000). 'Foreign Aid and Rent-Seeking', *Journal of International Economics*, 51: 437-461.

World Bank (2011). *World Development Indicators. Online Database.*

13

Consumption Inequality in India

An Analysis of New Trends

Ranjan Kumar Nayak

The important socio-political and economic ideals enshrined in the Constitution of India are to reduce inequalities and promote equality among all sections of Indian population irrespective of caste, colour, creed, language, religion, ethnicity and region. The planning era of Indian economy during 1950-1980 did not give up the objective, at least in rhetoric. However, introduction of neo-liberal policies seemed to have veered the nation into a different direction. Rising inequalities have been glaring. Several studies have indicated the effects of the policies and rising tide of inequality in the economy. Data limitations have always constrained inequality studies, while inequality is a multidimensional issue covering income, wealth, skills, education, health and even cultural aspects. Given data constraints, most studies examined consumption inequality, because of availability of NSS data. However, there are several ways of estimating consumption inequality. This paper is a modest attempt to examine patterns of consumption inequality and causes of inequality in India.

Since the onset of economic liberalization in the early 1990s, the facts suggest escalating inequality. The macroeconomic policies perhaps accountable for these trends include—fiscal tightening, expenditure cuts, regressive tax policies and financial sector reforms that reduced the flow of institutional credit to small producers and agriculturalists; leading to more regional imbalance and skewed investment patterns. Added to that, liberalization of rules for foreign and domestic investment and trade liberalization have affected livelihoods and employment generation.

Indian policymakers have always shown their concern on the reduction of inequality. However, between the First Five Year Plan after Independence in 1947 and at the turn of the century, Indian economic policy making went through a sea change. After independence and for an episode of about forty years, India followed an economic intervention policy based on central planning. The pace of policy change was, however, accelerated in the early 1990s, when the explicit adoption of neo-liberal reform programmes marked the beginning of a period of intensive economic liberalization and changed attitudes towards state intervention in the economy. As Chakravarty (1987) pointed out, one of the reasons for adopting an interventionist economic policy was the fear that total reliance on the market mechanism would cause in excessive consumption by upper-income groups, along with comparative under-investment in sectors vital to the development of the economy. According to Chakravarty (1987: 10), policymakers in India adopted a middle path, in which "there was a tolerance towards consumption inequality, provided it was not excessive and could be seen to result in a higher rate of growth than would be possible otherwise." In this framework, however, the macroeconomic understanding to inflation as fallout of growth reflected government concerns regarding the redistributive effects of inflation, which typically affected peasants, workers and the unorganized sectors more.

Contemporary Literature on Inequality Studies

Most studies have looked at inequality in terms of consumption expenditure and the unit of analysis is households. But there are some studies, which have tried to address the inequality issue through credit, human development index, income, physical and social infrastructure. The most important aspect here is the measurement. The commonly used inequality measure is Gini coefficient. Few studies have taken some different measures like coefficient of variation, Theil index, Atkinson's index, Population Weighted Gini index, Hoover's index, Couler's index, and log mean deviation, the logarithm difference of arithmetic and geometric mean and variance of logarithm. One of the studies has taken the Lorenz curve technique to analyze the inequality.

In the received literature, Deaton and Dreze (2002) have noted that the increasing inequality in 1990s is a new development in the Indian economy. They also have refuted the well known Kuznet's curve argument in favour of increasing economic inequality. According to them it is a graph with measures of increased economic development (presumed to correlate with time) on the horizontal axis, and measures of income inequality on the vertical axis hypothesized by Kuznets (1955) to have an inverted-U-shape. The argument is the trend of increasing inequality is short lived and it is as per expectation due to the liberalization.

On the other hand, Singh, Khare *et al.* (2003) have argued that the conclusion is sensitive to the measure of inequality taken by the specific study. They have used the consumption expenditure by taking data from the Planning Commission's National Human Development Report. They have used these data to perform a regression to test for absolute convergence in per capita consumption expenditure across states. They argue that between 1993-94 to 1999-2000 'the interstate disparities in well-being have not been worsened'.

In contrast, Sen and Himanshu (2005) provide evidence of increase in inequality in post-reform period. Their analysis based on the real mean per capita expenditure by fractile groups showed that while the consumption level of the upper tail of the population including top 20 per cent of rural population went up remarkably during the 1990s, the bottom 80 per cent of rural population suffered during this period. Another study undertaken by Dev and Ravi (2007) is also showing almost same trend as suggested. Bhalla (2003) has, however, shown that both rural and urban Gini coefficient of inequality have declined by 0.20 from 28.5 and by 0.31 from 34.31 between 1993-94 and 1999-2000.

A study by Sripad Motiram and Vakulabharanam (2011) has also highlighted the similar points as most of the earlier studies did by taking the measure Gini coefficient, and using the data from NSSO. Their result shows that inequality was decreasing between 1983 and 1993-94, although the decrease was very marginal. But later on the inequality has increased between 1993-94 to 2004-05. The Gini value of inequality was almost same between 1983 to

1993-94, while between 1993-94 to 2004-05 the Gini value reflecting inequality increased to a marked extent.

Motiram and Vakulabharabam (2011) had used the Indian Human Development survey data conducted by the National Council of Applied Economic Research (NCAER) for 1994 and 2004-05. Their findings show that the Gini coefficient of inequality in per capita income was 0.43 in rural India in 1994 but it increased to 0.50 in 2004-05. Similarly, in urban area the Gini coefficient of inequality in per capita income stood at 0.47 in 1994 and this had increased to 0.51 in 2004-05. The ratio of the income of the average person in the 10th percentile to the median was 38.89 per cent, whereas the ratio of the income of the average person in the 90th percentile to the median was 347.60 per cent (Motiram & Vakulabharanam, 2011). Pinaki Chakraborty (2009) also basically tried to portray how the rise in inequality in income and consumption can affect the access to various public services (like Health and Education).

Trends in Consumption Inequality in India

This study is based on secondary data. The required data have been collected from the National Sample Survey Organization (NSSO) on consumption expenditure, adapting it to the particular class structure used. The period of study is from 1983-2010. The indicators used for the purpose to find out the inequality trend are: (i) the ratio of urban-rural consumption, (ii) consumption ratio of different Groups, and (iii) growth rate related to average consumption of rural and urban. The study uses the Modified Mixed Reference Period MPCE (or MPCEMMRP) which is obtained by the consumer expenditure survey when household consumer expenditure on edible oil, egg, fish and meat, vegetables, fruits, spices, beverages, refreshments, processed food, pan, tobacco and intoxicants is recorded for a reference period of "last 7 days", and for all other items, the reference period is "last 365 days".

Then the combined ratio estimate ($\hat{R}$) of the ratio (*R= X/ Y)* is obtained as $\hat{R} = \hat{X} / \hat{Y}$. Where, $\hat{X}$ and $\hat{Y}$ be the overall estimates of the aggregates X and Y for two characteristics x and y respectively at the State/UT/all-India level.

The inequalities in consumption across the sectors and classes may be presented as follows:

Overview of ratio of urban to rural consumption, Rural per capita consumption, Consumption by urban groups, Consumption ratio of different groups, Growth rate of average rural consumption by decile groups in percentage, and Growth rate of average consumption by urban decile groups.

Fig. 13.1 shows that the average urban consumption (at constant 2009-10 prices) has been increasing much faster than rural consumption, and the latter, in fact, narrowed off in the most recent five-year period. The ratio of urban to rural consumption rose from 1.79 in 1983 to 1.96 in 2009-10, with the most rapid widening of the gap coming after 2004-05. But even within locations, there were significant differences between the upper and lower ends of the consumption spectrum in the matter of time trends.

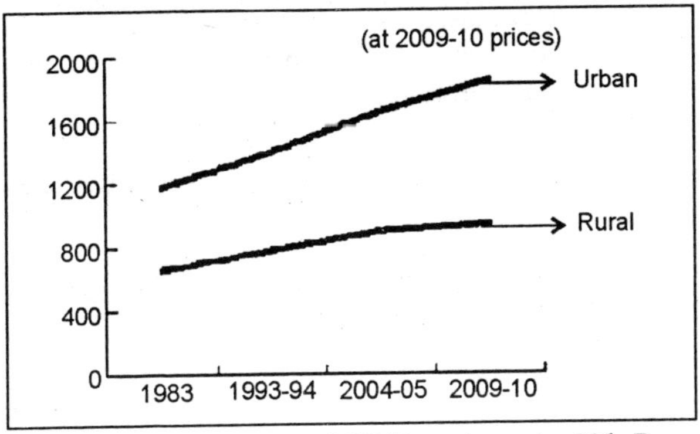

Source: Compiled from Various NSS Rounds up to 66th Round (July 2009 – June 2010).

Fig. 13.1: Average Per Capita Consumption (Monthly) in Rupees

As manifest from Fig. 13.2, in rural areas, it is actually only the top decile that shows noteworthy increases in per capita consumption after 1993-94. The relative constancy of consumption for all the other groups is remarkable, particularly given that this was a period of rapid GDP growth.

Unquestionably, there was hardly any change in per capita consumption of rural people between 2004-05 and 2009-10, not only for the lowest quintile of the population, but also for the next

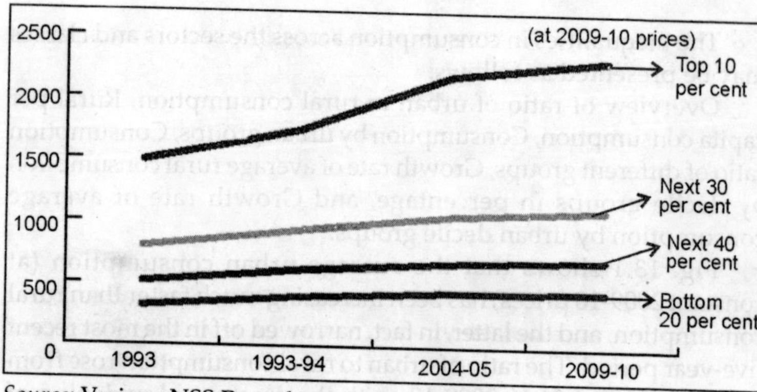

Source: Various NSS Rounds up to 66th Round.

Fig. 13.2: Rural Per Capita Consumption (Monthly) in Rupees

40 per cent and even for the following 30 per cent just underneath the top decile.

Within the rural areas, thus, only the top decile benefited from the aggregate income growth in a manner, so as to be able to increase their consumption appreciably.

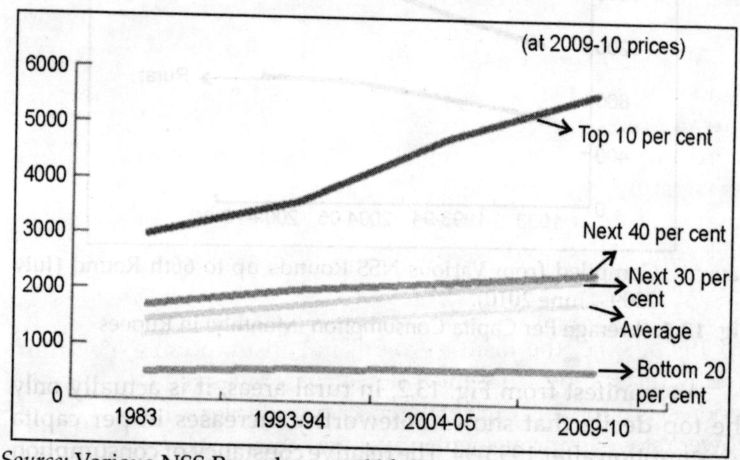

Source: Various NSS Rounds up to 66th Round.

Fig. 13.3: Monthly Consumption by Urban Groups

Fig. 13.3 indicates the degree to which the consumption of the top decile has zoomed far exceeding all the other groups. Incidentally, it should be borne in mind that the NSSO surveys generally and probably increasingly underestimate the consumption expenditure of the rich, so that the consumption of the top ten per cent is likely to be even higher than indicated here.

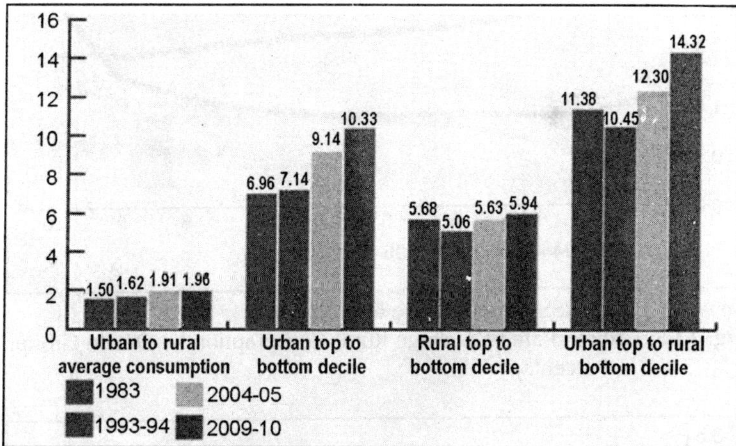

Source: Various NSS Rounds up to 66th Round.

Fig. 13.4: Consumption Ratio of Different Groups

Fig. 13.4 suggests that consumption process has not been smoothly steady through the whole period since 1983. Indeed, in rural areas, the gap between top and bottom deciles in consumption spending fell slightly and then increased only marginally, thereby remains broadly the same over the entire period. This is in sharp contrast to urban India, where the gap between richest and poorest deciles increased consistently and even sharply.

From Fig. 13.5, an exciting pattern emerges in the decade 1983 to 1993-94, i.e. the fastest growth in consumption expenditure (notwithstanding from much lower base) was registered by the poorest groups, and each of the successive deciles exhibited slightly lower rates of improvement in average consumption. This suggests a progressive pattern of consumption distribution at the margin. In both of the other periods (1993-94 to 2004-05 and 2004-05 to 2009-10) the pattern was reversed, with the richest deciles showing the fastest growth rates of consumption.

The pattern for urban areas, as evident from Fig. 13.6, is only slightly different. In the decade 1983 to 1993-94, the rate of growth

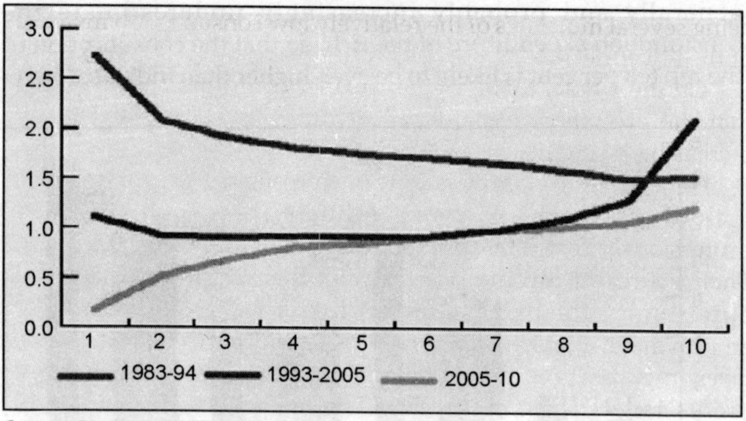

Source: Various NSS Rounds up to 66th Round

Fig. 13.5: Growth Rate of Average Rural Consumption by Decile Groups in Percentage

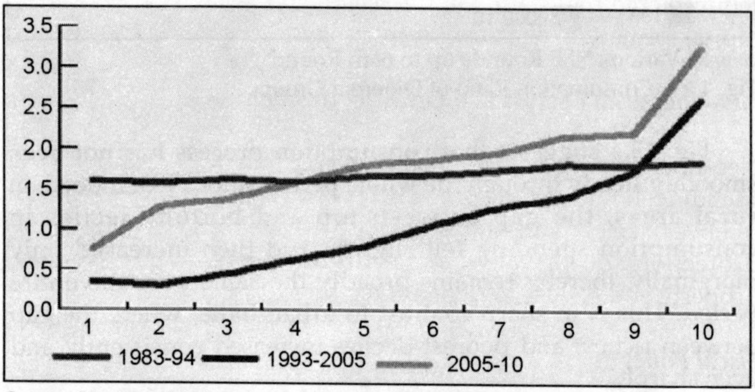

Source: Various NSS Rounds up to 66th Round.

Fig. 13.6: Growth Rate of Average Consumption by Urban Decile Groups

of consumption increased with decile (rising from the lowest to the highest) but only marginally, so that the difference in rates of growth across consumption decile were not significant, as indicated by the relatively flat line in Fig. 13.6.

However, in both of the other periods, the trend of accentuated inequality was marked with increasing trend—with the rate of growth increasing quite sharply as one moved across consumption deciles, and the rate of growth of consumption of the top deciles being several multiples of the relatively low consumption increase of the lower deciles.

On the whole, this provides further confirmation of the fact that the growth process of recent times has been marked by increasing inequality.

Generally top class constitute businessmen, top professionals including doctors, lawyers, industrialists, managers, IT professionals, real-estate brokers, politicians and the bureaucrats. Their source of income rise faster in their business. Increased opportunity for private sector, increased casualisation of employment, reduced tax rates, decreased customs and excise taxes, privatization, deregulation, etc. all these would increase profits, reduce share of wages and on the other hand corruption by giving land to mining companies creating financial booms.

The factors that account inequality between urban and rural consumption are declining in terms of trade, reduced subsidies, reduced credit allocation to the sector, and reduced government capital formation, neglect of technology.

Neo-liberalism Factors and Growing Inequality

Neo-liberalism principles include government's reduced deficit spending, limit subsidies, reform tax laws to broaden the tax base, remove fixed exchange rates, open up markets to trade by limiting protectionism, privatize state-run businesses, allow private property and restore deregulation.

Fiscal Policy

A vital element of the economic reform process adopted in India was the belief that a high fiscal deficit level was responsible for the 1991 crisis, and the deficit should, therefore, be brought down to a certain pre-determined target. It was argued that a high fiscal deficit is bad for an economy because it can be inflationary, can give rise to external deficits, can lead to high interest rates and therefore, crowd-out private investment, and can put an unsustainable interest rate burden on an economy through accumulation of public debt[1].

It can be concluded that the fiscal policy measures initiated in the reform period did not allow the government to build up productive capacity in the economy. Lack of public investment dampened aggregate demand, negatively affected private investments, created infrastructure bottlenecks to future growth, and adversely affected the provision of important public services. Moreover, in a developing country, where capital expenditure on infrastructure and social services tends to crowd in private investment, reduced expenditure on these sectors led to the crowding out of private investment. As a result of reduced public and private investment, there was inadequate productive employment generation, both in rural and urban areas. This was a key factor behind the increased inequality and slows down poverty reduction in the country.

Financial Sector Reform

Financial liberalization was considered to bring about the following objectives: (a) make the central bank more independent; (b) relieve financial repression by freeing interest rates, and introduce various new financial instruments and innovations in the Indian financial system; (c) reduce directed and subsidized credit; and (d) allow greater openness and freedom for various forms of external capital flows. It should be noted that these objectives were not realized in full, and indeed, the lack of completeness of such financial liberalization has been one important reason for the relative financial stability of the country, unlike several other 'emerging markets'.

The most unfavourable effects of financial liberalization on inequality came from policies which eased 'priority sector'[2] lending norms for nationalized banks. Until the 1980s, nationalized banks had obligations to fulfil priority sector lending targets. But in post-liberalization, the priority sector definition was widened to include many more activities, and the emphasis on banking shifted towards maintaining the capital adequacy level prescribed by the Basle accord. As a consequence, most banks now evade lending to small farmers and small scale industries, as they are supposed to be less creditworthy customers. This has had vivid effects on the viability of cultivation and small enterprises, which are the largest employers in the country, and has, therefore, indirectly impacted income distribution and poverty reduction.

It has been observed that there is reduced credit allocation to the small scale industries and small farmers which results in decline in their income and leads to decrease in consumption level and patterns.

Liberalization of Foreign and Domestic Investment

Enormously skewed inter-state distribution of domestic and foreign direct investment (FDI) has also contributed to increased inter-regional disparities in India. There is also a strong regional disparity in the pattern of FDI flows, with the southern and western states faring much better than the other parts of the country. Three southern states (Andhra Pradesh, Karnataka and Tamil Nadu) received more than 20 per cent of total FDI, while Maharashtra and Gujarat (both in Western India) received 17.35 per cent and 7.7 per cent of FDI respectively. In contrast, the seven North-Eastern states together received only 0.03 per cent of total FDI during the same period. This unequal distribution of FDI across states in India is not unexpected, as FDI inflows tend to move towards states with better infrastructure and development. The concentration of FDI in a few pockets in India, therefore, did not help to reduce inequality during the reform period.

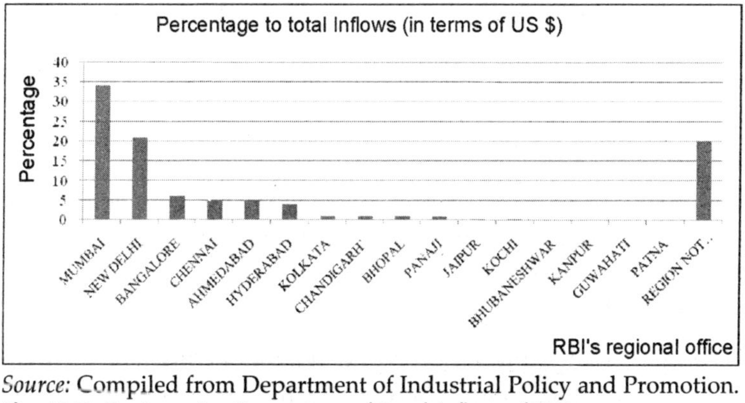

Source: Compiled from Department of Industrial Policy and Promotion.
Fig. 13.7: Region-wise Percentage of Total Inflow of FDI

The regional distribution of FDI inflows in Fig. 13.7 shows highly concentrated patterns. Five regional offices received around more than 70 per cent of Indian FDI inflows. Mumbai, New Delhi, and their surroundings include almost the half of the FDI received by India since 2000. The areas of Bangalore, Ahmedabad received 6 per cent and 5 per cent respectively and Chennai and Hyderabad each with 5 per cent. Then there are places surrounding Kolkata, Chandigarh and Panaji received around 1 per cent each of FDI investment and the rest by other regions/states of India.

Trade Liberalization

Trade is basically inequitable in nature since it distributes income in favour of the export sector and beside the import competing sector. Unless the gains from trade are redistributed, trade liberalization will always change income distribution, which may imply higher inequality. In India, an analogous phenomenon can be observed, but not necessarily along the lines predicted by traditional Hecksher-Ohlin trade theory. The more employment-intensive sectors have been adversely affected, rather than encouraged by trade liberalization. Opening up trade has helped certain sub-sectors, both in manufacturing and services, where India is internationally competitive, but mainly in activities using relatively skilled labour in the Indian context. By expanding the markets for these sectors, trade liberalization has definitely created some pockets of prosperity in India, but on the other hand, it has negatively affected most other manufacturing sectors and agriculture.

The decline terms of trade are another cause of increase in income inequality because the income elasticity of demand for manufactured goods is greater than that for primary products—especially food. Therefore, as incomes rise, the demand for manufactured goods increases more rapidly than demand for primary products that the rural people consume more.

Conclusion

In India, although there are claims that inequality has decreased in the post-liberalization period, careful analysis of data shows that these views are mostly unsubstantiated. Several authors have also pointed out that though the richer sections of the population benefited in the post-liberalization period, there has been a stagnation of incomes for the majority, with the bottom rung of the population severely negatively affected by this process. There is also evidence that, both at the national and the state levels, income disparities between the rural and urban sectors increased during this period. Thus, in nutshell we may say that adoption of neoliberal policies has led to an increase in economic inequality in India.

NOTES

1. Neo-liberal arguments against high fiscal deficits.
2. Small and medium scale enterprises and agriculture.

REFERENCES

Bhalla, Surjit S. (2002). 'Imagine there's no Country: Poverty, Inequality and Growth in the Era of Globalization', *Institute of International Economics.*

Chakraborty, Pinaki (2009). 'Intra Regional Inequality and the Role of Public Policy: Lesson learnt from Kerala', *Economic and Political Weekly*, 44(26 & 27), 27th June.

Chakravarty, Sukhamoy (1987). *Development Planning: The Indian Experience*. New Delhi: Oxford University Press.

Deaton, Angus and Jean Dreze (2002). 'Poverty and Inequality in India; A Re-examination', *Economic and Political Weekly*, 37: 7th September.

Dev, Mahindra S. and C. Ravi (2007). 'Poverty and Inequality: All India and States, 1983-2005', *Economic and Political Weekly*, 42(6), February 10-16.

Motiram Sripad and Vakulabharanam Vamsi (2011). 'Poverty and Inequality in the Age of Economic Liberalization' in Dilip Nachane (ed.) *India Development Report*, 2011, New Delhi: Oxford University Press.

Patnaik, Utsa (2007). 'Neoliberalism and Rural Poverty in India', *Economic and Political Weekly*, 42(30), July 28- 03 August.

Sen, Abhijit, and Himanshu (2004). 'Poverty and Inequality in India', *Economic and Political Weekly*, 39(38): 4247-63, 18-24 September.

Singh, Nirvikar, Laveesh Bhandari, Aoyu Chen and Aarti Khare (2003). 'Regional Inequality in India: A Fresh Look', *Economic and Political Weekly*, 38: 1069-73.

Vakulabharanm Vamsi (2010). 'Does Class Matter? Class Structure and Worsening Inequality in India', *Economic and Political Weekly*, 45(29), 17th July.

14

Post-Reform Closure and Sickness of Plantation Industry

Marginalisation of Workers and Vulnerability of Women and Children in Jalpaiguri, West Bengal

Biswajit Ghosh

Since economic liberalisation, the plantation industry of West Bengal (and other parts of the country) has witnessed major crises. Most of the gardens witnessed fall in production and profit due to low and inferior quality yield from ageing tea bushes as well as their inability to sell the products in the international market. Despite reopening of many closed gardens since 2007, they are yet functioning under the constant shadow of closure. The immediate upshot of sickness and closure of tea gardens fell directly on the workers, their family members and particularly children belonging to socially and economically marginalised tribal and non-tribal communities. Even though cases of starvation deaths have become rare today, a cursory visit to any tea garden would reveal that along with hunger, poverty, inequality and unemployment, problems like casualisation, unfair wages and non-payment of statutory benefits, non-implementation of provisions of Plantation Labour Act, drop-out of children, malnutrition and diseases are rampant. A combined effect of such vulnerabilities has further contributed to unsafe exodus and consequent trafficking of children and women in large proportions. As the 'enclave economy' of plantation industry provides very little alternative for the adolescent boys and girls, commission agents and touts have found it easy to expand their 'business' in the name of lucrative job placement. It is in this context that this paper, based on field research, tries to assess marginalisation of workers and vulnerability of women and children in 12 sick and closed tea gardens in Jalpaiguri, West Bengal. It would also try to suggest possible remedies to prevent such marginalisation and vulnerabilities.

Introduction

India's economic reforms introduced since early 1990's have left deep imprint on several aspects of its society and culture. It has by now become clear to many of us that *market globalism*[1] has failed to provide solutions to some of our major problems as it excludes many and includes only a few. Gains of globalisation have been grabbed and cornered mostly by certain specific classes, industries, states and regions leading to incremental inequality and disparity. There is consequent rise in rural-urban divide along with growth in structural inequalities despite high growth of GDP during the last few years. Inequality in opportunity is also evident among the rich-poor, skilled-unskilled, educated-uneducated, user and non-user of technology, men-women, low caste-high caste people and the like. Notwithstanding the existence of inequality in pre-liberalised India, our life today is characterised by sharp rise in inequities of multidimensional nature. Even though the income of a section of the poor working in the informal sector has experienced some rise during the last two decades, there is consensus about the fact that due to galloping inflation such rise in not reflected in better quality of life for them. Hence, even protagonists of reforms and supporters of 'inclusive growth' model today acknowledge that consumption inequality has sharpened deeply within and across regions despite some reduction in poverty. There are, however, sharp divisions among social scientists about the extent and nature of poverty in India and the methodology to calculate that. As statistical exercises related to calculation of inequality including estimates of GDP and GNP often leads to suppression and misrepresentation of facts, it is now being realised that even matter like poverty can be and should be measured qualitatively (Ghosh, 2012: 27). Any arithmetic measurement of quality of life including vulnerabilities of marginalised people and victims of disparity, distress, discrimination and displacement is neither possible not desirable. As Panini (2012) argues, 'vulnerability is a serious issue not just for the poor who are the victims of vulnerability but also for those above the poverty line...even relatively better off segments of farmers have been turned into vulnerable sections because the social and economic contexts have altered drastically.' For a nuanced understanding of emerging inequities, we therefore need to introspect into the processes of marginalisation as well as vulnerabilities of selected groups of people from qualitative points of view. The contention of this paper is to do so and it is based on the experiences of tea garden workers and their family members of 12 closed/sick gardens from Jalpaiguri district of West Bengal. Such field-based micro studies might not be very helpful to understand the totality of the situation; nevertheless they have the strength to expose the limits of macro analysis and thereby make us aware by the complexity of the situation.

Background of the Study

Since economic liberalisation, the tea industry of the Darjeeling hills, Terai and Dooars region of West Bengal (and other parts of the country as well) has witnessed major crises including the compulsion of the competitive international market. Like similar other labour concentrated traditional industries of the country like jute and engineering, economic reforms have exposed the workers to the vagaries of the market. Despite re-opening of many closed gardens since 2007, the problem of sickness and the consequent threat of closure could not be mitigated. Workers of many tea gardens witnessed recurring see-saw between closure/ abandonment and reopening. The immediate upshot of such sickness and closure fell directly on the workers, their family members and particularly children belonging to socially and economically marginalised tribal and non-tribal communities. It has been documented that in the first decade of the current century, many garden owners abandoned their tea gardens leaving behind large debts. Closure of tea gardens has brought to the fore starvation deaths, cases of workers being mauled by wild animals, trafficking of abandoned widows and children, increasing suicides and smuggling of contraband and burglary. Even today the tea garden workers on the whole live a life of destitute. The condition of workers in so called 'good' tea gardens is no different as poverty regime is ubiquitous under the 'low-wage system'.

The overall impact of such destitution on the family members and particularly on children and women is unimaginable. It has by now become clear that the situation of workers and their family members in the sick and closing tea gardens in the Jalpaiguri district is grim and it is fast deteriorating. A cursory visit to any tea garden would reveal that along with hunger, poverty and unemployment, problems like illiteracy, drop-out, malnutrition, and diseases are rampant. A combined effect of such vulnerabilities has further contributed to trafficking of children and women in large proportion. One would be surprised to stumble on countless stories of brutal exploitation of missing children including rape and death by unscrupulous agents and employers at far-off places. Astonishingly these stories constitute a significant part of public discourse at tea gardens even though protest against such heinous crimes is yet wanting. As the tea garden workers themselves are struggling for alternative means of livelihood to supplement their paltry income, boys and girls in the age group of 14-20 have developed a tendency to leave studies and go to places like Delhi or Kashmir for earning some cash. Evidently, the 'enclave economy' of Jalpaiguri tea gardens provides very little alternative for these unskilled and semi-literate boys and girls. Such vulnerability exposes them to the well built networks of trafficking agents working openly in the disguise of 'placement agent' within and outside the gardens. Surveys conducted on the tea gardens earlier (Talwar *et al.*, 2005, Dacholia *et al.*, 2006) including an assessment survey by *Save the Children* in recent times show a very grim picture of child and women trafficking particularly from the sick and closed tea gardens. What is more alarming is that there is absolute apathy amongst the parents and other stakeholders on this issue.

Methodology

It is in this context that this research[2] was carried out during May-July 2011 to assess the extent of marginalisation of workers and vulnerabilities of women and children in 12 sick and closed tea gardens in Jalpaiguri of West Bengal (*see* Table 14.1), one of the richest districts of India in terms of production of tea. These gardens were first selected after discussion with members of research teams and experts, and finalised after field visits on the basis of accessibility and initial status report. Till now, issue of vulnerabilities of tea garden workers and family members has not received due and appropriate attention though visual media centres and local press have sporadically shown/published reports about child trafficking. It is high time that we give serious attention to the issues faced particularly by women and children in the tea gardens of Jalpaiguri district and seek remedial actions to mitigate their sufferings.

Table 14.1: Names, Location and Status of Tea Gardens Studied

Sl. No.	*Name of Tea Gardens*	*Location (Block)*	*Current Status as on 31-7-2011*	*Date of Closure*	*Date of Re-opening*
1	Indong Tea Garden	Matelli	Sick	23rd November 2007	8th January 2008
2	Grassmore Tea Garden	Nagrakata	Sick	Closed for 3 days in August 2003	Not Applicable
3	Red Bank Tea Estate	Dhupguri	Sick	Abandoned in March 2003	13.3.2011
4	Chulsa Tea Garden	Matelli	Good	Not Applicable	Not Applicable
5	Nayasaili Tea Garden	Nagrakata	Sick	Not Applicable	Not Applicable
6	Samsing Tea Estate	Matelli	Sick	23.9.2005	17.8.2009
7	Bharnobari Tea Garden	Kalchini	Sick	30.12.2005	28.4.2008
8	Dheklapara Tea Estate	Madarihat	Closed	22.8.2002	Not Applicable
9	Radharani Tea Estate	Kalchini	Sick	18.3.2009	23.3.2011
10	Rahimabad Tea Garden	Kumargram	Sick	17.4.2002	4.5.2004
11	Raimatang Tea Estate	Kalchini	Sick	28.1.2005	13.8.2010
12	Satali Tea Garden	Kalchini	Good	Not Applicable	Not Applicable

Source: Field Study, July 2011.

As the objective of the research was to collect qualitative data about the nature, extent and dimensions of different types of vulnerabilities of children in particular, we have decided to collect specific data and opinion through the use of research tools like In-depth Key Informants Interviews (IKII), Participatory Rural Appraisal (PRA), Focused Group Discussion (FGD) and Case Study Method. It was not possible for us to conduct house-to-house survey in huge tea gardens each covering nearly 670 hectares (67 lakh square metre) on an average and having 1500 workers per garden on an average. Moreove, our research objective did not support such household survey. The study began by interviewing important stakeholders from the community. This was deliberately done to collect prior data on some critical issues before beginning the PRA and the FGD. Secondly, the PRA strategies (Body Mapping, Mobility Mapping, and Cause-Effect Matrix) allowed us much greater accessibility to certain issues of local community. The use of open-ended, adaptable visual methods within a flexible, interactive learning process generated important often surprising insights. A total of 36 PRAs were conducted for this study involving 310 participants and school girls constituted 80 per cent of them. For the FDGs, four groups of stakeholders from each tea garden, namely fathers, mothers, elders and children (boys/girls) were selected for intense debate and discussion on critical and sensitive issues like trafficking. Apart from the use of these research tools, case studies of trafficked victims were collected from victims, their family members, neighbours, school teachers, friends and others. In all, nearly 90 cases of trafficking of children and women were collected. On the whole, we conducted 180 IKII involving important stakeholders from the community apart from 3 PRAs and 4 FGDs from each garden making the total number of PRAs 36 and FGDs 48. The total number of formal informants in this study is 874 combining IKII (180), PRA (310) and FGD (384) participants together. This list does not include those who supplied us information informally. Despite some limitations, this study has been able to reveal and expose several unknown facts and facets about the vulnerabilities of workers and their family members in sick and closed tea gardens and analyse them in the overall context. It has combined different methods to overcome the limits and collected data from diverse sources to reach at certain general conclusions.

Closure and Sickness of Tea Plantation Industry since Economic Reforms

North Bengal has about 450 tea gardens spread out in the Darjeeling hills, Terai and Dooars region. A large number of tea gardens of Jalpaiguri and Darjeeling districts produce the famous "Dooars tea" and in Jalpaiguri itself there are nearly 160 tea gardens. It is estimated that more than 25,00,000 people are dependent directly or indirectly on the tea industry in the region. Demographically, Jalpaiguri is the largest district in North Bengal and is bounded by Bhutan (north) and Bangladesh (south). The economy of the town is centred on the tea industry. It is also one of the richest districts of India in terms of production of tea. Both the districts of Jalpaiguri and Darjeeling produce 20 per cent of India's tea with Jalpaiguri producing around 15 per cent. But with the onset of economic liberalisation in the country since 1991, the tea industry of the region has witnessed major crises. The high vulnerability of the tea industry of Jalpaiguri producing average tea then became evident due to surging competition from countries like Kenya, Sri Lanka, China, Indonesia, Vietnam and Turkey. Tea exports to big markets like Russian Federation, Iraq, United Arab Emirates, Afghanistan along with Europe and US declined sharply due to weaker demands (Dutt, 2007). Along with external reason, many internal factors have played critical role in exposing the workers of tea plantation to the vulnerabilities of the global market. Most of the gardens becoming sick and getting closed particularly after 2001 witnessed fall in production and profit due to low and inferior quality yield from ageing tea bushes. As per one estimate, more than 50 gardens had closed during 2000-2007 affecting a huge section of the workforce (NTUI, 2011). For any average tea bush, peak production period is generally considered to be when these are between 35 to 50 years old. But, many tea gardens in Jalpaiguri, including the ones we have studied, are more than 100 years old. Moreover, bushes give good yields only if they are properly maintained and nourished. But, as tea gardens have witnessed frequent changes in ownership particularly during the last two decades, a cursory visit to many of the gardens would let anyone feel that old bushes are neither cared, nor re-plantation is done on a large scale to replace them. Investment in machinery and factories and re-plantation had also been quite minimal in the past although

Government provides economic incentives for new plantation. Hence, re-opened gardens normally tether on the brink of closure now and then. It is, therefore, claimed that 50 per cent of the 318 gardens in the Terai and Dooars region in the state are sick (Gupta, 2008).

Despite reopening of many closed gardens since 2007 with the special financial assistance from the Government of India, they are yet functioning under the constant shadow of closure. In fact sickness is omnipresent in the tea plantation industry of Jalpaiguri. Table 14.2 reveals the existing liabilities of selected tea gardens. It appears that all gardens except a few 'good' ones have huge liabilities and workers doubt whether such dues would really be paid! Surprisingly, enough closed and re-opened gardens like Dheklapara and Raimatang do not have even any formal record of liabilities. One of the reasons for this is change in management of gardens. The new management shows no concern about the dues of the old. It may fairly be argued that there is hardly any qualitative difference between a 'sick' and 'closed' garden so far as the plight of workers are concerned. Except daily wages, all other statutory benefits are occasionally provided to a few workers in the sick gardens. The sea-saw between sickness and closure or between sudden opening of a garden to reap a harvest during the peak season (April-September) and abandonment during the slack season has become a common story of this industry. It has, however, been argued that 'sickness' of plantation industry is a 'good business' that promotes 'myopic profit motives' (Nagarik Mancha and NESPON, 2010). This is because, if any garden is declared 'sick' by the competent authority, it becomes eligible for 'rebate on salami' admissible in terms of a Government Order of 2004. The owner then is also absolved of his duty to pay provident fund or other dues of the workers temporarily. There are also instances of established companies declaring them 'sick' on the ground of huge liabilities so as to evade income tax.

One would be surprised to know in this context that The Tea Act, 1953 empowers the Central Government with special powers of investigation when the tea plantation is 'being managed in a manner highly detrimental to the tea industry or to public interest' and it can even take over the management of a tea plantation if the owner of such plantation has 'habitually made default in the payment of wages, or provident fund dues, of workers and other

Table 14.2: Total Liability of Sick and Closed Tea Gardens

Sl. No	*Name of Gardens*	*PF (Rs.)*	*Gratuity (Rs.)*	*Salary (Rs.)*
1.	Indong	No Record	No Record	No Record
2.	Grassmore	Rs. 88,56,293 approx	Rs. 43,12,121	No Record
3.	Red Bank	Rs. 85,24,000 approx	Rs. 57,57,300 approx.	Rs. 33,94,400
4.	Chulsa	Not Applicable	Not Applicable	Not Applicable
5.	Nayasaili	Rs. 2,88,77,345	50,12,914	Not Available
6.	Samsing	2 crore 50 lakh	Rs. 1 crore 50 lakh	Rs. 1 crore 20 lakh
7.	Bharnobari	2 crore Approx	Rs. 1.12 crore approx.	Not Available
8.	Dheklapara	No record to OMC	No record to OMC	No record to OMC
9.	Radharani	Rs. 71 lakh approx	Rs. 14.3 lakh approx.	No Record
10.	Rahimabad	Rs. 51,27,775	Rs. 18,53,499	Nil
11.	Raimatang	Not Available	Not Available	Not Available
12.	Satali	Not Applicable	Not Applicable	Not Applicable

Source: Official records till 31st July 2011

employees, or rent of the land, or duties of excise, or in the payment of such other dues as are obligatory under any law for the time being in force'. Furthermore, the Supreme Court in its order in August 2010 had directed the Central Government to invoke the Tea Act, 1953 to take over the gardens that are closed within six months. But, the Central Government has not only failed to stop closures in the industry, it has also failed to implement the Supreme Court order. Hence, owners continue to abandon their gardens and no action is initiated against the defaulters for the recovery of dues by the Tea Board or the Central Government as required by the law. A few of such gardens are, however, run by the Operative Management Committees (OMCs) – a committee initiated and formed with the workers of the garden to pluck tea leaves during pick season for providing survival sustenance to the workers. These OMCs, however, cannot mitigate the problems of workers as they offer a much lower wage (Rs. 45 per day) as compared to the officially declared wage of Rs. 67 a day (till 31st March, 2011).

Hence, this experiment only offers a stopgap arrangement rather than a solution to the ills of tea gardens.

Challenges of Tea Plantation Workers and their Family Members in Jalpaiguri

The immediate result of industrial sickness and consequent deprivations can be perceived on the life of the workers, their family members including children belonging to socially and economically marginalised tribal and other communities. When any owner abandons his tea gardens leaving behind large debts, workers are immediately deprived of their job and facilities required for their sustenance. As a corollary, closure of tea gardens has caused many starvation deaths in the past (Lahiri, 2006; Chowdhuri, 2007; Dean, 2007; JESA, 2007; Mitra, 2007). Cases of trafficking of abandoned widows and children and suicides also became a reality. It has been estimated by CHDR (2006: 26) that more than 3,000 workers of abandoned tea gardens of North Bengal have succumbed to starvation deaths in between 2002 and 2006. Studies also show that 70 per cent of the people of closed tea gardens are in the Chronic Energy Deficiency III stage (Biswas and Others, 2005). Surveys conducted on these closed gardens in the past also reveal that welfare schemes, the public distribution system and basic amenities like safe drinking water, healthcare, primary education and electricity are practically non-existent in those gardens (Choudhury *et al.*, 2007). Such pathetic working and living conditions led to large scale exodus of out of job labourers from these gardens to far off states and in the metropolises (Beck, 2007). Consequent upon several survey reports and press coverage of starvation deaths, sufferings, malnutrition and human trafficking as well as interventions by many stakeholders including the judiciary, the Central government had announced the Financial Assistance to the Workers in Locked-out Industrial units scheme (FAWLOI) for providing financial assistance to every worker of closed gardens. But, even such scheme did not extend the same benefit to the *bigha* or casual workers whose ratio to the permanent workers is now almost at 1:3 and is ever increasing with the managements moving towards more induction of casual workers especially in the cases of plucking for the inferior CTC tea. There are also instances of FAWLOI not implemented on time to provide the needed support to the fasting workers. In February 2009, a Commission led by Smt. Urmila Singh, visited some tea gardens in Jalpaiguri. The Commission had also noted that the 'major problems relating to tea gardens pertain to lack of educational and medical facilities, inadequate supply of drinking water, less representation of tribal people at local level in Government jobs, administration of tribal areas and deficiencies in implementation of various schemes under NREGA, lack of sports facilities etc.' (Report on the visit of the Commission 2009).

Ray (2012) has noted that while tribal economy of West Bengal has witnessed a decline in the number of household industry over the years, the 'other workers' category, that includes jobs in the tea gardens, in the offices or other organised sector, did not grow expectedly. Even in the Jalpaiguri district, which accommodates most of the tea gardens, the growth of jobs has only been 16 per cent during the last four decades. The slow growth of jobs in 'other worker' category has to be understood in the light of stagnation and the planters' refusal to recruit permanent worker—a feature termed as 'feminisation of workforce'. He, however, has noted that despite the widely talked 'crisis' in the tea industry in North Bengal, there has been a sharp increase in the number of tea plantation in the region: the increase has been from 343 in 1995 to 1540 in 2000 (Roy, 2009). Such rise did not contribute to any increase in the number of permanent workers as many of the small plantations today survive on 'bought leaf factories', a new development in the tea industry (Gupta, 2009). In other words, tea business did not shrink in Jalpaiguri though investment in machinery and workers has declined sharply. This typically reminds us about the onslaught of post-Fordist strategy of industrial restructuring that dominates the neo-liberal agenda of 'development'.

The fact that 'flexibility' and inequality has made inroad into the plantation industry can be proved by the findings of the present study. Thus, the average number of workers in 11 operating tea gardens is 1,500 though a few employed more than 2000 workers. Among the workers employed, 56 per cent are women and most of them (68%) are temporary (*see* Figures 14.1 and 14.2).

This supports both the casualisation and feminisation theses. It is worth noting here that 78 per cent of workers in the gardens are classified as 'permanent' even though most of them work on 'daily basis'. It should also be added that office and factory workers

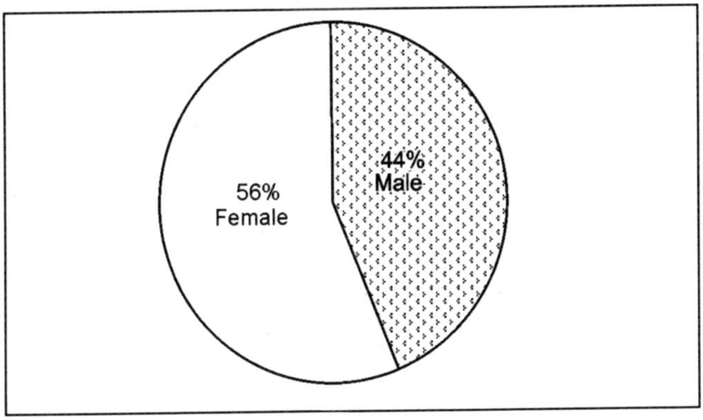

Source: Official records till 31st July 2011.

Fig. 14.1: Percentage of Workers Employed

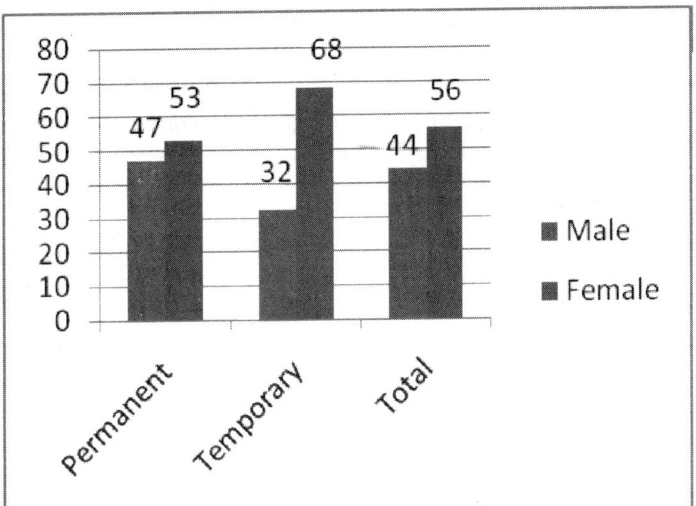

Source: Official records till 31st July, 2011.

Fig. 14.2: Types of Workers in 12 Tea Gardens

are mostly males and they receive better wage and non-wage benefits. An analysis of our field data also shows that while minimum daily wage is paid to all workers in running tea gardens, benefits like provident fund, gratuity and pension are paid to the permanent workers. The rate of bonus paid to workers also varies depending on the bargaining strength of the dominant trade union in a garden. The process of casualisation is also strengthened by increasing employment of children[3] during the season to pluck tea leaf on reduced rate (half of the wage of an adult worker). It appears that with growing constraints in the plantation industry, women and children are replacing the erstwhile male workers who migrated to these gardens three generations ago. This could also be due to the constant migration and mobility of young male workers from the garden.

The issues related to unfair wages and non-fulfilment of statutory benefits are matters of great concern today in the plantation industry. First of all, the *Plantation Labour Act, 1951* (PLA) classifies tea industry as industrial operations, yet the minimum wages paid to tea workers are lower than those of even agricultural workers (Dacholia and Others, 2006). The wages for the tea industry workers in North Bengal are determined through an industry-wise tripartite wage settlement that takes place after every three years. It has been shown by scholars working on the field that the wages of the workers in West Bengal (and in Assam) are the lowest among all other tea growing states of the country (Roy, 2009: 18; Bhowmik, 2011a: 26). This gives rise to the claim that employment conditions in the tea industry in West Bengal are highly exploitative. Unlike the industrial workers, the minimum wage of a tea worker comprises components of cash and kind. The cash component, as of 31st March, 2011, was Rs. 67 a day. The factory workers are provided some extra incentives. By any standard, the combined monetary value of both the cash and non-cash components would not be more than Rs. 90 a day. This is far below a need-based minimum wage paid to workers under the MGNREGA in March 2011. It has been calculated that a daily worker earns slightly above Rs. 1,700 a month during the pick season (April to September) as they are not paid for Sundays. During lean season, their income drastically comes down to between Rs. 800 to 1,000 a month. This being the condition of workers in tea garden, different trade unions have recently demanded manyfold increase in the minimum daily wage rate of workers. It is also demanded, for the first time, that wage increase should look into the length of service of a worker. This is important because whenever the minimum wage is revised, all workers, irrespective of their seniority, get the same wage (Bhowmik *ibid.*, 28). Finally, after seven months of hard negotiations, a tripartite agreement was signed between the trade unions, management and the state government on 4th November, 2011 (Anandabazar Patrika, 2011). As per this agreement, the wage rate has been increased to Rs. 85 for the first year, Rs. 90 for the second year and Rs. 95 for the third year. The contending parties have also agreed to introduce 'variable dearness allowance' (VDA) within six months.

Secondly, there are serious complaints about non-cash benefits being ignored by the management. These non-cash component include: (a) subsidized ration for wife and two dependent children for a male worker and only two dependent children for female workers; (b) firewood entitlement of two and half piles to each permanent worker per year; and (c) housing entitlement consisting of *pucca* and *non-pucca* houses among others. Interestingly, an employer is supposed to ensure these non-cash provisions along with many others like fringe benefits like free medical care, safe drinking water, electricity, transport, support for children's education, crèches, house repair etc., as per the PLA. In view of the geographically secluded nature of tea plantations, the PLA mandates that employers should provide these fringe benefits to workers and their family members. Considered one of the finest pieces of labour legislation for ensuring good working conditions, this Act was the result of a long drawn struggle by tea workers. But, it has been time and again demonstrated that many employers dither on meeting these basic needs resulting in poor living conditions of the workers. Table 14.3 gives a brief view of the non-wage and fringe benefits actually provided to the workers of 12 gardens. It is a pity that illiteracy and ignorance of migrant tribal workers, multiplicity of trade unions, geographical isolation, apathy of the governments and fragmentation of workers on ethnic lines (Adivasi *vs*. Nepali) in recent times have allowed a safe and free hand to the owners. Bhowmik (2011b) has, therefore, argued that in the plantation industry of West Bengal low wages were built into the system and the workers were helpless in this regard. He has further argued that largely due to their ethnic status and isolation within the plantations, the workers have remained marginalised over the years (Bhowmik, 1981, 2011a: 26). The *adivasi* workers, who constitute the majority in the plantation industry, are the worst sufferer due to a combination of several economic and social factors.

Table 14.3: Non-Wage and Fringe Benefits Actually Provided to the Workers

Sl. No.	*Name of Tea Gardens*	*Casual Leave (Yearly 10 Days)*	*Maternity Leave (90 days, wage for 42 days)*	*Sick Leave (Yearly 14 days)*	*Holidays (14 National & Festival Days)*	*Annual Leave (1 day for 20 working days)*	*Non-cash/Fringe Benefits (Ration, Tea, Firewood/ kerosene, Apron, Umbrella, Chappal etc.)*
1.	Indong	Office Staff only	Yes, but one has to bargain	2/3 of wage for daily workers	Permanent Workers only	Permanent Workers only	Ration Irregular, Other benefits occasionally provided
2.	Grassmore	Office Staff only	Yes, but one has to bargain	2/3 of wage	Permanent Workers only	Permanent Workers only	Irregular
3.	Red Bank	Nil	Nil	Nil	Nil	Nil	Nil
4.	Chulsa	Office Staff only	Yes	2/3 of wage	Permanent Workers only	Permanent Workers only	All Benefits provided
5.	Nayasaili	Office Staff only	Yes	2/3 of wage	Permanent Workers only	Permanent Workers only	Irregular
6.	Samsing	Office Staff only	Yes	2/3 of wage	Permanent Workers only	Permanent Workers only	Nil
7.	Bharnobari	Office Staff only	Yes	2/3 of wage	Permanent Workers only	Permanent Workers only	Nil; Ration not given for last 6 months, other benefits not given since 2005
8.	Dheklapara	Nil	Nil	Nil	Nil	Nil	Nil
9.	Radharani	Office Staff only	Yes	2/3 of wage	Permanent Workers only	Permanent Workers only	Benefits yet to be given
10.	Rahimabad	Office Staff only	Yes	2/3 of wage	Permanent Workers only	Permanent Workers only	Nil; After 24kgs of tea plucking Rs. 1 per kg.
11.	Raimatang	Office Staff only	Yes	2/3 of wage	Permanent Workers only	Permanent Workers only	Benefits given, Stipend for students from Tea Board
12.	Satali	Office Staff only	Yes	2/3 of wage	Permanent Workers only	Permanent Workers only	All Benefits provided

Source: Official records of the Tea Garden Managements, OMC and Trade Unions (till 31st July, 2011).

It must also be noted here that as per the PLA, all tea gardens are supposed to appoint Labour Welfare Officer (LWO) to look after the general well-being of the workers. But except a few, they are not appointed. For instance, among the gardens studied only Satali has a LWO. Also, there is a provision for appointment of Labour Commissioners at every sub-division of the district by the government to see whether the legal framework and rules/ regulation are maintained or not. But, many of such posts are lying vacant and it is also alleged that these bureaucrats collide with the management and don't pay any heed towards blatant denial of human rights to the workers and their families.

It may be noted that problem of non-availability of ration and fringe benefits arises as and when a garden becomes sick and faces shortages of fund to meet essential requirements. Additionally, whenever any new management takes over the responsibility of a garden, it does not care for the outstanding entitlements of ration or other benefits. On the whole, therefore, non-fulfilment of non-cash entitlements adds up to the miseries of the parents and their children. When a worker does not receive ration and other non-cash benefits on time, it literally becomes difficult for him to meet even the food requirements of the family. The onus falling on the children is felt more if the parents are alcoholic, family is large[4], someone is very sick or if there is only one income earner in the family. It is in such a context government schemes like MGNREGA may turn out to be significant for the poverty ridden workers of plantation industry. But, as our field experience reveals, except a few cases, progress made in implementing this flagship scheme during 2009-10 is far from appealing[5]. There is, therefore, every reason to argue for the rights of plantation workers and their children living and growing under the shadow of threat, vulnerabilities and uncertainties.

The district administration has, however, attempted to open seven tea gardens with the package of Mahatma Gandhi National Rural Employment Guaranty Act (MGNREGA) in between July 2009 and March 2010. Another three gardens were opened by October 2010 (District Magistrate, 2011). Hence, the administration claimed to have solved the 'most glaring problem of the district and regenerate the old economy' (District Magistrate, 2011). But, 'all is not found to be well' and this study reveals the cavity of the claim in several respects. There are also claims regarding wage violation of NREGA in the tea plantation in the district (Radical Socialist, 2011). We have also witnessed large scale violation of the rights of plantation workers despite public outcry and adequate media attention. For instance, in Dheklapara Tea Estate – a remote and closed (since 2002) garden at Madarihat block of Jalpaiguri – the distress of 484 families of workers did not draw proper attention of the authority. Both the Central and the State governments are yet to show any real commitment towards the basic issues of poor. Hence, reports about starvation deaths intermittently flow from tea gardens (Chaudhury, 2011; *The Times of India*, 2012).

Quality of Life in Selected Tea Gardens

The prevailing economic hardship, social backwardness, absence of life supporting facilities, dearth of viable employment alternative and geographical isolation – all have collectively created an environment of catastrophe and disgust in the plantation industry. One direct consequence of this is poor performance of children in the realm of education. Dropout is rampant in the tea gardens. In Hasimara Hindi High School, for instance, 154 tribal girl students are enrolled in class five. The figure goes down to 88 only in class eleven. For the tribal boys, the figures are 151 and 43 for both the classes respectively. Lack of educational infrastructure including shortage of qualified teachers within gardens is the most important reason for this. Also poor parents cannot afford books, writing material, private tutor's fees and transportation costs. The illiteracy and ignorance of alcoholic parents, large size of family, unwillingness of children to study, lack of facilities like electricity road, and gender preference for the girl child are the other important reasons for poor educational performance of the children. During closure and consequent non-payment of essential benefits also, parents prefer to cut costs on education. Table 14.4 shows the availability of educational facilities within the gardens. Right to education is a basic human right and the blissfully the zeal for education has also reached the younger generation of *adivasi* workers today whose parents were mostly illiterate. Despite the craze for better education among the youngsters, Raimatang has only one Sarba Siksha Kendra (SSK) meant for beginners. Among others, three gardens have educational infrastructure for secondary students (MSK) and another two have higher secondary schools. It is obvious that after class four, many children of tea gardens have to travel to distant location to continue their studies. Lack of proper transport also puts obstacles for daily movement of students and labourers to other places of work. Only four tea garden owners (Chulsa, Radharani, Rahimabad and Satali) have so far arranged transportation of students by bus. But students have to pay for this. Given the economic conditions of worker's families and teeming modes of transportation, this appears to be a very difficult barrier for the children.

Table 14.4: Educational Facilities Available within Garden

Sl. No.	Name of Tea Gardens	Sarba Siksha Kendra (SSK)			Primary Level (Class 1-4)			MSK (Class 5-10)	High School
		SSK	No of teachers	Mid Day Meal	Primary School	No of teachers	Mid Day Meal		
1.	Indong	2	4	Yes	1	6	Yes	0	0
2.	Grassmore	3	6	Yes	1	3	Yes	1	0
3.	Red Bank	3	6	Yes	1	3	Yes	1	0
4.	Chulsa	2	4	Yes	1	7	Yes	0	0
5.	Nayasaili	2	4	Yes	1	4	Yes	1	0
6.	Samsing	4	8	Yes	1	10	Yes	0	1
7.	Bharnobari	2	8	Yes	1	10	Yes	0	0
8.	Dheklapara	0	0	Yes	1	4	Yes	0	0
9.	Radharani	1	3	Yes	1	2	Yes	0	0
10.	Rahimabad	0	0	0	1	5	Yes	0	1
11.	Raimatang	1	4	Yes	0	0	0	0	0
12.	Satali	2	6	Yes	1	3	Yes	0	0

Source: Data collected from SSK, Primary, MSK and High schools within respective tea gardens, July 2011.

Along with education, health conditions of workers and their children bear the imprint of acute distress. Non-availability of required health facilities within tea gardens is a prime issue to children and their family members. Figure 3 provides a glimpse of health facilities available within selected gardens. We were shocked to find that for an estimated population of 70,000, there are only two doctors in equal number of gardens and hence the task of treating patients in ten other gardens is left to some nurses and staff. In case of Dheklapara, the condition is even worse and people there have to depend on a health sub-centre located at a

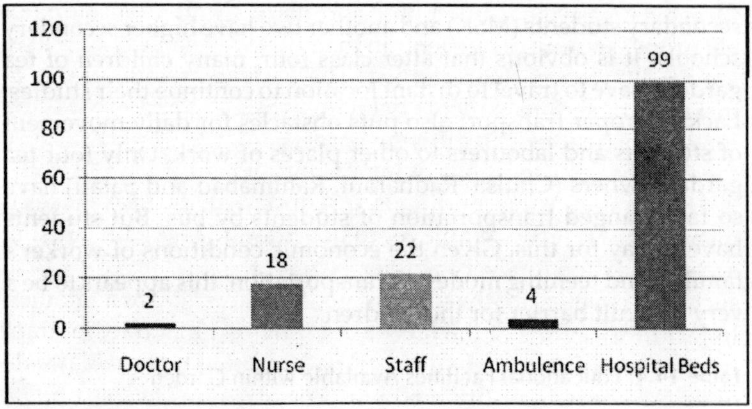

Source: Data collected from Health Centres/Dispensaries, July 2011.

Fig. 14.3: A Glimpse of Health Facilities Available within 12 Tea Gardens

distance of 2 km from the garden. It is also expected that a patient requiring continuous medical care would remain under the observation of doctors within a garden hospital. But, such facility is not there in four tea gardens (Grassmore, Nayasaili, Dheklapara, and Satali) and Bharnobari has only two seats for patients. Again, only four gardens have ambulance to take serious patients out. There are also complaints about the quality of services provided by health professional including the medicines given. It has been complained by many that garden health professionals, if available, give the same medicine for different types of diseases. This clearly reveals that there is acute shortage of medicines at garden hospital or dispensary. Considering the fact that tea garden workers are exposed to several occupational diseases like TB and the gardens are located far away from government hospitals, absence of proper medical facilities including qualified doctors is a matter of major concern for workers and their family members. Furthermore, those seeking medical services outside have to run from pillar to post to reimburse their bills. Surprisingly, conditions of so-called 'good' gardens do not differ strikingly in this respect.

It has been observed that along with tuberculosis, diseases like cholera, diarrhoea, typhoid are common here. Children equally suffer from water borne diseases due to consumption of impure and infected water as well as poor sanitation inside gardens. Again, drains are all *kutcha* (temporary) and these are not cleaned.

Moreover, garbage is piled here and there. Children also do not get proper amount of nutrients in their diet. Vegetables and pulses are hardly seen in their diet list. There are, therefore, plenty of instances of serious patients delaying treatment and even dying for want of treatment in different gardens. All these clearly expose the poor health conditions of inhabitants of tea gardens.

So far as housing conditions are concerned, the PLA makes it mandatory for 'every employer to provide and maintain housing accommodation for every worker'. Under the 'low-wage' system, such help is a must for the safety of poor workers and their families. In fact this was one of the incentives provided to attract migrant tribal workers since early days. It may be noted that *pakka* (made of brick) houses constitute 60 per cent of houses as per official records of managements of 12 tea gardens. Surprisingly, however, even though workers are provided some accommodation by the employers, we found many of them in depleted conditions. This is because employers on an average did not take care to repair the houses for years together. This forces the workers to carry out very essential repair on their own. In case of only two gardens, repair work is undertaken by the employer and in another, some BPL families got grant to construct houses under the Indira Awas Yojana (IAY) in recent times. Astonishingly, such grant to construct house under the IAY was not extended to many other BPL families of other gardens.

It is obvious that if basic and life supporting facilities like medicine and qualified doctor are hardly available at tea gardens, other additional facilities would be non-existent. And the irony of fate is that workers also don't expect their employers to pay attention to issues. Hence, they just laughed at us when questions related to existence of permanent crèche, sanitation or conservancy were asked. Though some employers have recently introduced the concept of 'mobile crèche', children of mothers working in the garden are mostly provided temporary shelter under a tree by spreading a polythene sheet. Even this type of 'shelter' is not extended in all the gardens. Table 14.5 provides a brief status of some of the residual facilities that a plantation worker is entitled under the existing laws. The presence of health workers in varying degrees under the Integrated Child Development Services (ICDS) and Accredited Social Health Activist (ASHA) of the government in all the gardens is the only element of satisfaction for the parents

Table 14.5: Other Facilities Available within Select Gardens

Sl. No.	Name of Tea Gardens	Health Workers (Number)		Crèche	Drinking Water Source	Drainage	Electricity	Unemployment Assistance	Transportation facility	Any Other
		ICDS	ASHA							
1.	Indong	15	1	Mobile	Tap	Kutcha	Nil	Nil	Nil	Nil
2.	Grassmore	4	2	Mobile	Tap, well	Kutcha	Street Only	Nil	Nil	Nil
3.	Red Bank	6	1	Nil	Tap	Kutcha	Nil	Nil	Nil	Nil
4.	Chulsa	17	1	Temporary	Tap, well	Kutcha	Nil	Nil	Yes	Nil
5.	Nayasaili	7	5	Mobile	Tap	Kutcha	3 out of 6 lines	Nil	Nil	Nil
6.	Samsing	30	0	Temporary	Tap	Kutcha	Nil	Nil	Nil	Nil
7.	Bharnobari	23	3	Nil	Tap	Kutcha	Nil	Nil	Nil	Nil
8.	Dheklapara	1	1	Nil	Tap, well	Kutcha	Nil	Yes	Nil	AAY Ration
9.	Radharani	8	1	Temporary	Tap	Kutcha	Yes	Nil	Yes	Nil
10.	Rahimabad	8	3	Nil	Tap	Kutcha	Yes	Nil	Yes	Nil
11.	Raimatang	5	1	Temporary	Tap, hand pump	Kutcha	Nil	Nil	Nil	Nil
12.	Satali	14	0	Temporary	Tap, well	Kutcha	Nil	Nil	Yes	Nil

Source: Data collected from Garden management and Gram Panchayat, July 2011.

and children. Unemployment assistance is paid by the district administration to some workers of closed Dheklapara garden only though one may trace many unemployed persons in all the gardens. This is because the garden employer is bound to provide employment to only one adult member of a family.

Among others, absence of safe drinking water and electricity are the major issues for the inhabitants. Parents and children cutting across labour lines and gardens have complained about insufficient as well as very poor quality of drinking water provided to them by the employers. As the water tank supplying water to the workers is not cleaned regularly by the company, there are grievances against the management for gross violation of human rights of all. In certain gardens, the company has provided tube wells or hand pump to overcome the problem of drinking water. But these are few in numbers and cannot meet the demands of workers and their families. Similarly, electricity is available to the workers of only a few gardens. But even those few consumers having electricity at home have to pay huge monthly bill from their wages. It has been learnt that individual electric subscribers are not provided with any personal metres and the monthly rent is calculated by the company by dividing the total units consumed by all the users equally. This has shot up the rent for workers as office, managers and staff quarters using heavy electric gazettes pay equal to the sum paid by a poor worker using only two or three electrical points for some limited hours at night. Surprisingly, there are instances of management not paying the electric bills to the government even after deducting exorbitant amount from the workers' accounts. Some of such facts came to limelight only after the company became bankrupt and electric lines were removed by the government. Needless to say that most of the employers have also failed to ensure street lights in labour lines. Hence, just after the dusk, life within tea gardens becomes repetitive and boring. Excessive consumption of alcohol by the workers may also be explained from this point of view. The decline of plantation has accompanied the rise of alcohol industry within the gardens. Some of the unemployed workers have taken lead to unearth this alternative. But, it is equally true that after work the insiders have no opportunity to go for social mixing in a club, community hall, panchayat office, or even a trade unions office as these 'extension facilities' are located far away from the garden. Confinement within a limited circle has also promoted alcoholism, backwardness and ignorance among the parents who are mostly illiterate. Absence of electricity and similar other facilities like high schools, transport etc., in the gardens have also been a driving force for youngsters to abandon studies and go out in search of a life outside which appear to be promising, entertaining and colourful.

Exodus and Trafficking of Children and Women from Tea Gardens

For the younger generation, such a deplorable state of affair with no hope for any improvement in near future is intolerable. Even environment within home is often deplorable and domestic violence is not uncommon. It has, therefore, become a common practice for the adolescents to migrate to far away destinations often with the obvious knowledge and support of their parents, friends and neighbours. The PRA participants of this study have estimated that nearly 3,500 children have migrated from 12 tea gardens in 2010 alone. Among the key places of destination, Delhi attracts most of the job seekers followed by Kerala, Sikkim, Punjab, Bangalore and Bhutan. Table 14.6 shows that on an average nearly 300 children per year from each tea garden, nearly one-third of whom are girls, go out to different destinations in search of alternative livelihood. From closed and sick gardens, such mobility is very high obviously due to push factors. More importantly, the PRA findings disclose that not all children going out return home and nearly 8 to 10 children go 'missing' out of hundred migrating every year as they remain untraceable even after several years. It may happen that a few of the children missing have actually settled in their place of work. But, the stories of more than 70 missing children corroborate the close link between missing and trafficked children. There is no reason to believe that an *adivasi* settling in the place of work would not love to come back to see family members, take part in the community festivals or even maintain contact with friends over phone. Hence, it may strongly be argued that a large number of those 'missing' are actually trafficked. The experience of local NGOs and other stakeholders also corroborate this. It is worth noting here that agents, spreading their wings inside gardens, recruit child and youth by either luring them or fooling their parents. It is this network which manages trafficking silently and effectively.

Table 14.6: Mobility of Children by Sex from Tea Gardens from 12 Tea Gardens during 2010: Perception of PRA Participants

Sl. No.	Places where children go the most	Number of Children by Sex					
		Children Moving (Migration)			Children Missing		
		Boys	Girls	Total	Boys	Girls	Total
1.	Delhi	307	406	713	38	94	132
2.	Kerala	515	31	546	10	4	14
3.	Sikkim	230	180	410	15	25	40
4.	Punjab	302	100	402	12	10	22
5.	Bangalore	275	80	355	10	12	22
6.	Bhutan	225	42	267	18	12	30
7.	Siliguri	108	45	153	1	1	2
8.	Jalgaon	110	40	150	0	0	0
9.	Chandigarh	57	25	82	1	2	3
10.	Pune	80	0	80	3	2	5
11.	Ootty	45	15	60	2	1	3
12.	Nagaland	15	45	60	1	4	5
13.	Kalimgpong	20	40	60	3	6	9
14.	Rahimpur	20	40	60	0	0	0
15.	Kashmir	45	5	50	5	2	7
16.	Mumbai	10	35	45	1	5	6
17.	Hyderabad	30	0	30	3	0	3
18.	Kolkata	15	10	25	1	1	2
19.	Indore	20	0	20	1	1	2
20.	Lucknow	5	3	8	1	1	2
21.	Saudi Arab	10	3	13	5	3	8
	Total	2444	1145	3589	131	186	317

Source: Data collected from field through 36 PRA during May-July 2011.

As a corollary, a large number of our research participants have identified child and women trafficking as a 'major' problem in their area in the post-reform period. It is true that the problem of human trafficking, particularly trafficking in children and women has emerged as an important social issue in recent times in many parts of the world. In particular, India has the world's largest labour trafficking problem with hundreds of thousands of sex trafficking victims and millions of bonded labourers including forced child labourers (Ghosh, 2009: 720). More alarmingly, the State of West Bengal, lying in the Eastern part of India, serves as a source, transit and destination for national and international trafficking in women and children. A study conducted earlier by the UNICEF and Government of West Bengal has identified certain districts of West Bengal including the districts of North Bengal as 'endemic' for child trafficking (Ghosh, 2007: 55). Increasing instances of trafficking of women and children from Jalpaiguri tea gardens should also be perceived in such a context. Reasons for this are obvious: poverty, unemployment, lack of awareness and illiteracy of parents, promise of better job and comfortable life elsewhere, broken family, large family, domestic violence, lack of social and police support and fear of social criticism (in case of sexual exploitation of the girl child). The prime targets of trafficking are the *adivasi* children and women from poor and large families. As compared to the *adivasis*, Nepalese are found to be more conscious, organised, argumentative and better placed economically. Many of them also hold important positions in the power hierarchy (called 'super-staff' as compared to the 'sub-staff' meaning workers) of tea gardens. By virtue of their relatively better position within the tea gardens as well as numerical majority in the Dooars and Terai regions of North Bengal, the Nepali workers on an average are socially and politically well organised. Despite the formation of Akhil Bharatiya Adivasi Vikash Parishad (ABAVP) and consequent ethnic polarisation as well as movement by this outfit, consciousness level of the common tribals including their level of exploitation do not demonstrate any qualitative change and the grave vulnerability of children continues unabated. Contrarily, instances of trafficking of Nepali children are found to be few. Rather, we could collect names of many Nepalese working as 'placement agents' in the gardens along with some *adivasi* agents. Involvement of Nepali agents is also found to complicate the issue as any protest against such agent often takes an ethnic turn.

While exact estimation of the volume of child trafficking was not the objective of this research, the perception of FGD participants reveal that on an average 11 children and women are trafficked from each tea garden every year and many of children are girls. Perceptions of both PRA participants and In-depth Key Informants also come close to this figure. Our field experience also reveals that many of those who have returned home 'safely', also complained about 'money not paid as promised' or other types of 'exploitations' like denial of food, clothing and shelter, physical assault, verbal abuse, and excessive work pressure. Technically speaking, these cases also come under the term 'trafficking' as the 'end purpose' of such transportation is exploitation. Even if children opting for work have expressed 'manifest consent', it is in fact, a facade of consent and not 'informed consent' as the victim is lured, cheated, falsified, deceived and often coerced (Ghosh, 2009: 717-18). It may therefore be safely concluded that the volume of trafficking is much larger than common perceptions of stakeholders. The issue of child trafficking along with trafficking in women therefore appears to be very alarming in the tea gardens of North Bengal. Surprisingly, there is hardly any protest movement against trafficking in the tea gardens.

Conclusion

The findings of this study speak about the volume of marginalisation of tea garden workers and consequent vulnerability of children and women including trafficking since economic liberalisation. The fact that trafficking in women and children along with some other gender crimes have increased since economic reforms have been documented in several other research. It is in this context that assessment about the impact of economic reforms must take into cognisance these experiences as growth has often been accompanied by 'new inequalities' and susceptibilities of vulnerable sections of our population. The experience of plantation workers reveals that people involved in the traditional sectors of our economy are the worst sufferer. It may, however, be argued that sickness and closure of the plantation industry were natural consequences of managerial policies followed in the pre-liberalised period. The planters were neither serious about re-plantation and investment in machinery and factories, nor did they bother about changes in the quality of production of tea world-wide. Similarly, even after liberalisation, planters have favoured certain post-Fordist managerial strategies like casualisation, feminization, subcontracting and flexibility in order to grow the volume of tea business in the region despite sickness and closure. Surprisingly, state response to such catastrophe and faulty policies has been noticeably feeble. Hence, it may be argued that emerging marginalisation and vulnerabilities are not merely socio-legal issues in the context of deepening crises of plantation industry. These are symptoms of a much deeper malice in our society and we need to identify these symptoms in order to measure inequality in post-reform India.

This study has clearly exposed that there are profound economic, social, ethnic, geographical, administrative and political issues faced by the tea garden workers and their children in particular. Hence, there cannot be any instant remedy for such a problem. The difficulties in detecting and measuring vulnerability like trafficking make the task of prevention much more challenging. Nonetheless, several immediate and long term measures are suggested by the stakeholders. As the issues involved are multi-dimensional, their solutions also lie in following a multi-dimensional approach for prevention.

Recommendations

In a context when tea garden workers are struggling for alternative means of livelihood to supplement their paltry income, preventions of different types of vulnerabilities of children and young people depend much on reviving the economy and meeting the basic needs of workers. And the state has to come forward to take leadership in this respect. Even strong supporters of economic reforms today would agree with me that globalisation should not result in complete 'retreat of the state' as the latter may play a greater and a different role to regulate speculative and unscrupulous activities, mediate between interest groups and protect the marginalised people. Our experience during the last two decades has taught us this lesson.

Keeping such broad perspective in mind, we may present the views of our research participants on what is to done? Children participating in the PRA proceedings have collectively identified 'proper employment of parents' and 'removal of poverty' as the two main strategies even to tackle problems related to education. Additionally, steps like proper transportation facility, appropriate infrastructure for school education, awareness and education of parents, and incentive schemes like free books, writing materials, uniform and scholarships are listed by the children. Also steps like small family, vocational training including formal education for secondary and higher secondary students, and the facility of electricity are identified by the children. The necessity of an appropriate health infrastructure and requisite facilities is an imperative in the present context. It is recommended that in view of the failure of the garden management to meet life supporting facilities, government and non-government agencies should come forward to share the burden.

So far as the question of preventing child trafficking is concerned, majority of FGD participants have identified poverty reduction and employment creation as the foremost steps for this. Steps like awareness building, better education and community policing are also indentified by these participants in descending order. The Local Key Informants have also aired such views among others. Surprisingly, however, local key informants, many of whom were members of trade unions, political party, NGO, SHG or Panchayat, could not name any dominant agency or people who are currently working against trafficking in the area. Neither could they name any person/agency that may assist in preventing trafficking in near future.

In view of the above, this study stresses on the need to draw up a comprehensive strategy to fight vulnerabilities of children and women in the plantation industry as a whole. Such strategy includes short and long term plans related to the empowerment of children, parents, neighbours and other stakeholders under the following heads:

(a) Proper Employment and Capacity Development

- Steps by the district administration to improve vital aspects of living including infrastructure within tea gardens.
- Implement schemes of rural development, poverty alleviation and employment creation programmes rigorously.
- Develop alternative avenues of employment.
- Skill development for non-farm job placement.
- Need-based vocational training.
- Effective loan programme, training and income generation activities for women.

(b) Education and Empowerment

- Spread of quality education.
- Improve the process of access and retention of learners.

- Proper implementation of state incentives for SC and ST students.
- Incentives like free books, cycle and umbrella/raincoat to all students.
- Vocational education, special coaching classes.
- Enhancements of school infrastructure, teaching and office staff.
- Removal of communication impediments.

(c) Awareness and Motivation Building

- Formation of Garden Campaign Committee (GCC) to motivate and make parents aware.
- Use posters, leaflets and documentary films to campaign against child trafficking.
- Sensitise media and people about suspected placement agents.
- Awareness campaign on social issues like alcoholism, large family size, responsibility of parents, need for education etc.
- Regular and vigorous campaign to create awareness on gender issues including trafficking.
- Involve Self-Help Groups, NGOs, school teachers among others in the campaign.
- Introduction of schemes like 'Sabala', Ujjwala and the 'Rajiv Gandhi Scheme for Adolescent Girls' for the well-being and overall empowerment of adolescent girls.

(d) Administrative and Community Actions

- Strong administrative action to monitor labour conditions and implementation of PLA.
- Inclusion of all tea garden workers under the BPL category.
- Strengthening network of NGOs and other agencies, establishment of counselling centres, legal centres and help line.
- A grading system for panchayats on the basis of social indices with financial incentives.

- Formation of Anti-Human Trafficking Units (AHTUs) in all the tea gardens of Jalpaiguri and Darjeeling districts.
- Setting up of Neighbourhood Watch Groups in the vulnerable labour lines.
- Intensive training of law enforcement officers.
- Regular police raids, arrests of real traffickers and strict vigilance.
- Appointment of full time 'special police officers' and/or 'trafficking police officers'.
- Fix accountability of the law enforcing officials.
- Protection and rehabilitation of rescued victims.
- Setting up of Government hospitals/health centres within a cluster of tea gardens.
- Mobile health services and special health camps for tea garden workers.
- Periodic health camps by NGOs in labour lines.
- Registration of names of those migrating for job placement.

Acknowledgements: This is a revised version of a paper presented in the National Seminar on "Inequality in Post-Reform India: Measurement and Policy Issues", organised by Nabakrushna Choudhury Centre for Development Studies, Bhubaneswar in between 28-29th September, 2012. I am immensely benefited by the quality of discussion in the seminar by several eminent scholars including my esteemed teacher Prof. M.N. Panini that has helped me to revise some of my arguments.

NOTES

1. I used this term earlier to refer to the current process of globalisation as market driven impulses have guided our choices for 'globalisation from above' (Ghosh, 2003).
2. This study was sponsored by Save the Children and UNICEF. I am grateful to these funding agencies and the volunteers of two peer teams, namely of Rural Aid and Life Line Foundation for cooperation and help in conducting the research. Prof. Amit Hazra of Visva Bharati has helped me in carrying out the research.
3. The Plantation Labour Act of 1951 does not prohibit such temporary employment though it talks about certain conditions.
4. The average size of worker's families is found to be 5 in the survey. This means that most of the workers have more than 3 surviving children and some have more than 5 children.

5. The average working days in the selected gardens under MGNREGA were 31 during 2009-10. But, if we exclude Samsing (70) and Red Bank (60) from this list, the average working days comes to 24 only.

REFERENCES

Anandabazar Patrika (2011). 'New wage settlement for tea workers in Terai-Dooars' (in Bengali), November 5, Kolkata.

Beck, Renuca Rajni (2007). 'Conditions of Workers in Closed Tea Gardens: A Report on Jalpaiguri District of West Bengal'. Unpublished Report, Centre for Education and Communication, New Delhi.

Bhowmik, Sharit K. (1981). *Class Formation in the Plantation System*. New Delhi: People's Publishing House.

Bhowmik, Sharit K. (2011a). 'Wages and Ethnic Conflicts in Bengal's Tea Industry', *Economic and Political Weekly*, XLVI (32): 26-29.

Bhowmik, Sharit K. (2011b). 'Ethnicity and Isolation: Marginalization of Tea Plantation Workers', *Race/Ethnicity: Multidisciplinary Global Context*, 4(2), Winter: 235-253.

Biswas, Sarmishtha and Others (2005). 'Nutritional Survey of Tea Workers on Closed, Re-Opened, and Open Tea Plantations of the Dooars Region, West Bengal, India'.

Centre for Development and Human Rights (2006). 'Starvation Deaths in Tea Plantations in India', *Rights and Development Bulletin*, 1 (4): 26-28.

Chaudhury, Shibani (2011). 'Hunger in the Mine of Green Gold', Retrieved September 1, 2011, from www.tehelka.com/story_main31.asp?filename=Bu070707hunger_in.

Chaudhury, Sreerupa Mitra and Others (2007). 'The Tragedy of Tea: Starvation Deaths and Disasters Stalk Lives of Tea Garden Workers in West Bengal', Retrieved September 1, 2011, from *inttuc.blogspot.com/2009/05/save-tea-garden-save-workers.htm*.

Chowdhury, Sreerupa (2007). 'Death in your morning Cuppa', Retrieved September 1, 2011, from *www.tehelka.com/story_main33.asp?filename=Cr250807Death_in*.

Dacholia, Abhishek and Others (2006). 'Study on Labour Conditions in Tea Gardens of New Jalpaiguri' (Project Report). Group No. 9, Indian Institute of Management, Calcutta.

Dean, Nelson (2007). 'Tea pickers starve to death', *The Sunday Times*, September 16th, from www.timesonline.co.uk/tol/news/world/asia/article2461426.ece.

District Magistrate (2011). 'The Jalpaiguri Story: Innovative Application for Livelihood Security', Jalpaiguri, Government of West Bengal,

Retrieved September 1, 2011, from *www.nrega.net/csd/mgnrega-awards2011/write.../westbengal_jalpaiguri.pdf.*

Dutt, Himanshu (2007). 'The turnaround of Indian Tea Sector', in *Delhi Business Review,* Vol. 8, No. 1 (January–June): 117-120, www.delhibusinessreview.org/ v_8n1/v8n1 case_study.pdf, *accessed on 5010-2012.*

Ghosh, Biswajit (2003). 'Impact of Market Globalism – Indian Experience', in *Bharata Vidya,* Vol. III: 73-83.

Ghosh, Biswajit (2007). *Trafficking in Women & Children, Child Marriage and Dowry—A Study For Action Plan in West Bengal* (Edited & Compiled), Published by UNICEF and Government of West Bengal, Kolkata.

Ghosh, Biswajit (2009). 'Human Trafficking In India: Nature, Dimensions And Strategies For Prevention', in *The International Journal of Human Rights,* 13 (05): 716-738.

Ghosh, Biswajit (ed.) (2012). *Interrogating Development–Discourses on Development in India Today.* Jaipur: Rawat Publication.

Gupta, Ananda Das (2009). *Tea Plantation in India: Towards Sustainable Development.* Kolkata: Gangchil.

Gupta, Aparajita (2008). 'Poverty, starvation stalk Bengal tea garden workers', in *Thaindian News,* Retrieved September 1, 2011, www.thaindian.com/.../poverty-starvation-stalk-bengal.

JESA (2007). 'Starvation deaths due to closure of Tea Gardens in Jalpaiguri' Retrieved September 1, 2011, from www.jesaonline.org/index.php?...tea-gardens...jalpaiguri.

Lahiri, Souparna (2006). 'Bonded Labour and the Tea Plantation Economy', Retrieved September 1, 2011, http://www.revolutionarydemocracy.org/rdv6n2/tea.htm

Mitra, Maureen Nandini (2007). 'Workers starving due to closure of tea estates in North Bengal', Retrieved September 1, 2011, www.indiaenvironmentportal.org.in/node/40468.

New Trade Union Initiative (NTUI) (2011). 'Campaign for a Just Wage for Tea Plantation Workers launched', Retrieved September 1, 2011, www.radicalsocialist.in/.../403-campaign-for-a-just-wage-for-tea-pla.

Nagarik, Mancha and NESPON (2010). 'Annual Chronic Problems in North Bengal Ta Garden'. Retrieved September 1, 2011, *sanhati.com/excerpted/2112.*

Panini, M. N. (2012). 'Inequalities after Economic Reforms: A Sociologist's Perspective', Valedictory address given on 29th September, 2012 at the National Seminar organised by NCCDS, Bhubaneswar.

Radical Socialist (2011). 'Wage Violation in NREGA in tea plantations of District Jalpaiguri', West Bengal, 21 June, Retrieved September 1, 2011, www.raducalsocialist.in/.../404-*wage violation-in-nrega-in-tea-plant.*

Report on the visit of the Commission (2009), Retrieved September 1, 2011, from *ncst.nic.in/.../Tour_Report_12_17_Feb_2009_West_%20Bengal62685941*.

Roy, Sanjay (2009). 'North Bengal Tribes in Development Perspective', *Journal of Indian Anthropological Society*, 44: 5-27.

Roy, Sanjay (2012). 'The Adivasis in a Liberal Democratic Order and their Struggle for a Self', in Biswajit Ghosh (ed.), *Interrogating Development: Discourses on Development in India Today* (81-103). Jaipur: Rawat Publications.

Talwar, Anuradha, D. Chakraborty and S. Biswas (2005). *Study on Closed and Re-opened Tea Gardens in North Bengal*. Kolkata: Paschim Banga Khet Majoor Samity and International Union of Food, Agriculture, Hotel, Restaurant, Catering, Tobacco, Plantation and Allied Workers' Associations (IUF).

The Times of India (2012). 'Tea garden deaths spark starvation controversy', January 1. Kolkata.

Index